AGENDA FOR EXCELLENCE 2

AGENDA FOR EXCELLENCE 2
Administering the State

Edited by

B. Guy Peters
University of Pittsburgh

and

Bert A. Rockman
University of Pittsburgh

Chatham House Publishers, Inc.
Chatham, New Jersey

AGENDA FOR EXCELLENCE 2:
ADMINISTERING THE STATE

Chatham House Publishers, Inc.
Box One, Chatham, New Jersey 07928

Copyright © 1996 by Chatham House Publishers, Inc.

All rights reserved. No part of this publication may be reproduced, stored in a retrieval system, or transmitted in any form or by any means, electronic, mechanical, photocopying, recording, or otherwise, without the prior permission of the publisher.

Publisher: Edward Artinian
Editor: Christopher J. Kelaher
Production supervisor: Katharine F. Miller
Cover design: The Antler & Baldwin Design Group
Composition: Bang, Motley, Olufsen
Printing and binding: A to Z Printing

LIBRARY OF CONGRESS CATALOGING-IN-PUBLICATION DATA

Agenda for excellence 2 : administering the state / edited by B. Guy Peters and Bert A. Rockman.
    p. cm. —(Festschriften in honor of Charles H. Levine ; no. 2)
Includes bibliographical references.
ISBN 1-56643-016-X (pbk.)
    1. Public administration. 2. Administrative agencies—United States—Management. 3. United States—Politics and government. 4. Policy sciences. 5. Political planning—United States. 6. Levine, Charles H. I. Peters, B. Guy. II. Rockman, Bert A. III. Series.
JF1351.A29   1996
353.001—dc20
                                                     95-41827
                                                     CIP

Manufactured in the United States of America
10 9 8 7 6 5 4 3 2 1

Contents

B. Guy Peters and Bert A. Rockman
Preface
vii

B. Guy Peters
1. Introduction: The State of Public Administration
1

Lawrence F. Keller, Richard Green,
and Gary L. Wamsley
2. An Eleventh-Hour Attempt to Develop a Normatively Based Theory of Public Administration
12

H. Brinton Milward and Wendy Laird
3. Where Does Policy Come From?
38

James A. Thurber
4. Political Power and Policy Subsystems in American Politics
76

IRENE S. RUBIN AND BERNARD H. ROSS
5. Explaining the Growth and Contraction of Municipal Services
105

RONALD C. MOE
6. Managing Privatization: A New Challenge to Public Administration
135

HANS-ULRICH DERLIEN
7. Politicization of Bureaucracies in Historical and Comparative Perspective
149

BERT A. ROCKMAN
Conclusion
163

About the Contributors
179

Preface

B. Guy Peters and Bert A. Rockman

Completing this manuscript is at once a joyous and a sad occasion for us. The joy is a natural response upon completing a project on which we have worked for a very long time. Moreover, we feel that this book and the articles in it make some important statements about what has happened with public administration over the past decade and the many challenges that remain. The process of governance has changed substantially over that time period, and this volume should help the reader understand what has happened and what the implications of those changes are.

As much joy as there may be about the completion of this project, it is tempered by our even greater sense of loss. We might have assembled a book of this sort without the untimely passing of Charles Levine, but it is not likely that it would have been the same. This book is the second of two memorial volumes for Charlie. As such, it contains the works of several of his friends and addresses a number of the themes with which he was involved during his professional career. It attempts to integrate some of the concerns of academics with those of the practitioners of public administration, just as Charlie did during his lifetime.

The eclecticism of this collection reflects the range of Charlie's work and of his friends. Thus, it reflects his wide-ranging value to the study of public administration. Although there are any number of experts on subdisciplines such as personnel, budgeting, and organization theory, Charlie was important to the field in that he could converse with experts in all these subdisciplines and command their respect. Similarly, he could talk to both academics and practitioners and help each group understand the other (and themselves) better. Also, toward the end of his career, Charlie became interested in comparative and international administration, and he was especially adept at explaining the intricacies of American government to non-

Americans. Working as he did at the intersection of a number of components of this field of study, Charlie was able to develop a unique vision of the diverse enterprise we refer to as public administration.

That vision, which we have attempted to reflect in this volume, is complex, but it contains a number of simple and enduring truths about the field. Perhaps the most important of those truths is that the ultimate purpose of administration is governance. This point in turn implies that administration is more than simply management; it is management in the service of policy and in service of the state. Charlie's work for the Volcker Commission toward the end of his life was intended in part to remind some individuals then at the helm of the institutions of government that administration and administrators want to serve much more than they want to oppose. That having been said, he might have been among the first to argue for the responsibility of public administrators to exert principled opposition to actions they considered unlawful, inappropriate, or simply unwise. Governance is a very difficult value to create, but it is crucial for the success of a society.

The conflict between the responsibility of the civil service in the highest sense of protecting the public interest and the accountability of the civil service to higher legal authority provides one of the fundamental tensions in modern democracies. Charlie knew that, as the proverbial expression goes, civil servants had to be on tap rather than on top. However, he also understood that civil servants could not be aloof from the policy process; indeed, without their contribution, government would flail blindly and fail badly. Civil servants provide the reality principle to policy aspiration. Without their input and without respectful attention to their service in that role, politicians might only delude themselves in thinking they could achieve their policy goals. Connecting reality to direction was Charlie's concern in the face of political trends that have seemed to value rhetoric, symbol, and gesture more than real achievement.

At the end of Charlie's all too brief life, he committed himself to the work of the Volcker Commission as its staff director. His goal was to alert the attentive public to the dangers faced by the country if its public service failed. He was deeply concerned that delegitimation of the civil service and of the public sector would eventually take its toll on the quality of the public service, to the great detriment of the government as well as the citizens. How close that fear may be to becoming a reality remains a matter of controversy best explored through empirical examination. Charlie's concerns, however, were the product of his commitment to applied scholarship. He was a scholar and a citizen in the classical meaning of that term. His service to the Volcker Commission culminated a lifetime of commitment to the ideal of knowledge for public purpose.

In addition to our attraction to Charlie as a scholar, the participants in this volume shared a commitment to him as an individual. He was a loyal and valued friend to us all. He was that as well to a large number of other people in academia and government. Despite a heavy work schedule and a strong commitment to his family, Charlie was always ready to meet with his friends and acquaintances and to lend a hand with their intellectual or practical problems. For many of us, Charlie was a one-man clearinghouse of information about government and the people who worked in it and studied it. He knew who was doing what, and who needed what done, and he was able to get people together in order to advance their interests and the interests of the discipline as a whole. His passing left a huge hole in the discipline as well as a great sense of personal loss for us.

We have a number of people to thank for their assistance in completing this volume. The individual authors have responded well to our requests for changes and have been patient with the inevitable delays in completing the volume. Several other scholars offered chapters that could not be included because of space considerations, and we thank them for their interest. Also, several members of the secretarial staffs at the University of Pittsburgh, most notably Wiltraudt Grashoff and Christie Souders, have been of great help in preparing the final version of this manuscript. Finally, Edward Artinian and his staff at Chatham House have been helpful and supportive as we have brought this long-delayed project to fruition.

AGENDA FOR EXCELLENCE 2

I

Introduction: The State of Public Administration

B. Guy Peters

The study and interpretation of public administration is a large and extremely varied enterprise. This one field of inquiry includes a range of scholars, united loosely by their common concern with the manner in which the public sector operates, the means through which governments achieve their goals, and the role of public administrators in making the public sector more or less effective. Even this vague and seemingly innocuous statement describing the existence of common threads in public administration may provoke some members of the profession and cause others to question exactly what is being included and excluded in the statement. For example, who precisely is a "public administrator" in this definition? Does the term include only career public servants—the "bureaucracy"—or does it also include that large group of public officials appointed to office, often to exercise political control over the career officials? We can even inquire, given recent experiences with privatization and contracting, just what constitutes the public sector in the United States?[1] It may be that the increased intermingling of public and private activity has eroded the utility of any theorizing about the sovereignty of government in the United States.

The academic discussion of public administration is extremely varied and contains a number of contending approaches. One approach is to treat public administration as a political activity and as one major political institution involved in the making and execution of public policy.[2] An alternative approach is to treat public administration as the exercise of managerial functions within a public context, making its principal questions the same as those of business administration, despite markedly different contexts.[3]

Finally, other scholars focus on public administration as just another social activity and attempt to understand administration through the meanings that its human participants attach to it.[4] Each approach provides some important information about public administration, but the complementarity of the approaches is often ignored in the midst of conflicts over which is *the* best approach.

In addition to the academic squabbles that may arise over definitions, even vague ones, the field of public administration is further divided among academics and practitioners. The great divide among the members of professional organizations in this field is between those who believe that practice should follow theoretical developments (including those in the more basic social sciences) and those who believe that practice is the only meaningful standard for understanding public administration. Academics, especially those concerned with subjects such as organization theory and the politics of bureaucracy, regard most practitioners as addicted to the "nuts and bolts" of their profession and as incapable of identifying the interesting and important political and theoretical questions arising in public administration. Many practitioners, in contrast, consider academics to be hopelessly wooly headed and out of touch with the real issues that affect the lives and careers of public administrators. For these "pragmatists" in public administration, theory is just another way of saying that the writer does not truly understand the reality of the situation in government.

The above descriptions of both some committed academics and some committed practitioners are, to some extent, just caricatures of their real and more subtle positions in these debates. Although hyperbolic, these descriptions do capture some of the reality of the important differences between the two groups that attempt to coexist within the boundaries of this field of public administration. Adherents of these two orientations to public administration take their differences seriously and often appear to believe that real harm may come to the field if the other side becomes dominant.

In some ways, the wide diversity of views existing within public administration is a weakness for the field and makes it difficult to contend that it is a discipline in the usual academic meaning of that term. Public administration has been plagued by internecine warfare over just what is in and what is out of the field, and most fundamentally whether it should be an academic or an applied profession. This basic conflict has engendered, in turn, conflicts over the content and editorship of the journals in the field, over the direction of departments and schools, over the content of conferences and courses, and generally over who is permitted to define the boundaries of the field. Some conflict may be functional for a discipline, especially when academic politics have a tendency to force an excessively quick closure over a field's definition. At times, however, the conflicts within public administration have bordered on the extreme and the self-destructive. It often appears to outside observers that the social science least capable of administering its own affairs effectively ironically is public administration.

This book celebrates the career and contributions of a unique individual who was able to bridge the real or imagined gap between the academic and the practitioner worlds. He also was someone who was able to converse easily with academics representing many different persuasions and schools. Indeed, Charles H. Levine seemed to revel in the diversity of the field and to use that diversity as a mechanism for addressing a number of significant policy and administrative questions. The arguments he made were as relevant and meaningful to the practitioner community as they were to his fellow academics. It was, in fact, often difficult to determine who the intended audience for his work really was. Charlie made many contributions to the field of public administration that can be enumerated through lists of publications and speeches. In some ways, however, his most enduring legacy was the less visible one of offering a means to unite the strands of thought and action within the broad umbrella of public administration. This was a quest on his part that was both personal and professional. The articles in this book reflect the diversity of the field and therefore, to some extent, reflect the range of concerns that Charles Levine had about public administration as a positive force for improving American society. While the contributors to this volume—friends, colleagues, and admirers of Charles Levine—themselves display some of the diversity of the field, they are united in their appreciation of Charlie's efforts to cross-walk between the concerns of practitioners and the concerns of academicians in public administration.

Public Administration and Policy Formulation

The first aspect of public administration, and of Charles Levine's work, we discuss in this volume is the role that the public bureaucracy plays in initiating policy and in defining the agenda for government.[5] For many traditional students of public administration in the United States, the above sentence might seem heretical. To traditionalists, the notion that the administrators of government policy also would have an influential, even decisive, role in formulating public policy was not a part of the accepted wisdom. These defenders of tradition would argue that the role of administration (the bureaucracy) is to administer the policies decided on by the political institutions of government. Until those institutions act and give them a policy to implement, public administration has little or nothing to do.

In a strict sense, the defenders of administrative traditionalism are correct. Public administration is indeed founded on law, and its ultimate task is to implement the decisions made by legislatures and political executives. There are, however, a number of flaws associated with this argument, and these flaws present dangers for the efficient and effective management of contemporary governments. The most important flaw is the failure to recognize that administering a program inherently involves making policy. Every time the "cop on the beat" or a social worker or an OSHA inspector or a schoolteacher or any other "street-level bureaucrat"[6] makes a decision about an individual case, he or she is making public policy. In some policy areas (e.g., taxation), these decisions have been cumulated and constitute a body of precedent that is "policy" in any meaningful sense of that term. Rulings by the Internal Revenue Service on issues such as what is "income" determine the manner in which the tax laws apply. In other policy areas the impact of administrative decision making is less formalized and cumulative, but is nonetheless very real. That body of knowledge and practice derived from administrative practice is also transmitted to new members of the organization so that the organizational culture will persist unless authoritative actions are taken to alter it.[7]

Another aspect of the traditional dichotomous view of administration is that it fails to take into account the expertise and experience of the civil service. Many political leaders are amateurs in government, especially in the details of the policies over which they are given dominion. Because of their relative amateurism, they can usefully rely on their civil services for policy advice and leadership. The problem again is that some elective political leaders believe that having a political mandate and having an ideology is all that is needed for effective governing. There has always been some disjuncture between the possession of legitimacy and the possession of knowledge in government, but that gap has been perceived to be (whether it is or not) wider in the 1980s and 1990s than at any time in the recent past. With that gap, the ability of the public bureaucracy to supply the policy leadership that societies need is seriously compromised, with the possibility that government will make foolish errors, while it has within its own bosom the source of error correction. Three of the contributions to this volume deal directly with the political and policymaking role of the public bureaucracy and clearly document the inability—conceptually and empirically—to separate politics and administration. Brinton Milward and Wendy Laird make this point for the initial stages of making policy: defining the public agenda.[8] This stage is in many ways the most crucial element of the policymaking process because it tends to lock in future responses. The manner in which a policy is defined initially for subsequent resolution is likely to influence for a long time the manner in which government will attempt to "solve" the problem.

Introduction: The State of Public Administration

Indeed, the very recognition of public problems is a crucial and problematic aspect of the process. We cannot say that the many real problems existing in society naturally gravitate to the agenda of the political system; there is too much evidence to the contrary. Instead, public problems must be socially and politically constructed before they can be addressed through the policymaking process. The manner in which the drug problem has been constructed in the United States, for example, will determine that the question will be primarily one for law enforcement rather than education or social work. This need not have been the case, but the agenda-setting process went in a certain direction under the guidance of Presidents Reagan and Bush.

Milward and Laird's analysis points to the social construction of policy agendas and the manner in which public organizations become involved in that construction. Organizations within the bureaucracy are often active participants in the process of agenda building. The social construction of policy issues cannot be seen as irrelevant for administrative organizations, given that the nature of the construction will determine who will get the money, personnel, and responsibility associated with the newly defined or redefined policy. Even if they do not have intellectual or policy stakes in the agenda-setting process, organizations within the public bureaucracy may have a more pragmatic reason to be involved and attempt to impose their own definition of policy problems on the process.

A second contribution on the political role of public administration, that by James Thurber, discusses the close political connections between Congress and the public bureaucracy in the United States. This manuscript goes beyond the conventional discussion of "iron triangles," "issue networks," or "big, sloppy hexagons" to provide a nuanced picture of the relationships that exist in the federal government between the legislature and the organizations responsible to it for the implementation of policy.[9] In so doing, the manuscript points to several interesting features of American politics. The first is the independence of the agencies within the public bureaucracy. Whereas a European audience might be concerned with the role of ministries and with relatively large organizations that have direct ties to political decision makers in the cabinet, in the United States the linkages tend to be at the agency, subdepartmental level, with a consequent increase in the degree of fragmentation of American government.

A second point that Thurber raises is the significant degree of interdependence of the political and administrative institutions in the United States. Again, an extraordinary proportion of the literature in public administration has been devoted to the question of the separation, or lack of it, of politics and administration.[10] This article is another very clear indication that this separation may not exist in the real world of government and that the two forces are closely intertwined. A number of scholars have argued this connection over the years, but this paper offers clear evidence of the linkage, and just how crucial that linkage is for the performance of government. Indeed, we could argue that the best way to understand how American government actually functions is to understand the manner in which administrative organizations and Congress interact in making public policy. Not only do these interactions provide an adequate picture of government at any one time, but they also provide a means of looking at the important changes that have occurred in government. For example, as the relationships between Congress and the agencies have become less structured,[11] there has been greater indeterminacy and greater "gridlock"[12] in policymaking.

Values and Public Administration

A second section of this book deals with the values of public administrators and the need to reinvigorate our discussion of those values. Too often, public administration is considered to be just "nuts and bolts" rather than an integral part of the decision-making process within government. The choices made by public administrators—whether they are made at the peaks of administrative pyramids or by working directly with clients near the bottom of those pyramids—reflect values. Those values influence both the content of decisions and the procedures through which they are made. It is crucial, therefore, that members of public bureaucracies understand that they are acting in more than simply a technical capacity; they are acting in the name of the government and the people. Moreover, they must have some notions about the most appropriate values to implement through the public sector.

One value that traditionally has been important for public administration in the United States is that civil servants should be politically neutral. This concept replaced the spoils system during the latter part of the nineteenth century and has since attained the status of an assumption in public management.[13] One presumed function of political neutrality is to preserve stability in the public sector so that when there is a change in government, an entire new cadre of public servants does not have to be hired and trained. In addition, neutrality is presumed to ensure the fair treatment of all citizens by their government. The concept of neutrality at times has been taken to extremes, as in certain aspects of the Hatch Act, but most Americans still seem to prefer a neutral civil service.

The concept of civil service neutrality is, however, under attack in the United States and in many other industrialized democracies, as is pointed out very forcefully by Hans-Ulrich Derlien in his discussion of the "politicization" of public bureaucracies. Derlien first describes the changing concept of political involvement. Even in countries such as Germany and France that have had a political civil service for some time, there is growing concern about the ever greater involvement of politicians in the selection and promotion of their civil servants.

Derlien proceeds to discuss the potential effects of the changes he has observed on the management of governments. Again, even in personnel systems accustomed to political involvement, the increased level of politicization is likely to have significant impacts on governance and on the ability of the civil service to command the respect and cooperation of the public.

Keller, Green, and Wamsley take a somewhat broader view of the value systems important for effective public administration. They and other colleagues[14] have been involved for several years in advocating the centrality of administrative questions in American democracy and in proposing a set of crucial values for guiding the public administrators responsible for so much of governance. Their paper continues the work in that tradition by articulating a number of central concerns for the ethical and political analysis of public administration in the United States. In particular, these authors argue that public administration has made a fundamental error in adopting "science" as the basis of good practice, instead of depending more on normative concerns for guidance. The concentration on the technical and managerial aspects of the job of public administrators, combined with the denigration of political analysis in much "administrative science," creates the danger of an administrative apparatus composed of capable technocrats but devoid of sensitive public decision makers. The drive for technical competence is strong in many areas of American life, but Keller, Green, and Wamsley ask us to question those values and find alternative models of competence.

As well as providing an evaluation of what they consider to be the unfortunate condition of the contemporary public administration profession, Keller, Green, and Wamsley offer ideas as to how to rescue the field of public administration and its practitioners from the perceived trap of "mere" technical competence. The most fundamental of their suggestions for change is to return to many of the original ideas of the profession of public administration in the United States. Correspondingly, a revitalization of public administration requires greater emphasis on its social mission and calling, rather than merely to be in the service of technical rationality. In their view, the United States might be better served in the long run by individuals with less technical training but with a much stronger grounding in the legal and constitutional basis of government in a democracy. Although unstated, it appears that the same argument is meant to apply to public administration in any democratic regime.

Public Management

The final set of concerns about contemporary public administration expressed in this volume are with the managerial aspects of the contemporary public sector. In contrast to Wamsley and others concerned with the ethical aspects of governance, some students of public administration are concerned that there may not be enough technical competence in the public bureaucracy. Public administrators are the principal cadre of managers for government, and a good deal of attention has been focused in recent years on the managerial aspects of government, especially as contrasted to management in the private sector. Critics from inside and especially from outside government have argued that public-sector management practices are wasteful and could be improved by importing the practices of the private sector. Also, it should be remembered that management issues need not be confined to the "nuts and bolts" of administration or to practical and pragmatic issues. To some extent, managerial concerns extend across the range of public-sector activity and therefore must address questions not only of how things are done in government but also of what functions should be performed within government.

As well as having to cope with political pressures to improve their performance, public organizations must cope with change. Some of that change comes from within the organizations, as they attempt to improve their performance, to adjust to new economic and technological demands, and to satisfy the needs of their clients and their own employees. Irene Rubin and Bernard Ross examine the manner in which public organizations have adjusted to one major change—changes in the external resource base available to them. Their paper clearly follows in the tradition of research on cutback management in the public sector that Charles Levine pioneered.[15] Rubin and Ross focus on decisions taken at the municipal level about whether to expand or contract public services. Although we tend to think about the experiences of the 1980s and 1990s in terms of cutback management, there is a long history of local governments attempting to adjust their service levels to the varying availability of financial resources in the public sector. Rubin and Ross provide both a useful analysis of the cycles of expansion and contraction of municipal services in the United States and an interpretation of those cycles. The authors point out clearly that managers within the public sector, no matter how skilled they may be, cannot isolate their organizations from broad socioeconomic trends. Instead, they must learn to cope effectively with the pressures coming from their environment if they want to have any success in reaching important policy goals.

One of the most important political and managerial challenges to public administration in the 1990s is coping with the new, more privatized style of policy implementation being imposed. One of the central goals of the Reagan and Bush administrations was to reduce the size of the public sector and use private mechanisms for achieving public purposes. This strategy is by no means new in the United States, nor is it confined to the Republican Party,[16] but it did achieve much greater prominence during the administrations of these two presidents. The goals of privatization are to some extent political and at a macro level—to make government smaller, less costly, and less intrusive in the daily lives of Americans. These political goals and programs, however, have substantial administrative implications and require administrators accustomed to implementing policies directly to find ways of achieving the same goals by contracting out to private suppliers. This may well change the role of the public administrator from one of program manager into one of bargainer or negotiator with contractors in the private sector. While program responsibilities remain the same, the administrative capacity to meet those responsibilities may be diminished.

Ronald Moe addresses this issue of the increased use of alternative policy delivery systems at the federal level in the United States. Unlike most European countries, or even state and local governments within the United States, the federal government had relatively few public enterprises that could be sold off to the private sector, so the principal forms of privatization at the federal level involved changing delivery systems. Moe describes a range of those alternative implementation systems, especially "third-party government" and the contracting out of services. Those two strategies are argued by Moe to have a significant impact on the manner in which government does its business and consequently on the skills required of public servants. Public management becomes as much contract writing as the organization and motivation of personnel within an agency. Likewise, strategies for funding public programs must adjust to the increased utilization of user fees and the diminution of direct financial control within government.

As well as altering the nature of public administration in the federal government, Moe argues that privatization has had important, largely negative, impacts on the capacity of the federal government to perform its fundamental role in society. He notes that government agencies often find themselves in the position of not being able to perform legally mandated services because they lack adequate staff resources. Moreover, sensitive public functions such as trial proceedings and security checks are left to private contractors who may lack a sufficient concept of public service and propriety to perform those activities properly. Further, the privatization strategies have exacerbated the feeling that the public and private sectors are adversaries, rather than "symbiotically linked" components of the same economy and society. Moe argues that this divorce of the public and the private sectors will ultimately produce negative consequences for both sectors.

Conclusion

This collection of essays is designed to honor the memory of Charles Levine and provide some commentary on the breadth and impact of his scholarly contributions on the study of public administration in the United States. The contributions cover at least as wide a range as Charlie's work and share with his own writing a deep commitment to the importance of government and public administration in a free and democratic society. It is now generally popular to denigrate the contributions of government, especially of "the bureaucracy," to a capitalist and liberal society such as the United States. Our past several presidents have come to office by running against Washington, and the civil service that is seen to embody the enervated character of government. As popular as this strategy can be politically, it carries with it risks of making the failure of government a self-fulfilling prophecy.

As important as public administration is for the smooth functioning of government, we must always remember that its importance extends beyond "simple" management. Public administration is an inherently political activity that must be considered in the context of decision-making patterns within the public sector that affect the lives of all citizens. Individuals and organizations within the public bureaucracy are important repositories of information and policy advice. The public bureaucracy also has political interests, or at a minimum reflects the political interests of its clients, that must be pursued within the policy process. Finally, every time a member of a public organization makes a decision about an individual client, he or she is also to some extent making public policy. All these considerations combine to make the public bureaucracy a central political actor. Charles Levine never lost sight of that political role, and in the midst of all the discussion and conflict among other scholars in the field he was able to keep sight of that central fact and of the importance that the study of this field can make for the quality of government. These essays also point to the essential role of public administration and the contribution Charles Levine made to our understanding of the discipline.

Notes

1. Charles O. Jones, *The Reagan Legacy* (Chatham, N.J.: Chatham House, 1988).

2. Charles H. Levine, B. Guy Peters, and Frank J. Thompson, *Public Administration: Challenges, Choices, and Consequences* (New York: HarperCollins, 1990).

3. Hal G. Rainey and James L. Perry, "Building Public Management Research and Practice," in *Agenda for Excellence,* ed. Patricia W. Ingraham and Donald F. Kettl (Chatham, N.J.: Chatham House, 1992); and Hal G. Rainey,

"The Uniqueness of the Public Bureaucracy," in *The State of Public Bureaucracy*, ed. Larry B. Hill (Armonk, N.Y.: M.E. Sharpe, 1992).

4. Ralph Hummel, *The Bureaucratic Experience* (New York: St. Martin's, 1987).

5. Charles H. Levine, "Where Policy Comes From: Ideas, Innovations, and Agenda Choices," *Public Administrative Review* 45 (1985): 255–58.

6. Michael Lipsky, *Street-Level Bureaucracy* (New York: Russell Sage, 1980); and Jeffrey M. Prottas, *People-Processing: The Street Level Bureaucrat in Public Service Bureaucracies* (Lexington, Mass.: Lexington Books, 1979).

7. James G. March and Johan P. Olsen, *Rediscovering Institutions* (New York: Free Press, 1989).

8. Roger W. Cobb and Charles W. Elder, *Participation in American Politics: The Dynamics of Agenda-Building* (Boston: Allyn and Bacon, 1972).

9. Hugh Heclo, "Issue Networks and the Executive Establishment," in *The New American Political System*, ed. Anthony King (Washington, D.C.: American Enterprise Institute, 1978); Michael M. Atkinson and William D. Coleman, "Policy Networks, Policy Communities and the Problems of Governance," *Governance* 5 (1992): 154–80; Jack L. Walker, "Policy Communities as Global Phenomena," *Governance* 2 (1989): 1–4; Jones, *Reagan Legacy*.

10. Colin Campbell and B. Guy Peters, "The Politics/Administration Dichotomy: Death or Merely Change," *Governance* 1 (1988): 79–99.

11. Jones, *Reagan Legacy*.

12. Charles H. Levine, "Human Resource Erosion and the Uncertain Future of the U.S. Civil Service: From Policy Gridlock to Structural Fragmentation," *Governance* 1 (1988): 115–43.

13. Paul P. Van Riper, *History of the United States Civil Service* (Westport, Conn.: Greenwood, 1976).

14. Charles T. Goodsell, *The Case for Bureaucracy: A Public Administration Polemic*, 3d ed. (Chatham, N.J.: Chatham House, 1994); Lawrence F. Keller, Richard Green, and Gary L. Wamsley, "An Eleventh-Hour Attempt to Develop a Normatively Based Theory of Public Administration," chapter 2 of this volume.

15. Charles H. Levine, "Organizational Decline and Cutback Management," *Public Administration Review* 38 (1978): 315–57.

16. Charles L. Schultze, *The Public Use of Private Interest* (Washington, D.C.: Brookings Institution, 1977).

2

An Eleventh-Hour Attempt to Develop a Normatively Based Theory of Public Administration

LAWRENCE F. KELLER, RICHARD GREEN, AND GARY L. WAMSLEY

> In light of current scholarly views of the nature of professionalism, the practice of public administration can hardly be ranked among the professions. It exhibits few if any of the attributes commonly associated with professional status. — Richard Schott

> What I propose is that we try to act as a profession without actually being one, and perhaps even without the hope or intention of becoming one in any strict sense. — Dwight Waldo

> We've always had the power to get back to Kansas: we've just needed to believe in ourselves. — Dorothy, in *The Wizard of Oz*

Confusion is rampant over the definition of *profession*. Nearly everyone wants to be a member of a profession or at least to be referred to as a professional—and certainly to be paid like one. Yet the relationship between public administration and professionalism is a troubled one. Our field, like others, assumes that we should be a profession and have more professionalism. But some say that we can never meet contemporary definitions of a profession.[1] Others assert that professionalism in the public service constitutes a threat to public administration and our democratic republic.

This essay tries to clarify the thinking on profession and professionalism as it applies to those who work in public administration. Our main purpose, however, is to reestablish a normative basis for a supervening or "follow-on" profession of public administration. We hope to articulate an approach to professionalism that not only attracts precareer students, but provides a normative grounding for midcareerists in specialized occupations or professions when they move into the ranks of public management and administration. What we propose is not a profession with a specific set of behaviors, skills, and "recipe" knowledge to be inculcated in new members, but a cluster of values that public administrators can use as a reference as they work within the framework of the special knowledge required of their specific agency and its policy milieu. In doing so, they become what we refer to as "agential leaders."[2]

Contrasting Concepts of a Profession

Some of the debate over the concepts and implications of profession arises from the fact that the nature of professions and their place in society are undergoing considerable change. There seem to be two principal ways of defining and conceptualizing a profession. One of them, which we label "modern sociological," is prevalent today. The other we call "classical normative." It is less common, but it is much more in keeping with centuries-old meanings and derivations of the word. Despite its lack of currency, this latter concept has a number of aspects that are urgently needed by public administration today.

THE MODERN SOCIOLOGICAL CONCEPT

This concept of profession evolved mainly out of twentieth-century empirical studies that indicate that modern professions have claimed expertise in some key societal roles or functions on the basis of systematic or scientific knowledge. The undergirding assumption has been that this systematic knowledge could be developed only in extended formal training. This claim to special knowledge has provided a basis for corporatism in these professions, and a claim to some degree of control over entrance, self-regulation, and autonomy in behavior. Aspiring professionals have buttressed this claim with special entrance examinations and codes of ethics. Often a formal organization has been developed to foster the corporate interests. Special language and rituals also have developed, apparently designed to foster exclusivity and awe. Some modern professions have claimed to have a service ethic, and a few might hold notions of a social ideal. But service to society is largely overshadowed by self-deserving behavior.

Sociological studies have also noted that professionals tend to be highly educated and come from high socioeconomic strata. Professions are thus viewed as a functional response to the increasing differentiation of complex, modern, industrializing society.[3]

There is nothing wrong with this modern concept of professions as a description of what they have become. It is, however, devoid of any concern for values and ignores the service ethic or social ideals of profession. Furthermore, Vollmer and Mills[4] indicate that such descriptive studies have unwittingly yielded a prescriptive "ideal type," that is, the description of what modern professions have become is increasingly taken as a prescription for what they should be. The distortion, according to Vollmer and Mills, is analogous to the way Weber's heuristic ideal-type of bureaucracy is often mistaken for a prescriptive model.[5] The result is a model of professionalism that takes on normative power without any normative reflection or argument.

Among contemporary writers, only Samuel Huntington gives serious attention to the responsibility of a profession to society in his work *The Soldier and the State: The Theory of Politics of Civil/Military Relations*.[6] Perhaps this is because the military cannot escape that which we seem to be forgetting in terms of other professions, namely, that acceptance of claims to autonomy and discretion ultimately hinge on perceived responsibility to society. In the military it is not just a matter of legitimating discretion, but more fundamentally of gaining and keeping basic societal acceptance. The difference between a military professional and a mercenary or hired killer is simply the degree to which one is perceived to be in service to society and the state. The military as a profession must take more than usual care to sustain acceptance. These professionals, who after all are public administrators in uniform, offer an important lesson for their civil counterparts.

The modern sociological concept of a profession neglects such normative concerns because of its epistemological stance. As a result, its outlook fosters a particularistic and micropolitical view of the world. This has made the development of a normatively grounded profession of public administration problematic at best. The consequences have been disastrous to the reputation of public administration. It is viewed as weak, bungling, self-serving, and dangerous at a time when it should be playing a strong and legitimate role in governance.

THE CLASSIC NORMATIVE CONCEPT

This concept of a profession is not as easy to articulate, in part because it is hard for us to grasp the context and the notions of knowledge and epistemology in which it developed. The roots of the word *profession* are interesting because they consistently point to origins in religion and learning. Bruce,[7] drawing on several sources, feels that the word comes out of late Latin religious usage and down to us through the French, probably with the creation of the university systems in the fifteenth century. Another source[8] suggests that the distinctive aspects of the word's usage center on personal and public avowal and semisacred, or bounded knowledge sets. Bruce concludes therefore that "vocations" and "calling" and "speaking the fates" are deeply rooted in the concept. The core meaning of the word seems to include both calling and knowledge.

Etymology is an imprecise art, but it is nevertheless useful in demonstrating how far we have departed from original meanings. The concept was once rich with values, ideals, and sacred tones that were gradually eroded by our naive but growing belief in the efficacy of science. Today, an emphasis on *knowledge* (narrowly and rigorously defined) has overwhelmed the notion of *calling*. Historical studies indicate that the classical normative concept of profession was dominant from at least the Middle Ages to the early nineteenth century. The modern sociological concept began to emerge as early as the late seventeenth century[9] and became dominant by the late nineteenth century.

Elliot[10] and Marshall[11] described the classic professional outlook as one preoccupied with classical education, social and economic independence, high status, and the ability to live a leisured and cultured life. Service was the focus of work; and competition, advertising, and profit were discouraged. As Elliot explained, "for most of those who went into politics or government service, the ideology simply called on them to keep their distance from business."[12]

Law, medicine, and clergy are commonly referred to in studies of these old "status" professions, and much of the research focuses on their development in England. But it is somewhat misleading to think of them as singular and distinct occupations in the sense that we do today. Instead, they represented something like avocations to which broadly educated persons of means applied themselves as their interests, aspirations, and ways of life directed. Moreover, these occupations exhibited internal stratification. For example, in medicine there was the Royal College of Physicians, followed by surgeons and apothecaries. In law there were the lawyers admitted to the bar by Inns of Court (barristers), followed by attorneys, solicitors, and proctors. Only the top ranks of each vocation held professional status, with members of the lower ranks seeking advancement and admittance to the top.

The old professions emphasized social status. They were populated mainly by gentlemen and were considered among the most important and prestigious pursuits in political society. It was believed that this class supplied persons with the best character, classical learning, and wealth.[13]

Wealth was an important aspect of this concept of profession for several reasons. It allowed for greater independence from employers and clients, partisan and economic pressure, and so on. Independence provided essential support for wise judgment and prudent action. Wealth also accorded substantial leisure time for service to the society. Leisure and service, like property and virtue, were inseparable ideas in this context. "The professional man does not work in order to be paid; he is paid in order that he may work."[14] Furthermore, there was a general awareness that wealth tended to tie one's self-interest to broader interests, particularly to national interests and the ways of life engendered therein. Private and public life were connected by communal conceptions of property and citizenship. This helped them steer a middle course between altruism and parochialism. Finally, wealth accorded time for cultivation of character and learned study.

The presumed relationship between virtuous character and learned study were central to the classic normative concept of profession. The two were supposedly mutually reinforcing. For our purposes, the important point is that they were symbolic of a person so thoroughly schooled in his own political culture that he could both sustain and enhance it through his professional work.[15] Ideally, the gentleman embodied all that was noble about his country. Character and learning were therefore considered inseparable criteria for membership in the class and professions. Moreover, character and learning tied the person and the vocation back to a political order—an established way of life. That life entailed significant meaning insofar as one's work contributed to the furtherance of that way of life. A person held high status because he embodied a way of life, not because of the specific job or occupation held.

From our point of view, the classical education of the gentleman involved some interesting and benign paradoxes. In order to teach him about his own culture, he had to learn about others. The study of history, languages, great lives, literature, philosophy, religion, and many other subjects simultaneously highlighted his culture and linked it to others This broad education also enabled him to dabble in a variety of pursuits, including more than one profession. Some gentlemen made important contributions to several fields beyond their main professional identity.[16] Amateur accomplishment was highly regarded. Specialization seemed neither necessary nor desirable.

Broad education played a part in character building—indeed, in maturation and the development of the whole individual, from what we can learn of the products of such education, they emerged more often than not as mature, integrated, and self-aware personalities who were reflective, reflexive, and prudent. They were men who thought and acted with a sense of proportion.[17]

Their education and profession were important articulations of political orthodoxy. Indeed, they were "strategically crafted arguments"[18] providing rationale for why these gentlemen and their professions played leading roles in society. These "arguments" were so deeply embedded in societal structure that few questioned them; the professions were simply accepted as an integral and essential part of political life. The gentleman's life and profession were thus a part of a long and rich political discourse.

Highlighting the Contrasts

Our purpose in this historical review is not to romanticize a concept of profession more appropriate to the times of Sir Thomas More, the estimable "man for all seasons." Whatever that conception's merits might be, we would not wish to return to days when professions were the birthright of a leisured class of gentlemen. That kind of blatant, class-bound elitism is unacceptable in today's world (though some would argue the professions of today are no less elitist, simply more subtly based on "merit" than class). Our aim is to contrast the normative nature of the classical concept with the rather sterile and misleading sociological model and in the process identify some directions to take in constructing a normative model appropriate to the present day.

Today, the faith in reason engendered by the Enlightenment has run to its logical extreme. The resulting explosion of information, education, and technology has led to a contemporary cast of mind and a corpus of theory and knowledge built on technical and disciplinary specialization. Unfortunately, we are no longer concerned about the embodiment of general political culture and knowledge in our professionals. Instead, we value a secularized training founded on scientific/analytic proof or estimation and amenable to organizational routinization. In contrast with the classic professions, modern professions lack the ability to maintain a sense of proportion and direction for themselves that serves the good of the greater society. Today's professionals are trained in specific "scientific knowledge" and skills that overshadow concern for imparting such ephemeral things as social responsibility, general cultural values, norms of political culture, virtue, or good judgment.

The linkage between a profession, the meaning of the profession for the individual and for a way of life, is gone, and this creates grave doubts about the centrality of professions to the structure and functioning of society. Moreover, this substantial change in the foundation and structure of our knowledge is marked by attention to creating analytically clear boundaries that preserve zones of discretion and behavior.[19] Specialized knowledge then becomes a form of property for a profession, and professional responsibility focuses on maintaining exclusive control over that property.[20] The connection between private and public matters is greatly weakened in the process. Because specialized knowledge rests on claims of scientific foundation, methodological standards overshadow ethical standards. Ethical standards are pushed to the margins, attending mainly to definitions of inappropriate behavior. This highlights the boundaries of a profession, but detracts attention from its positive uses of discretion. We watch for sins of commission and tend to ignore sins of omission. Public life and vision suffer accordingly.

These trends in modern professions contribute to the erosion of public philosophy and feed extreme forms of economic individualism that lead to institutional and societal drift and unconstrained technicism.[21] With the weakening of any integrative public vision, the professions descend into directionless practices that emphasize nothing more than pursuit of narrowly conceived self-interest. The sense that professions constitute strategically crafted arguments about appropriate political institutions and processes is lost in a maze of calculative, technical rationality that seeks legitimacy in varying degrees of methodological precision. Those negative characteristics of the contemporary professions that theorists such as Mosher criticize become increasingly pronounced as the decline continues.[22]

Individual and collective strategies for private, economic advantage stifle attention to higher public values, and the role of professions in political life comes to be seen as "just one more interest group." Thus it is increasingly true that professions such as law and medicine are better characterized as "business" professions than as "public" ones. There was a time when such a characterization would have been insulting. Correspondingly, there was a time when these professions had widespread respect. No more. The volume of malpractice suits against medical doctors is but one doleful reminder of the decline.

Regardless of what we think of these developments in professions, we cannot abide the same for public administration. The erosion of confidence and legitimacy in governing institutions cuts into the heart of the polity and its capacity for peaceful and orderly change; it enervates its capacity to better the collective lives of its citizens. And yet this is inevitable unless we develop a normatively grounded, supervening profession of public administration, one in which the values of service and responsibility to society are embodied in the mature professionals of which it is comprised.[23]

Implications for Public Administration and Governance

As American public administration began the process of self-consciously defining itself at the turn of the century, an error of colossal proportions was made in trying to follow the headlong rush of other professions (extant and emergent) to embrace science. It was probably inevitable given the inextricable ties of public administration with the Progressive and Urban Reform movements.

American reformers were belated but true children of the Enlightenment. Rationality and morality seemed to them to be bound together in beneficent symbiosis. They not only believed rationality would answer all questions but that it also grounded morality. They felt morality was doubly assured because it could be created by education. As they saw it, an educated person could reason and thus come unambiguously to the "best" method to do anything—the right course of action. But the mounting complexities of modern and industrial America necessitated an amendment to the simple faith in education that sustained the Jeffersonian democratic ideal. Now the reformers were forced to an amendment to their faith that held that the *more* education and the *more* scientific expertise one had, the better one could ascertain the "best" method or course of action.

We do not mean to belittle the reformers. Their fervent belief in science and progress enabled them to challenge old institutions and create new ones. They believed they could ground key institutions in science, rather than superstitions, myths, or tired traditions. Rationality, they were certain, would provide answers that could restructure and direct society. It followed that they would believe that experts, those with the requisite education, should lead. Questions of policy, they were certain, could be answered by positivist methods rather than by politics, the antithesis of reason in their eyes. If positivism was applied universally, they were convinced everyone would be better off. The public interest could then be determined and achieved.

And as they applied their science to the tasks of making steel, running railroads, building urban infrastructure, and manufacturing autos, their faith in science was reinforced. Life seemed to improve in quantum leaps. It was only natural that the "coulds" and "woulds" of lecture halls and the campaign trail easily became "shoulds." Science, it seemed, not only indicated what could be done, it mandated what *should* be done.

Administration from this perspective should be nothing less than the clear-headed, no-nonsense direction of the state by experts. It was not just coincidence that political science and management science came into existence in this heady atmosphere—and the names were not meant to connote merely the scientific study of these subjects, but their practice as well. Scientific experts gained legitimacy as they increased their education. They were perceived as "objective," and therefore unswayed by individual and group considerations that "infected" politics.

There thus developed a general but confused belief in an objectivity that transcended political life. The politics/administration dichotomy was founded on that belief. Despite decades of academic critiques of that dichotomy, we still find public administrators trying to act out role behavior based on it—the administrator as objective actor, the embodiment of neutral competence. Outside administration, the belief in an objectivity that transcends politics has led to a kind of politics/profession dichotomy on much the same naive grounds. Professional decisions in many fields are held to be above or beyond "merely political" decisions.

The potential for professions constituting strategically crafted arguments about appropriate political institutions and processes is lost in a maze of calculative, technical rationality. As Stone points out,[24] it does not matter whether such rationality proceeds from rational comprehensiveness or successive limited comparison.[25] They both ignore the political values and arguments inherent in their approaches, seeking instead for legitimacy in differing forms of methodological proof. The crisis of legitimacy that public administrators and other professionals now experience flows directly from their studied ignorance of this point.

Professionals in the modern sociological mode are trained to fit into organizations and bureaucracies. They encourage as well as follow the tilt toward the elaboration of formal, top-down, "scientific" management systems. Indeed, one of the primary indications of career advancement in "established" modern professions is elevation in hierarchical organizations to management ranks. Compared to the explicit linkage to politics in the classical professions, this is a dangerous form of sublimated politics. Professional associations and employing organizations lose sight of the consequences of their actions for higher politics (at the level of polity and society) with itstroubling paradoxes and "wicked" problems.[26] In fact, modern professionals tend to deny their political roles altogether. Accordingly, they lose sight of proportion, balance, moderation, and sense of place. Their way of life is no longer rooted in a sense of concern for the political order and therefore devolves into the unhealthy parochialism we refer to as bureaucratic or organizational politics or interest-group liberalism.

This negative view of politics has been consistent since the reform era. Politics was seen by the nascent profession of public administration as an unfortunate intrusion into the domain of rationality. Politics had to be constrained or the public interest could not be achieved. This mode of thinking swept the field of all alternatives. Management was viewed as a potent tool of science for expert administration. When coupled with the morality of reform, its appeal was irresistible to those who wished to create a profession of public administration. Management offered a set of universal principles for directing organizations; a tool they claimed was neither culturally biased nor time bound.

In retrospect, it must have been easy to believe that cities, states, and even the national government could be managed or administered just as "scientifically" as they believed corporations were. To protect "scientific" managers—these new professionals—from illegitimate political interference, civil service systems had to be created. Managers required tenure in their careers that would put them beyond removal for "purely political reasons."

This innocently idyllic picture could not long withstand confrontation with reality. What early reformers had assumed to be science could not pass muster as a more sophisticated understanding of science developed.[27] The notion of universal management principles thus proved a chimera; "government was different" from business, and administration could not be separated from politics.[28] But just what kinds of professional role behaviors would be appropriate for public administrators under these changed conditions and perceptions was unclear.

Saying that the modern concept of profession had negative implications for developing a normatively based profession of public administration is not to say that we cannot and should not build such a profession. If we can clarify our thinking on professionalism, it might yet be possible to establish an appropriate normative foundation.

A Second Diagnosis of "The Professionalism Problem"

Before working on the establishment of a normative grounding for professionalism, we need to reaffirm that professionalism is part of the solution, not the problem, as some would seem to suggest. There is a considerable literature in public administration that worries about the spread of professionalism and its impact on the democratic norms of public employees.[29]

Though there is little agreement on a definition of professionalism, there ironically is considerable agreement that the American workforce in general, and the public-sector workforce in particular, is increasingly dominated by it.[30] Mosher's treatment is typical.[31] His concern is that professionals, instead of being elected, are placed in key positions because of their needed skills. Their growing influence, he feels, is therefore a problem for representative government. He also notes that they come to government with certain biases and that these may warp their perceptions of public wants and needs. As he colorfully puts it: "Except for those professionals who grow beyond their field, the real world is seen as by a submariner through a periscope whose direction is fixed and immutable."[32] Mosher also worries that the "basic drive of every profession" is "self-government in deciding policies, criteria, and standards for employment and advancement" and that this will result in a "delegation of real personnel authority ... to the professions and professionals themselves."[33]

Although there is plenty to worry about in the professionalization of key positions, our worries need to be kept in perspective. After all, one can and should also worry about the presumed antithesis, that is, deprofessionalization and creeping "managerialism," which, according to some, impoverishes pluralism, vitiates strong autonomous sources of professional judgment, and reduces professions to mere instruments of the state.[34]

Mosher's concerns make better sense at the level of organizational/institutional analysis than they do at the level of polity and governance. Indeed, he describes his analysis as "organizational" and speaks cogently of the trichotomy of organizational control: "management, workers, and professionals."[35] In organizational/institutional analysis one can clearly trace the effects and implications of the "periscope view." Even here, however, it is simply not clear whether the concern is borne out by empirical findings. Several empirically based studies have searched for correlations between degrees of professionalism in public administration and such variables as negativeness toward politics and citizen participation (both deemed relevant concerns by Mosher).[36] Unfortunately for the hypotheses suggested by Mosher and others, the studies came up relatively empty, with largely negative correlations.[37]

The problems of those concerned with the impact of professionalism on representative government go beyond a misguided choice in their level of analysis. They extend to conceptual and definitional problems. Again, Mosher set the tone and the terms of the discussion by what he describes as a "liberal" definition of profession: "1. a reasonably clear-cut occupational field, 2. which ordinarily requires higher education at least through the bachelor's level, and 3. which offers a lifetime career to its members."[38] This definition is so incredibly broad it encompasses most college graduates (with the possible exception of English majors) who can hold a job for any duration.

The data sources Mosher used further cloud the issue. He draws on the U.S. census and bases much of what he has to say on figures concerning "professional, technical and kindred workers." Mosher admits that this includes occupations that "some might not consider professional," such as applied scientists, athletic coaches, embalmers, writers, artists, and entertainers. Yet we find it incredible that his definition excludes others that might be considered professional, including all those who describe themselves as managers, officials, proprietors (of whom governments employed some 1,170,000 in 1978), military officers, and police.[39]

Our purpose here is not to dismiss the concern raised by Mosher and many others about the professionalization of government. Instead, we mean to suggest that this concern needs to be treated cautiously and subjected to more thorough examination. Little is gained by using extremely broad definitions of a profession that make a problem seem more serious than it may in fact be. Nor do we shed much light by raising concerns at the governmentwide level of analysis but then shifting to the organizational level, where we can make arguments or uncover findings more suited to the alarms raised in part by a broad definition. Clearly occupations that meet more stringently and thoroughly defined criteria will constitute a significant concern, especially at an organizational/institutional level of analysis. But how great an overall threat they pose to representative government is by no means as clear as some writers have been suggesting.

Focusing on the Right Problem

The more pressing problem for public administration is a lack of a properly conceptualized professionalism that is normatively grounded. Much of what Mosher has laid before us is relevant, but for altogether different reasons than he suggests. It is indeed true that at all levels of government there is an incredible and growing occupational and professional diversity, and this does create problems at the organizational level. But the greater problem of professionalism is its lack of a legitimating normative foundation, one that persons moving out of their occupational specialties or original professions can use as the basis for their reflexivity and growth as agential leaders as they move into administrative positions.

American public administration suffers because we do not see administration as a calling distinct from substantive occupations and professions. We see it as simply "being boss" or "being in charge." Thus we take persons scientifically trained in their specialty or profession, successful and happy in their practice, and esteemed by their peers and then make them and everyone else miserable by promoting them to managerial or administrative positions with little or no preparation. In 1988, for example, 53 percent of the Senior Executive Service was drawn from "specialist professions," 41 percent of which came from three areas—engineering, law, and science. About 26 percent of the appointees in 1986, and 15 percent in 1987, had no training or development activity in the five years before appointment to prepare them for executive responsibilities.

Not only do individuals pay a high price, but the consequences for the institutions to which they belong can be serious. Everyone loses because of our assumptions (1) that the most important thing to have is the scientifically based, specialized, occupational or professional training; and (2) that supervising, managing, administering is something one can just "pick up" if one has the other.

If, as we believe, this is the principal pathology of American management, then the problems associated with it are increased exponentially in the public sector. Americans, even those who spend a career in the public service, find it difficult to grasp that administering in the public sector means that they do not operate in a monocentric and hierarchical system of power presumed to be typical of the corporation. The public sector involves multiple centers of responsibility and polycentric power, as required under the Constitution. Perhaps even more confusing and frustrating is the fact that public administrators are expected to operate in both simultaneously; or in one system (hierarchical and monocentric) early in their careers, only to find that expectations, demands, and rules change on them unannounced as they advance in their careers. An Oliver North has hierarchy and chain of command drummed into him during at least half or more of his career, only to find that the concept is too simplistic and is of little utility in guiding actions at higher levels.[40] The results, as Colonel North is now painfully aware, can be disastrous.

There may not be a cure for this American managerial disease. If such a cure is to be found, however, it will not come from trying to reverse our cultural proclivity for science and technicism. It has to be found in our grasping the fundamental nature and complexity of governance as a distinct moral endeavor.[41] We must recognize that public administration demands normatively grounded understanding and judgment. Only then may we be able to conceptualize public administration as a follow-on or supervening profession.

Dynamics of Professionalism in Complex Government

Yet, even if we speak of a normatively grounded supervening profession, the public administration comprises a universe too vast, heterogeneous, and complex to allow it to be encompassed within one profession with any kind of corporateness.[42] But those who therefore conclude that a profession of public administration is impossible need to give more attention to the way professionalism plays out in big government.

It is important to understand that not everyone in government must belong to the administrative profession or be socialized to the same degree in order for that profession to have significant normative impact. The military segment of public administration numbers 1.2 million men and women. Only a segment of the military could meet Huntington's definition of a profession: most of the officer corps and significant parts of the senior noncommissioned officers. Yet the military qualifies as a profession by definition. Thus it is nonsense to say that the public administration can never become a profession because of its size and diversity. Not everyone in the public administration has to meet Huntington's definition of a profession in order for one to develop and flourish.

Following James D. Thompson, we think that most social constructs of intended rationality (SCIRs, e.g., bureaucracies, organizations, institutions, agencies)[43] have three discernible levels: technical, managerial, and institutional.[44]

These levels, which differentiate responsibility and role behavior, also have a rough correspondence to "three worlds of public service occupations" described by Wolf and Bacher—the job, the career, and the vocation.[45] They describe these three "worlds" as social realities experienced by persons from many occupations in the societal labor force into the field of public administration.[46]

The world of a "job" is experienced as a "9-to-5" means to economic success and security. The self is defined outside the job, and the job is merely a means to that end.

The world of the "career" is a social reality in which the self is developed within the occupation. The individual finds self-identity in growing competence, social standing, prestige, and responsibility within the career.

The social reality of "vocation" is one experienced as a "calling," something transpersonal in which the individual finds self-fulfillment in contributing to the common good and in responding to a "sense of values and beliefs outside oneself."

Juxtaposing Thompson's three levels of responsibility with Wolf and Bacher's three worlds reveals a rough but natural correspondence. Persons entering the public service do so with a wide variety of outlooks, preparation, skills, and motivation, but the greatest proportion of them will enter at the lower technical level. At least initially, they will have less intense commitment and connections to their work, or in keeping with the modern concept of professionalism they may be committed, but to a narrowly defined, scientific or technologically based professional or occupational specialty—one without a transcendent sense or social responsibility. The job will more often be viewed as instrumental to acquiring the vast array of material things consumer capitalism offers. This is true whether they are trained as lawyers or secretaries.

There are, no doubt, a significant number of persons in entry-level cohorts who are highly idealistic about their scientifically based profession and its potential contributions to society. If we follow any entering cohort for five to ten years, however, we begin to see them "sort out" and (given the nature of professions today) their idealism drain away. Some will continue in the world of the job, while others will begin to perceive of and experience their work as a career—the pursuit of ambition without collective purpose. This latter group is eventually recruited into positions at the management level. They no longer will be involved so directly in the work of the SCIR. Instead, their positions will entail the coordination of *other* persons engaged in the work of the SCIR. For some, this creates great disillusionment and a crisis of identity, confidence, and career. Others who find sufficient challenge or fulfillment of ideals may begin to experience their work in yet a different way—as a vocation (or calling). Normatively their numbers could be expected to comprise the largest proportion of the cohort moving into the institutional levels of SCIRs. These persons would naturally become less mobile and develop stronger identities within the SCIRs to which they belong. Our current "quiet crisis" in the federal service is in large part reflective of the fact that, for a variety of reasons, fewer and fewer persons reaching the final stages of their career have been able to view what they do as a calling.[47]

None of the above is meant to suggest that dedication and calling are qualities intrinsic to those found at the institutional level; we are speaking of functional segregation and valences here, not of individuals or innate qualities. Most important, we would argue that all three of the social realities experienced are interrelated and have an impact on one another. The values and behavior of professionals who experience their occupation as a vocation will set the tone and conditions for those experiencing the world of work as careers or jobs. The levels of SCIRs and the social realities of work are also interrelated because of the necessary mobility and permeability between them. A significant number of each cohort will move from one to another.

We have previously indicated that we think a meaningful conception of a public administration profession must reestablish the linkage between the special knowledge or expertise of the profession and the notion of calling and the responsibility to serve society. The special knowledge of how to administer in a public context of polycentric power accumulates as a cohort moves through Thompson's layers from the technical to the institutional. At least it would do so if our political system were not in its current state of "quiet crisis."

The technoscience or other specialized knowledge of traditional professions should, in the normal course of events, become less and less useful to persons as they move into the managerial and institutional levels of SCIRs. More general and intuitive wisdom about people and the political system becomes progressively more important. The fact that Americans as a people have failed to recognize this makes it no less a necessity. It is central to an effective system of governance.

Given the dynamics between SCIRs and professionalism sketched above, the size and diversity of public administration is not an insurmountable obstacle to the development of a supervening profession. One need only examine the variety of doctors and related health-care occupations or professions, or lawyers, or soldiers and their amazingly esoteric specializations to see that incredible ranges of specialization and circumstances of practice did not prevent the development of professions in those fields.

Recall also that our historical analysis revealed several status levels in the "old" or classical professions. One can also readily see that only a fraction of our military, our legal system, and our health-care system consists of professionals by Huntington's definition. Yet those significant or "strategic" professional fractions have tremendous normative implications and practical consequences for these fields—implications and consequences out of all proportion to their numbers. We submit therefore that a normatively based supervening profession of public administration is possible and need not include everyone whose salary is paid from the treasury, nor need they share the same level of professional commitment.

Normative Foundations: Constitutional Governance

THE FOUNDERS AND THE PROFESSIONS

The Founders were largely influenced by the classical orientation to professions. Most were considered gentlemen, dabbled in more than one profession, and held political and administrative office. Most received classical education and paid great attention to status, honor, and character. Good character was the central concern of early American professions, and this carried over into government employment. "Fitness of character" was the first criterion for appointments to office in the founding period.[48] Competence and experience were secondary in comparison, though certainly not considered unimportant.

There was a corresponding attachment to public service and public trust. The Founders devoted their lives to public endeavors. Their disdain for parties and factions reflected their concern for independent judgment. Most of the Founders either inherited enough wealth and estate to maintain substantial independence from compromising interests or worked in lucrative professional practices and businesses until they achieved such independence. Their constitutional design reflects an effort to nurture independent judgment in public office. Separation of powers, checks and balances, filtered elections, and appointments during good behavior exemplify their concern.

Despite this classic orientation, the Founders lived at a crossroads of history that compelled many of them to recognize substantial changes in ways of living, working, and thinking. First, and most significantly, they were constructing a new regime, and on a basis quite different from their European counterparts. The organic constitutions of Europe, with their traditional classes and governing institutions, could not be mirrored in the United States. Our ways of life had yet to develop and mature. Our direction of development clearly indicated moves toward greater equality, individualism, and a conception of liberty cut loose from the Old World restraints of duty and public service.

Second, important changes were occurring in Western thought concerning commerce, industry, science, and innovation. Business was enjoying elevation in status. Technical innovation was changing daily life. Political economy was emerging as a new and vitally important field of study.

These circumstances gave great impetus to occupational specialization and technical innovation. Trades and other occupations not previously considered professions were gaining in prestige. The hierarchies in the old professions were being leveled or broken up. Specialization and innovation made technical training necessary. The benefits of such training were becoming more apparent, particularly in military, medical, and financial affairs. A classical education was no longer sufficient by itself, and in some cases seemed entirely inappropriate. Organization, system, and calculative detail became necessary elements of social and political structure.

Hamilton as Exemplar of Classical and Modern Fusion

The Founders contributed to these changes, and yet displayed ambivalence and restraint in the process. They stood with one foot in the Old World and the other in the New. Among them, Alexander Hamilton exemplified the resulting fusion in some ways that are instructive for modern professionalism in public administration.

Hamilton was one of a few Founders who understood the importance of technical expertise in the changing world. He developed specialized knowledge and discipline in military affairs, finance, economics, and public management. He applied this knowledge as a military officer in the new Revolutionary War and later as politician and administrator under the new Constitution.[49] His reports on public credit, banking and finance, and mixed economies reflected state-of-the-art expertise that mystified most people at the time. He used Prussian military experts to train troops during the war. He urged the creation of a professional diplomatic corps, military schools, and a national university that would train people for public service. He also expressed the desire to write a treatise on public administration and no doubt would have done so had he lived longer. He clearly advocated self-aware public administration.

In his reports to Congress, Hamilton also expressed a desire to see rapid development of specialized trades and occupations. He wanted a cadre of engineers, inventors, tradesmen, scientists, and businessmen who could build an innovative and self-sufficient political economy. Hamilton was an ardent exponent of general commercial development and technical innovation. In these things he clearly demonstrated enthusiasm for a new and modern world, one that certainly involved specialized occupations and professions.

Like many of his counterparts, however, Hamilton also demonstrated a strong devotion to the norms of classical professionalism. He attended to classical learning as well as technical expertise. He dabbled in many different occupations and avocations and made significant contributions to their development. More significantly, he embodied a commitment to public service. He sought wealth and leisure in order to work and serve. His career in public service reflected more a calling than an inducements/contributions contract.

Hamilton's administrative philosophy employed the norms of classical professionalism as a base from which his more modern orientation proceeded. For example, he tried to use the emerging business mentality in Americans for public benefit in much the same manner as the mentality of the landed gentry had been cultivated for public service in Europe. Wealthy businessmen had vested interests in a stable and prosperous political economy much like landed gentry. Hamilton sought to broaden their self-interest to accommodate public interests.

Where wealth failed to provide for independent judgment and action, Hamilton (and Madison) strove to guarantee it through constitutional structure. He believed judicial independence and review (*Federalist* No. 78), and executive energy (single heads of office, long duration in office, competent powers, and adequate compensation) would greatly enhance and protect wise judgment and action in government (*Federalist* No. 72). This belief was, of course, buttressed by the assumption that classical learning and inculcation of character or public virtue would continue alongside the growing interest in specialized training and occupations. This was not an unreasonable assumption. Elliot, Calhoun, and Geison indicated that, as the new professions emerged in the nineteenth century,[50] their leaders emulated the old professions' concern for classical learning. Occupational groups seeking professional status made classical education a prerequisite.

This orientation dissipated in the mid-nineteenth century, in part because educational disciplines began to specialize and concentrate on methodological purity. Positivistic norms led to a rejection of old ways of thinking and learning. Learning moved away from cultural embodiment and wisdom and toward austere theoretical consistency and technical analysis of data.

As indicated earlier, these modern developments impair our praxis because they impair our judgment. Praxis based on scientific criteria seeks to make good decisions self-evident through the accumulation of data. Methodology becomes central, while politics comes to be seen as an obstacle—it is "irrational" and narrowly "self-interested."

Jurisprudential Praxis

The Founders, and Hamilton especially, based their praxis on what can be described as a broad jurisprudential approach. That is, they stressed the ability to make good judgments in a legal context about things that remain problematic, not self-evident. They held to the idea that paradoxes and dilemmas characterize much of political and administrative life. These, they believed, were perennial, enduring, and perhaps subject to amelioration but seldom to final solutions.

Legal education and legal processes during the founding period reflected the orientation of classical professionalism. Law was not a narrow, technical subject, but constituted a legitimating focal point for moral and political philosophy, empirical enquiry, and reasoned persuasion in governance. Legal reasoning focused the classical concern for character, learning, and culture on questions pertaining to governance as a whole, not simply adjudication. Legal reasoning and process were understood as a basic and legitimate means of applying enduring values (that shape fundamentally our ways of living) to changing times.[51]

The common law embodied these jurisprudential dynamics. Under this system, perhaps the most striking characteristic of English settlements, law was made in incremental stages by judges utilizing juries to apply enduring values in formulating resolutions of disputes. These values were thus adjusted to changing times but always according to the customs and traditions of the people. The early English kings astutely used their unique system to unify England. The system clearly tied the law to the life and values of their people.

The efficacy of the common law and its jurisprudential qualities can be seen in the early American states. One observer, for example, has noted that the "remarkable similarity that is found among the various state constitutions" is in great part a result of "Blackstone-trained lawyers."[52] It was, of course, Blackstone who delivered the first university lectures on the common law, and these were later collected into his famous commentaries. The lectures were laced with lessons about government and its structure. A common-law attorney was indeed more than a legal technician armed with specialized knowledge and a license from the state. Blackstone eloquently expressed it in the following words: 'For I think it an undeniable position, that a competent knowledge of the laws of that society in which we live, is the proper accomplishments of every gentleman and scholar; a highly useful, I had almost said essential, part of a liberal and polite education."[53]

Jurisprudential praxis was especially important to the Founders because they could not build on the kind of organic or traditional constitution found in Europe. Instead, the Founders' Constitution was an abstract paper creation that could at best embody some general principles, values, and structures from which a proper way of life could emerge and evolve. The Founders had differing visions about proper ways of living, but they were unanimous in their support of a legal framework within which these political visions should be developed. Wisdom and judgment, along with ideology and technology, were mediated through constitutive legal process.

Hamilton's report and administrative actions were rooted in this jurisprudential orientation. His encouragement of occupations, specialization, innovation, technical expertise, and economic development were carefully couched in terms of public benefit and constitutional propriety. They flowed from his assessment of an emerging political character in the people and nation and from the extrapolation and projection of latent attributes into a sense of real potential. He merged legal and political feasibility with community planning and development. In all this, he applied the law, with its attendant values and processes, as a legitimating tool. His approach to legal interpretation and to the role of law in general were tied to his concern for building and sustaining a great political culture. His sense of profession was rooted in the same milieu.

A PROFESSION CONSISTENT WITH OUR FOUNDATION

The Founding Fathers lived their praxis in a world of transition from the classical normative conception of profession to the modern sociological conception. Many, like Hamilton, sought to fuse elements of both. The system they conceived and established might function better if the profession of public administration we develop is based on the better elements of both conceptions.

As a field, we are still establishing our origins. We use the term "establishing" advisedly. There is ample evidence that we founded public administration as a self-conscious field in the business and scientific ethos of the Progressive reform era simply because we did not realize the significance of earlier origins at the very founding of our nation-state.[54] These could have, and can today, provide a solid basis for refounding the field and a normative-based profession. The legitimacy problems inherent in Progressive dogma have led many in the field to search for better grounding. It is still possible, therefore, to establish our professional origins with an altogether different and more appropriate grounding.

As part of that grounding, the public administration should present itself as a profession devoted to (1) maintaining those constitutional processes that result in viable policies (a constitutional balance wheel) and (2) providing the critical impetus in those processes that lead to the public interest being defined as broadly as possible (a constitutional mainspring). It should be a profession, therefore, that finds its raison d'être in sustaining the capacity of our political system to act and more significantly to govern.

That requires the ability to administer in a political and governmental context where power is polycentric and responsibility is diffuse, an ability to act as an agent for multiple principals. An agent for multiple principals is left with considerable discretion that cannot be contracted or specified to a degree that will satisfy all (or perhaps any) of the principals. That discretion must in large part be constrained or guided by normative grounding—by internalized norms that legitimate such discretion.

This is where jurisprudential praxis must supplant scientific and technical expertise. Public administrators must here demonstrate the ability to relate enduring, legitimizing values to specific and often-changing decision contexts. They must make decisions that uphold and nurture the polymorphous constitutional framework as well as the public interest. A legion of business executives who have encountered great difficulties while holding public office have testified to the importance of such competence.[55] We need to avoid the trap of scientism and technicism by giving new emphasis to the calling of our profession to norms of stewardship, agential leadership, and constitutional prudence.[56]

A profession grounded in this jurisprudential perspective would refrain from claiming specialized knowledge and expertise as the primary basis for independent judgment and action. Constitutional prudence, agential leadership, stewardship, and commitment to public interest are overtly political justifications for power. They are therefore also problematic—subject to continual political debate and strategically crafted argument.[57]

A normatively based, supervening profession of this sort obviously has important implications for teaching and research in public administration, our professional associations, and our educational curricula. A detailed analysis of these goes beyond the scope of this chapter, but some general points will indicate appropriate directions of development.

The interests promoted by any formal professional association should relate to legitimating the profession's discretionary role in governance on political rather than scientific premises. The profession should emphasize the responsible use of discretion and avoid the tendency toward self-serving guild protectionism. The tendency of other modern professions to make exclusive claims over a specific methodology or corpus of theory and knowledge are inappropriate for public administrators. Instead, we should favor methodological diversity and the cultivation of wisdom and prudence in decision making. The paradoxes and dilemmas of political life are perennial and are not subject to singular interpretation or final resolution.

Nor should the education and training of public administrators simply be multidisciplinary. They must learn to integrate multidisciplinary knowledge and bring it to bear on behalf of political/administrative purposes and do so within varying forms of political identity—national, state, and local.

Educational curricula should therefore shift primary emphasis to ethicist-based learning, to steeping administrators in subjects rich with the values on which our political communities and society rest.

Education and training must also be reintegrated in the context of law. Not so much in technical legal training currently emphasized in law schools, but in its broader jurisdictional aspects. Public administrators must learn to approach the law as the point at which abstract but profound regime values and cultural knowledge are focused on specific situations demanding concrete decisions. Therein lies the path to legitimacy for public administration.

Conclusion

This chapter has tried to sketch the basics for a normatively grounded public administration profession, one that can capture the loyalties and provide values for persons already trained in a technically based profession or specialized occupation, yet who have the potential or need to broaden that background and enter the reality of public vocation—a calling to public service. We think this is crucial for a variety of reasons, but mostly because only a normatively grounded professionalism—one that clearly manifests a sense of societal responsibility reflected in principled behavior—will result in professional integrity and efficacy and in an accorded legitimacy necessary to meet the challenges inherent in governance. The profundity of these challenges necessitates a search for what Walter Lippmann called "the public philosophy."[58] A public without a public philosophy can provide little if any guidance to meeting these challenges, but a public administration steeped in a public philosophy inspires hope in the competence and fairness of our political system. That is surely reason to begin anew the task of constructing a theory of public administration in American government.

Notes

1. Richard L. Schott, "Public Administration as Profession: Problems and Prospects," *Public Administration Review* 36, no. 3 (May/June 1976): 253–59.

2. Gary Wamsley, "The Social Construction of Agency," paper presented at the annual meeting of the American Political Science Association, Atlanta, Ga., 31 August–4 September 1989.

3. Magali Sarfatti Larson, *The Rise of Professionalism: A Sociological Analysis* (Berkeley: University of California Press, 1977).

4. Howard M. Vollmer and Donald L. Mills, *Professionalization* (Englewood Cliffs, N.J.: Prentice Hall, 1966).

5. Alfred Diamant, "The Bureaucratic Model: Max Weber, Rediscovered,

Reformed." Mimeographed, n.d.

6. Samuel Huntington, *The Soldier and the State: The Theory of Politics of Civil/Military Relations* (New York: Vintage Books, 1957).

7. Ray Bruce, correspondence with the authors, 1988.

8. Mario Pei, *The Families of Words* (New York: St. Martin's Press, 1962).

9. Geoffrey S. Holmes, *Augustan England: Professions, State and Society* (London: Allen and Unwin, 1982).

10. Philip Elliot, *The Sociology of the Professions* (New York: Herder and Herder, 1972).

11. T.H. Marshall. "The Recent History of Professionalism in Relation to Social Structure and Policy," *Canadian Journal of Economics and Political Science* 5 (1939), 325–40.

12. Elliot, *Sociology of the Professions*, 53.

13. Daniel H. Calhoun, *Professional Lives in America: Structure and Aspiration, 1750–1850* (Cambridge: Harvard University Press, 1965); Elliot, *Sociology of the Professions*; Erwin C. Hargrove, *Professional Roles in Society and Government: The English Case* (Beverly Hills: Sage, 1972); Holmes, *Augustan England*; W.J. Reader, *Professional Men: The Rise of the Professional Classes in Nineteenth-Century England* (New York: Basic Books, 1966).

14. Marshall, "History of Professionalism," 325.

15. Elliot, *Sociology of the Professions*, 32.

16. Ibid., 21–22.

17. David K. Hart, "The Honorable Bureaucrat among the Philistines: A Reply to Ethical Discourse in Public Administration," *Administration and Society* 15, no. 1 (1988): 43–48; and J. Budziszewski, *The Resurrection of Nature: Political Theory and Human Character* (Ithaca: Cornell University Press, 1986).

18. Deborah A. Stone, *Policy Paradox and Political Reason* (Glenview, Ill.: Scott, Foresman, 1988).

19. Elliot, *Sociology of the Professions*, 16; and Gerald L. Geison, *Professions and Professional Ideologies in American* (Chapel Hill: University of North Carolina Press, 1983).

20. Larson, *Rise of Professionalism*, xvi.

21. Theodore Lowi, *The End of Liberalism: Ideology, Policy and the Crisis of Public Authority* (New York: Norton, 1979); Robert N. Bellah et al., *Habits of the Heart: Individualism and Commitment in American Life* (New York: Harper & Row, 1985); Orion F. White, Jr., and Cynthia J. McSwain, "The Phoenix Project: Raising Public Administration from the Ashes of the Past," in *Images and Identities in Public Administration*, ed. Henry D. Kass and Bayard L. Catron (Newbury Park, Calif.: Sage, 1990), 23–59; and Lauren A. Wollan "Lawyers in Government: The Most Serviceable Instruments of Authority," *Public Administration Review* 38, no. 2 (1978): 115–22.

22. Frederick C. Mosher, "Professions in Public Service," *Public Administration Review* 39, no. 2 (March/April 1978): 121–26.

23. William M. Sullivan, *Reconstructing Public Philosophy* (Berkeley: University of California Press, 1982), and George Will, *Statecraft as Soulcraft: What Government Does* (New York: Simon and Schuster, 1983).

24. Stone, *Policy Paradox*.

25. Charles E. Lindblom, "The Science of Muddling Through," *Public Ad-

ministration Review 19 (Spring 1959): 79–86.

26. Michael M. Harmon and Richard T. Mayer, *Organization Theory and Public Administration* (Boston and Toronto: Little, Brown, 1986).

27. Herbert A. Simon, "The Proverbs of Public Administration," *Public Administration Review* 6, no. 4 (1946): 53.

28. Paul Appleby, *Big Democracy* (New York: Knopf, 1945).

29. Robert L. Wynia, "Executive Development in Federal Government," *Public Administration Review* 32 (July/August 1974); James Thompson, *Organizations in Action* (New York: McGraw-Hill, 1979); Stephen M. Neuse, "Citizenship Participation: Variations in Bureaucratic Attitudes," *Midwest Review of Public Administration* 14 (December 1980): 252–69; Frederick C. Mosher, *Democracy and the Public Service* (New York: Oxford University Press, 1968); Mosher, "Professions in Public Services."

30. See, among others, Mosher, *Democracy and the Public Service;* and Charles Levine with Rosslyn S. Kleeman, "The Quiet Crisis of the Civil Service: The Federal Personnel System at the Crossroads," Occasional Paper (Washington, D.C.: National Academy of Public Administration, 1986).

31. Mosher, "Professions in Public Sector."

32. Mosher, 1978, 108.

33. Ibid., 124.

34. Curtis Ventriss and Helen J. Muller, *Public Health in a Retrenchment Era: An Alternative to Managerialism* (Albany: State University of New York Press, 1985); William G. Scott and David K. Hart, *Organizational America* (Boston: Houghton Mifflin, 1979); Lauren A. Wollan, "Lawyers in Government: The Most Serviceable Instruments of Authority," *Public Administration Review* 38, no. 2 (March/April 1978): 115–22.

35. Mosher, "Professions in Public Service," 111.

36. Ibid., 108–9.

37. Thompson, *Organizations in Action;* Neuse, "Citizenship Participation"; Gregory Streib, "Professionalism in Public Administration: Does It Really Pose a Threat to Democracy?" Paper prepared for the 1985 meeting of the American Society for Public Administration, Indianapolis.

38. Mosher, "Professions in Public Service," 106.

39. Ibid., 199n.

40. Ben Bradlee, Jr., *Guts and Glory: The Rise and Fall of Oliver North* (New York: Fine, 1988).

41. Hart, "The Honorable Bureaucrat."

42. The combined federal workforce as of 1992 numbered around 4.3 million; unformed armed services, 1.2 million; postal workers, about 792,000; and the legislative and judicial branches, about 67,000. The executive branch, including civilian employees of the Department of Defense, employed over 3 million (DOD nonuniformed employees accounted for 37 percent, or 1.1 million, of these). Of the 3 million paid civilian employees of the federal government, approximately 2 million in professional, administrative, technical, and clerical occupations, came under the General Schedule pay and classification system. U.S. Department of Commerce, *Statistical Abstract of the United States 1994* (Washington, D.C.: U.S. Government Printing Office, 1994).

43. SCIR is meant to refer without specificity to either bureaucracy, organi-

zation, institution, or agency. Each of these words has considerable theoretically specific content and connotations. In our view they should not be used interchangeably but only when we mean to be theoretically specific. The words "social construct" avoid any theoretic specificity, and yet the words "intended rationality" set them off from families, social clubs, and other social constructs that do not purposely intend "means-end" rationality as a product of cooperation among members. The word "intended" is meant to set aside for the moment questions of whether or not we can characterize behavior in these social constructs as rational or irrational in a particular sense of the word.

44. Note that this organizational complexity perspective resonates with the model developed by James Svara in his analysis of the roles within the council-manager system. Svara contended that the politics/administration dichotomy was too simplistic and ignored other critical function roles. He identified four functions: articulating mission, setting policy to achieve mission, creating administrative structures to effectuate policy, and management for carrying out tasks. These functions necessitate a greater range of administrative roles than are suggested by a politics/administration dichotomy. Svara portrayed city managers as major actors in all these activities, even that of mission articulation, that is, specifying the nature and function of the local government. City managers as appointed chief executives may be the clearest example of how the view of professionalism we are proposing facilitates administrators playing critical *system* roles. It should be noted that the profession of city management has avoided a prescribed curriculum or degree, yet had adopted a code of ethics around chief executive roles.

45. James Wolf and Robert Bacher, "The Public Administrator: The Worlds of Public Service Occupations," in Wamsley, *Refounding Public Administration*.

46. Ibid., 5, 6.

47. Paul Volcker, "Leadership for America: Rebuilding the Public Service," paper prepared for the President's Commission on the Public Service, April 1989.

48. Leonard D. White, *The Federalists: A Study in Administrative History* (Westport, Conn.: Greenwood, 1948); Paul P. Van Riper, *The History of the United States Civil Service* (Evanston, Ill.: Row, Peterson, 1958); Lynton K. Caldwell, *The Administrative Theories of Hamilton and Jefferson* (New York: Russell F. Russell, 1964). The Founding Fathers focused on public character rather than private character. This distinction accounts for what may strike us as an incongruity between the standards to which a person was held in conducting a public office and his private life.

49. White, *The Federalists*; Caldwell, *Theories of Hamilton and Jefferson*; Broadus Mitchell, *Alexander Hamilton: The National Adventure, 1799–1914* (New York: Macmillan, 1957); Gerald Stourzh, *Alexander Hamilton and the Idea of Republican Government* (Stanford: Stanford University Press, 1971); and Richard T. Green, "Oracle at Weehawkin: Alexander Hamilton and the Development of the Administrative State," Ph.D. dissertation, Virginia Polytechnic Institute and State University, 1987.

50. Elliot, *Sociology of the Professions*; Geison, *Professions and Professional Ideologies*; and Calhoun, *Professional Lives in America*.

51. Richard T. Green, "Constitutional Jurisprudence: Reviving Praxis in Public Administration," paper delivered at the annual meeting of the American

Political Science Association, Atlanta, Ga., 31 August–3 September 1989.

52. Blackstone, "The Great Ideas Today," *Encyclopedia Brittanica* (Chicago, 1989).

53. Ibid.

54. Leonard D. White, *Jacksonians: A Study in Administrative History, 1929–61* (New York: Macmillan, 1954); Paul P. Van Riper, "The American Administrative State: Wilson and the Founders," in *A Centennial History of the American Administrative State,* ed. Ralph Chandler (New York: Free Press, 1987); and John Rohr, "Professionalism, Legitimacy and the Constitution," *Public Administration Quarterly,* Winter 1985, 412–19.

55. Graham T. Allison, Jr., "Public and Private Management: Are They Fundamentally Alike in All Unimportant Respects?" in *Public Administration: Concepts and Cases,* 3d ed., ed. Richard J. Stillman, 453–66 (Boston: Houghton Mifflin, 1983); George Romney, "A Businessman in a Political Jungle," *Fortune,* 29 January 1979.

56. Henry D. Kass, "Stewardship as a Fundamental Element in Images of Public Administration," *Dialogue: The Public Administration Theory Network* 10, no. 2 (Winter 1988): 1–48; Terrence R. Mitchell and William C. Scott, "Leadership Failures: The Distrusting Public and Prospects of the Administrative State," *Public Administration Review* 47 (November/December 1987): 445–52; McSwain and White, "Phoenix Project"; Gary Wamsley, "Imagining the Public Administrators as Agential Leader," paper prepared for the American Society for Public Administration meeting, Portland, Ore., 1988; and Richard T. Green, "The Hamiltonian Image of the Public Administrator," paper prepared for the first annual symposium on Public Administration Theory, Portland, Ore., 15–16 April 1988.

57. Stone, *Policy Paradox.*

58. Walter Lippmann, *Essays in the Public Philosophy* (Boston: Little, Brown, 1955).

3

Where Does Policy Come From?

H. Brinton Milward and Wendy Laird

Several years ago, Charlie Levine published a review essay in *Public Administration Review* entitled "Where Policy Comes From: Ideas, Innovations and Agenda Choices."[1] In a few short pages he succeeded in capturing our attention and directing our research effort to a problem we had often discussed: the relationship between ideas and public policy. The literature he reviewed in that essay represented a new concern with agenda setting and the politics of ideas. The focus was on the process by which ideas come into and out of "good currency," that is, how unconventional notions are converted into conventional wisdom and public policy.[2] He contrasted this with the dominant political science models, which dismiss ideas as, at best, window dressing for interests.

Levine's review asked four basic questions: (1) Where do policy ideas come from? (2) What ideas get taken seriously? (3) How do ideas become public policy? (4) How do ideas fade away? The four questions Levine asked are especially pertinent today given the striking success of the governing ideas of the Reagan era, such as supply-side economics, deregulation, privatization, and the Star Wars initiative. The importance of research on the relationship between ideas and policy is highlighted by how quickly these ideas became public policy.

What Charlie Levine found most interesting in this literature was the general finding "that ideas are often more important than the push and pull of interest groups in affecting the substance of public policy."[3] This finding is significant because it departs from conventional wisdom in political science, which gives interest groups the seat of honor in the policymaking process.

What follows is a review of the agenda-setting literature as it relates to ideas and interests and how succeeding authors have changed initial theories of agenda setting to accommodate changes in our understanding of the relationship between interests and ideas. Finally, we perform a comparative analysis of the diffusion of five issues that move from "ideas" to "policy" after gaining access to the policy agenda. This comparative case analysis will be used to develop the elements of a theory of agenda setting.

As was so often the case, Charlie Levine pushed scholars in a direction that he recognized as important. This chapter is a small part of our intellectual debt to him.

Recent Literature on Agenda Setting
MODELS OF ISSUE DIFFUSION AND AGENDA SETTING

In this section we review the agenda-setting literature, specifically that part that attempts to develop at least verbal models of the agenda-setting and issue-diffusion processes. Cobb and Elder were the first political scientists to explicitly adopt agenda setting as a focus for their research on participation in American politics.[4] Their focus was on how issues move from the "systemic" agenda to the "formal" agenda. The systemic agenda is that set of issues discussed by the public in the media and on the streets, while the formal agenda is the set of issues on the legislative agenda of some level of government. Issues on the formal agenda are viewed as being "legitimate" because they have made it to a stage where government may or may not choose to address them.[5]

Cobb and Elder argue that an issue is a conflict between two or more identifiable groups over procedural or substantive matters relating to the distribution of positions or resources. Conflict occurs because, in a "policy dense" world, almost any new proposal will benefit some and hurt others. Hence, Cobb and Elder argue, there is some conflict over almost all issues. This leads to Cobb and Elder's basic model of how the "conflict" is initiated, or how the agenda-setting process begins (see figure 3.1).

In the Cobb and Elder model, a group or policy entrepreneur initiates the agenda-setting process. This occurs when an event "triggers" interest in a new issue. The triggering event can be cataclysmic, like Chernobyl, or it can be a slower, growing awareness, like the greenhouse effect. As the issue begins to diffuse across the systemic agenda through the media, and if public opinion and interest-group pressure is strong enough, the issue will be thrust onto the "formal" or "institutional" agenda, where the item is deemed serious enough for congressional consideration. Cobb and Elder argue that the number of gatekeepers, or those who will consider the plight of the issue and give the issue its imprimatur, will affect its chances for adoption. Cobb and Elder also state that political parties play an important role in translating issues into agenda items.

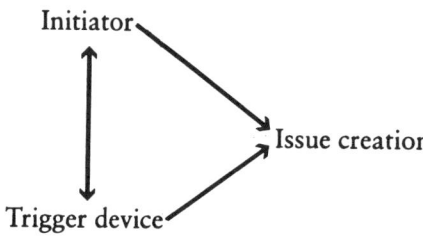

FIGURE 3.1

Cobb and Elder have had a powerful impact on scholars who study the agenda-setting process, but several of their assertions have been modified to accommodate changes in the political process. For example, political parties now share the agenda-setting process with an ever increasing number of interests tied to neither the Republican nor Democratic parties. Cobb and Elder had as an example Lyndon B. Johnson's Great Society. We have the recent example of policy stalemate as the White House and Congress are controlled by different parties. Special-interest groups, ad hoc coalitions, and caucuses are now as often the vehicles for policy change as political parties.

Change has had an impact on another Cobb and Elder hypothesis. Their assertion that the larger the number of gatekeepers required to approve an issue, the lower the probability that the issue will get on the agenda is no longer valid. The democratization of Congress after 1973 created a greater number of "gatekeepers," destroying the iron-fisted old southern committee chairmen (e.g., Wilbur Mills) who ruled their domains like feudal barons. Because of this reorganization, an issue today is opposed or supported not by one gatekeeper but by many. Power is no longer concentrated in one actor but decentralized to many. One individual cannot easily, singlehandedly keep an issue off the agenda. The greater number of gatekeepers has served to increase the likelihood an issue will make it to the institutional agenda, rather than hamper its arrival. Conversely, it has made it more difficult to get the issue adopted into law. In addition, ideas and the media play less of a role in Cobb and Elder's model than they seem to play today. The density of policy entrepreneurs, academics, think tanks, the print and electronic media devoted to public policy simply did not exist in the 1960s to the same degree they do today.

Cobb and Elder's assertions about the overall characterization of the agenda-setting process remain basically correct. While the agenda-setting process is relatively open with multiple levels and points of access, there remains a great imbalance in the power of various actors in the process, and there is no "equal opportunity" in agenda setting; ideas supported by powerful groups are easier to move onto the institutional agenda than those supported by less powerful groups. Compare the speed with which the savings-and-loan bailout passed with the torturous ten-year stalemate over amending the Clean Air Act.

Addressing some of the inadequacies of their earlier model, Cobb, Ross, and Ross proposed three different models of agenda setting that detailed the strategies social actors might use to get issues on the formal agenda and institutionalized as public policy. The Outside Initiative Model is the process by which groups outside government articulate grievances and pressure governmental elites to place issues on the institutional agenda. The Mobilization Model is the process by which political elites propose a policy or float an issue and then attempt to create mass support, or the illusion of mass support, to spur the government to do something about the issue. The desired solution in this model of agenda setting is usually attached to the issue. Finally, the Inside Initiative Model is described by Cobb, Ross, and Ross as the process by which political elites seek to initiate a policy proposal by means of a private decision within the ranks of the government.[6]

This basic framework has proved useful to scholars ever since the Cobb, Ross, and Ross models, built on the earlier Cobb and Elder model, appeared in 1976. As Barbara Nelson noted, the Cobb and Elder distinction between the systemic and formal agenda needed modification to maintain an important distinction raised by Cobb, Ross, and Ross. Nelson divides the agenda into a professional agenda discussed and defined in policy communities by experts and specialists within one policy domain; a popular agenda, which is what the media are discussing at any one time; and a public agenda, which is what some level of government is considering acting on at any given time. "Determining what is legitimately public is precisely the question posed by agenda-setting, and many issues achieve a governmental agenda without popular legitimacy."[7]

Nelson's point is precisely the point Cobb, Ross, and Ross make when they discuss the "inside access" model. The systemic agenda is a global concept. It is better redefined as consisting of any number of professional agendas developed in policy communities. Both Jack Walker's and Barbara Nelson's studies clearly demonstrate the critical role played by a policy community in forging an issue within a professional reference group and easing its entry onto the popular agenda and later placing it on the public agenda.[8]

It is possible to "cut the cake" a bit finer. There is a world beyond the professional agenda, but short of the popular agenda that the *New Republic* derisively calls "The World of High Chat." This is the agenda of the policy elite whose purview spans a number of policy domains. It might be differentiated broadly into such areas as "defense," "social policy," and "science policy." These communities are in turn served by a set of journals that purport to make sense of various specialized areas to a broader but very knowledgeable audience. The *Public Interest, Commentary,* the *New Republic,* the *Atlantic, Harpers,* the *New York Review of Books* are some of the journals of "High Chat" that serve as the anvil on which the policy elite's agenda is forged. These journals and those who write for them are very explicit about the role they play. They argue that their role is one of helping to define issues the government should attend to and to which the public will listen. These journals also serve as a forum for debate where an issue can be developed within a policy elite.

Donald Schon wrote *Beyond the Stable State* in 1971.[9] Although the book deals with how societies move from steady states into periods of rapid change, he focuses on the role "ideas in good currency" play in facilitating social change. He has a stage model which can be graphed as an S curve of the diffusion of the idea over time. The importance of Schon's book lies in his treatment of ideas as innovations and the role that functional networks play in their diffusion. He believes that "ideas obey a law of limited numbers" and that there are many more ideas than can ever be dealt with on the agenda. He is interested in which ideas are chosen and why. A logical question that flows from his work is, What is the nature of the relationship that exists between ideas and interests? Does a kind of coupling occur (e.g., an idea with an interest) to pull the idea into good currency and onto the public agenda? "As these ideas surface networks of individuals and interest groups gravitate to and galvanize around the new ideas. They in turn exert their own influence on the ideas by further developing them and providing them with a catchy slogan that provides emotional meaning and energy to the idea."[10] The key point here is that ideas cannot change policy unless they get on the public agenda, where they can be used by individuals and interests to channel resources toward specific policy solutions. The resources enhance or create legitimacy for the idea, as do the reputations of its sponsors. What Schon's work adds to our understanding of agenda setting is the centrality of ideas as the rallying point around which collective action mobilizes.[11]

Schon is under no illusion that the collective action that mobilizes around ideas ever completely solves the problem. The problems that get on the public agenda are usually there precisely because of their intractability. In addition, the media and the public can only attend to any given problem for so long. As Schon claims, "old questions are not answered—they only go out of fashion."[12] These unfashionable ideas then lie on the sidelines of the policy debate until they come into good currency again—usually with a new descriptive shorthand phrase identifying them. Hence the environmental crisis of the early 1970s is transformed by the 1980s into the "greenhouse effect."

Schon believes that ideas "lose out" at every one of the stages. That is, they cease to have any more power to mobilize concern. Like Cobb and Elder, Schon sees ideas developing in response to some disruptive or triggering event. There are seven stages to his model: (1) a threatening, disruptive event occurs; (2) solutions surface; (3) networks are galvanized; (4) political debate occurs; (5) legitimation happens if the idea gains agenda status; (6) the idea is then taken for granted; and (7) the idea becomes a barrier to the emergence of new ideas.

What follows is a figure by Van de Ven that graphs Schon's model over time.[13] It shows the diffusion curve with the ideas that lose out literally falling off the graph (see figure 3.2).

What Schon adds to our understanding of agenda setting is twofold. First, he introduces the notion of the relationship between ideas to functional networks of people who share similar interests, and second, he gives us a life-cycle theory of agenda setting. Anthony Downs, like Schon, also presents us with a life-cycle theory of agenda setting.

Anthony Downs's contribution to agenda setting came in the form of an article he published in the *Public Interest* in 1972, "Up and Down with Ecology: The Issue Attention Cycle."[14] Downs argues that most policy issues follow a five-stage cycle. The first stage he proposes is the Pre-Problem Stage, where the issue festers before it is discovered. His second stage is the Alarmed Discovery and Euphoric Enthusiasm Stage, or the point at which the general public becomes aware of the nature and dimensions of the problem and media coverage is extensive. The third stage is the Realization of Costs Stage, where the costs of significant progress are realized and vested interests feel threatened by solutions to the problem that are not compelling because of their disruption of the status quo. Downs's fourth stage maps the gradual decline of public interest. In this stage a "MEGO Effect" occurs; no matter what the headlines say, people's eyes glaze over at the mention of the problem, and they turn the page or change the television channel. The final stage in Downs's model is the Post-Problem Stage, where the problem still exists, but we have made peace with it. If an issue reaches this stage, it may come back to the public's attention, but not at its former high level.

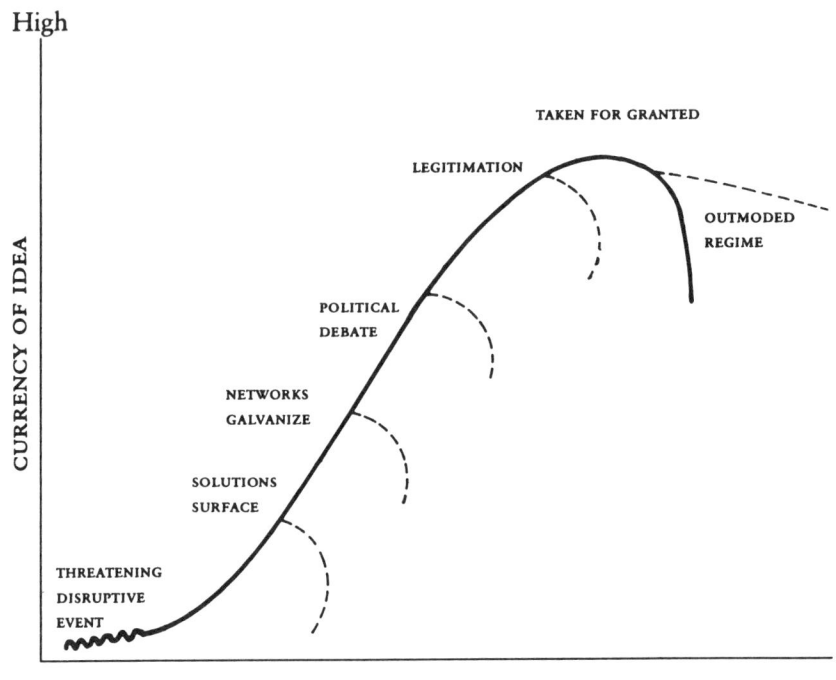

FIGURE 3.2. STAGES OVER TIME

SOURCE: Donald Schon, *Beyond the Stable State* (New York: Norton, 1971).

Downs's life-cycle theory handles the fact that most issues and social problems cannot be solved—only managed better or worse. He admits that some issues will complete only part of this cycle rather than be sufficiently resolved, and hence will be dropped from the agenda. His model works particularly well on the issue of ecology, an issue he used to build the model, and with the renewed interest in the environment in the late 1980s.

Downs's model is a stage theory concerned only with public opinion and not the governmental response, the action of political elites or interest groups to keep the issue on the agenda. What Downs is interested in defining are the kinds of problems most likely to go through the "issue-attention cycle." Downs argues that three basic characteristics describe this type of issue. The problem must affect a numerical minority. Suffering, caused by social arrangements, must provide significant benefits to a majority or a powerful minority of the population. And, the problem, while important, must not have intrinsically exciting qualities or must no longer seem to have them.

What Downs seems to indicate with these issue characteristics is that the issue is not defined in objective terms but is defined by the difference between our perception of the magnitude of the problem and our aspirations. Downs seems to be saying that the public manages the news by maintaining or losing interest in an issue.

Given the passage of more than twenty years since Downs wrote his article, there are a number of reasons for questioning the degree to which public opinion drives the model. One does not have to assume an autonomous mass media or a media controlled by a ruling class to come to the conclusion that there are interactive effects between government agencies, public interest groups, policy entrepreneurs, think tanks, and policy experts. Even utilizing a differentiated media model, one calls into question the simplistic notion that public opinion alone drives the issue in question.

In addition, since Downs wrote, news has become entertainment with shows like "Geraldo," "20/20," and "Prime Time." Interests and advocates fight fiercely to bring their issues to the attention of the media. This "fight" occurs because, as Schon recognized, issues obey a law of limited numbers. Only some of them can be attended to by a media with a limited number of column inches or time slots to fill.[15] The importance of this point is where Downs is weakest. The coupling that occurs between an issue and an interest is not mapped by his model. This we believe is the necessary, if not sufficient, condition for collective action to occur.

In 1985, Guy Peters and Brian Hogwood wrote "In Search of the Issue-Attention Cycle."[16] The article is a retrospective look at Downs's "issue-attention cycle," and it tests whether, in a variety of issue areas, there has been a governmental response.

Peters and Hogwood focus on what could be called the organizational attention cycle rather than the issue attention cycle. The data they use on organizational response come from the *U.S. Government Manual*. They measure structural change over time as the government responds to the issue attention cycle. This is measured by issues respondents view as salient in Gallup public opinion polls.

The conclusions of the Peters and Hogwood study are interesting and important for our work. They find that almost all policy areas have at least one clear "peak" decade of organizational activity and that the timing of the peak varies markedly between policy areas. Their evidence supports Downs's contention that problems that are going through the "issue-attention cycle" will have a higher level of attention after, rather than before, the peak. In addition, Peters and Hogwood find—although this seems somewhat problematic—that there is a linkage between public opinion and organizational, or what they term policy, change. Peters and Hogwood, like Cobb and Elder, use a model that triggers agenda setting by either an idea or an event. They find that issues triggered by "ideas in good currency" fit their model better than those triggered by events.

Jack Walker has conducted research on innovation diffusion and through this work came to study the process by which agendas are set. Walker developed a series of hypotheses related to agenda setting after completing a study of the process in the U.S. Senate.[17] He found that an item's attractiveness increases if it has an impact on large numbers of people; the more graphic and easily understood the issue, the more appealing the aspiring agenda item becomes; and the case for inclusion on the agenda is greatly strengthened if an easily understood solution exists for the problem being addressed. While these hypotheses are instructive about what can happen to issues that seek to become agenda items, they provide limited guidance as to what specific determinants will impact the inclusion of issues on the agenda and under what conditions.

John Kingdon's "garbage can" model of agenda setting, based on comparative case studies and interviews, partly addresses this concern.[18] He hypothesizes that issues rise on policy agendas when three separate streams join together. Borrowing from Cohen, March, and Olsen's "garbage can" model of decision making in organized anarchies, the streams of problems, policy solutions, and politics join when a "window of opportunity" occurs.[19]

Kingdon, like Walker and Schon, views agenda setting as including a broader policy environment than Cobb and Elder or Cobb, Ross, and Ross. Kingdon recognizes that much of the early stages of the agenda-setting process occurs in policy communities made up of policy professionals who work in government, think tanks, universities, and interest groups. Kingdon takes as a given that, in a policy-dense world, the policy network plays a key role in agenda setting. In addition, Kingdon does not believe that the media have an independent effect on agenda setting. He argues that the media reflect, rather than create, issues. The government, he argues, uses the media to advance its interests through strategic leaks and planted stories. Kingdon bases his conclusions on his interviews with policymakers who view the press as less important than either interest groups or academics in agenda setting. His findings support the proposition that the media can help shape and structure an issue, but cannot create it. Given the fact that he interviewed individuals involved in established policy areas (i.e., health and transportation), this analysis may be accurate. In newer policy arenas, however, or with issues that cut across issue areas, this finding may not be supported.

Kingdon rightly emphasizes the role played by the "official press" (e.g., the *New York Times,* the *Wall Street Journal,* and the *Washington Post*) in allowing key actors to communicate with one another. These newspapers are biased toward the institutions they cover, as they more often present the agency's or organization's view of an issue by virtue of the fact that the major branches of government are regular "beats" for journalists. Kingdon also points out that equally important is the role played by the "trade press," which runs the gamut from professionally produced publications like *Coal Age* to simple newsletters that serve to unite policy communities.

What Kingdon's approach to agenda setting handles less well are issues that are highly visual and thus diffuse very quickly. These issues burst on the policy agenda unattached and uncaptured by a policy community. The energy crisis is a good example of this kind of agenda item. Laumann and Knoke found that the energy policy domain was significantly less interconnected than health (one of Kingdon's areas).[20] A second example is the recent diffusion of drunk driving, which owes its rise on the agenda more to the media's account of tragic accidents and the airing of a docudrama about the founders of Mothers Against Drunk Driving (MADD) than to the influence of governmental or policy community actors.

Because Kingdon underplays nongovernmental factors associated with agenda setting, his model does not explain such events as the 1988 demise of the congressional pay raise, which was defeated by an unlikely alliance between Ralph Nader and a loose confederation of radio talk-show hosts.[21] While Kingdon's model handles consumer groups, public-interest groups, and environmentalists *after* they have become institutionalized, it does not explain how these groups are able to overcome the free-rider problem during the formative period.

In summary, John Kingdon has produced a fine model for explaining agenda setting by groups recognized as legitimate by the government (i.e., existing interest groups, government agencies, "the official press," and of course the Congress and the presidency).

The model makes two major contributions to our understanding of agenda setting. The first is that problems, solutions, and politics are incompletely coupled and are indeed separate "streams" that mingle in the "garbage can" called the agenda-setting process. The second contribution consists of adding policy communities that consist of governmental and nongovernmental actors in a policy domain to his model. In doing this, Kingdon follows the lead of Schon and Walker.

Fay Lomax Cook developed the "convergent voice" model that explains the process by which the same issue is independently articulated by different groups within and outside government at about the same time.[22] The issue is articulated in what she defines as a "ripe issue climate," which is equivalent to Kingdon's "window of opportunity." There are four stages in the Cook model, which are similar to Anthony Downs's "issue-attention cycle." The first stage she defines as the Ripe Issue Climate. Here the issue gains salience and is particularly aided if it is a "valence" issue or an issue that elicits a "single, fairly uniform emotional response."[23] The second stage is described by multiple sources that voice concern about the issue. Actors both within and outside government voice their concern about the issue at the same time. The "policy community," which consists of a network of policy interested parties, occupying positions both in the government and in interest groups, academia, think tanks and the media, begins to call for government action to solve the problem they have identified. These policy communities are largely specific to a policy domain.

Legitimization occurs in the third stage, where the media cover and document the extent of the problem. The government also gives grants to study the issue, and task forces are established to make recommendations for addressing the problem. In the fourth stage, policy specification and program development occurs. Bills are introduced in the legislature, signed by the executive, and implemented by executive agencies. At this point, the policy becomes institutionalized. Cook's convergent voice model fits the development of the issue of child abuse very well.

Barbara Nelson, in *Making an Issue of Child Abuse,* is interested in discerning the relationships between "conditions," "a social problem," and "a policy issue."[24] She is concerned with how a condition turns into a social problem and finally moves onto the public agenda as a policy issue. Her focus is slightly different from other authors and is closer to the social problem's tradition of sociology. Nelson focuses not on technological change (cold fusion) or on a triggering event (Chernobyl) as a way to bring issues to the agenda but on a cyclical process.[25] Child abuse is not a new problem, just a newly recognized one.

In studying child abuse, Barbara Nelson finds two basic groups of patterns into which the work on agenda setting fall.[26] First are organizational approaches and stage theories of agenda setting. These patterns focus on issue recognition, issue adoption, setting priorities among issues, and issue maintenance. Works displaying this pattern (including Nelson's *Making an Issue of Child Abuse*) focus on the actions of decision makers and the organizations they command in relation to the stages of the agenda-setting process. "By my definition," claims Nelson, "agenda-setting is the process whereby public officials learn about new problems, decide to give them their personal attention, and mobilize their organizations to respond to them."[27]

The second pattern is the issue cycles, careers, and clusters in which the agenda-setting literature focuses on social problems rather than whether to respond to the issue. Social problems seem to go through relatively predictable cycles, similar to Downs's issue attention cycle. Nelson modifies this in an important way. Child abuse, she argues, illustrates how the infusion of findings from professional and scientific journals help keep an issue on the agenda longer than Downs predicted.[28] Every time the issue started to decline, a new study or article appeared to keep child abuse on the public agenda.

Issue careers are a second aspect of this approach. Issue careers "focus not only on the legitimation of issues to the mass public, but also on the mobilization of groups and individuals around an issue," writes Nelson.[29] Policy entrepreneurs make careers out of issues, which they then invest in and become experts at, either as advocates or as heads of agencies devoted to alleviating the problem.

Within the context of the social constructionist, social problem tradition in sociology, Hilgartner and Bosk attempt to explain why some problems become very powerful ideas in good currency and have a very substantial impact on public policy.[30] In the past this differential impact has been ascribed to one problem's being more marketable than another. They point out that this begs the central question: why? Marketability also shifts over time. Bosso found that the Ethiopian famine that was so much in the news in 1984 had occurred annually since 1973-74.[31] AIDS was a very powerful agenda item after it was first diagnosed, but later faded somewhat when it appeared to be a "gay disease."[32] Hilgartner and Bosk view issues as the product of collective definition by social actors. "A theory that views social problems as mere reflections of objective conditions cannot explain why some conditions are defined as problems commanding a great deal of societal attentions, whereas others, equally harmful or dangerous, are not?"[33] Both the idea and the importance of the problem are viewed as contested concepts. Those with power and influence and those with an idea or policy innovation fight to define the issue for the public within the print and electronic media. Instead of emphasizing the stages of social problem development, Hilgartner and Bosk focus on competition: "We assume that public attention is a scarce resource, allocated through competition in a system of public arenas."[34]

Hilgartner and Bosk view their public arenas model as a step up from the Downsian natural history or stage models because many problems exist simultaneously in several stages of development in different arenas. At the same time, stage theories neglect the interaction among problems, which they view as central to the process of collective definition.[35] This means that if there is a "science beat" in the print and electronic media, both global warming and genetic engineering are competing for the same media space. This view constitutes an important extension of Schon's concept of ideas obeying a law of limited numbers. The social arenas model provides us with the mechanism by which the process occurs.

Issue Diffusion for Five Agenda Items

Design of the Research

The unit of analysis in this research is the *issue*. We follow Barbara Nelson's second pattern. The purpose of this section is to conduct a comparative case analysis of a set of issues in regard to agenda setting. The analysis will help construct a set of factors that can be used to develop an empirically testable model of agenda setting.

If we define theory as a deductively related and empirically testable set of explanatory propositions about the world, it is clear that there are no "theories" of agenda setting. In this essay we use theory to mean "a conceptual framework and analytical vocabulary in terms of which propositions about the world might be formulated."[36] This definition is particularly suited to agenda setting because gathering data in this area is not easy.

Our definition of agenda setting is simple. Following Cook and Skogan, we define agenda setting as the study of how issues come to receive serious attention by the public and policymakers.[37] In a limited way we are trying to do what Hogwood and Peters called for in studying policy dynamics—track the evolution of issues for a decade or more.[38] Here we concentrate on five issues: (1) the greenhouse effect, (2) drunk driving, (3) comparable worth, (4) supply-side economics, and (5) child abuse. These issues have been chosen carefully as each already has a rich descriptive, and in some cases, analytical case study. The "thick description" will help us explain, along with the literature we have reviewed, both similarities and differences among the five different issue cycles.

Supply-Side Economics

In 1981, less than six years after the term supply-side economics was coined, it became public law when President Ronald Reagan signed a three-year, 25 percent cut in personal income tax rates. This seems to be an unusually fast-paced journey through the agenda-setting process for an issue that did not result from a crisis.

At issue in the supply-side argument was, what was the driving force behind the economy? Keynesian economists, who held sway for a generation, argued it was aggregate demand. Demand, they claimed, creates supply. This is where the supply-siders joined the fight. The supply-siders argued that people produce not only because other people want to buy but because the producers want profits. The greater the after-tax rewards they can obtain, the greater their motivation to produce. Thus the supply-siders called for deep cuts in tax rates designed to make both work and investment more rewarding and stimulate production, increase the supply of goods and services, and cool inflation.[39] From the supply-sider's view, it was impossible to eliminate government deficits as long as high taxes stifled economic growth.

How did supply-side economics become a public issue? It emerged from the thinking of two economists, Arthur Laffer and Robert Mundell. Their ideas captured the imagination of Jude Wanniski, editorial writer for the *Wall Street Journal*. In the editorial pages of the *Journal* and in such opinion-setting journals as the *Public Interest,* Wanniski tirelessly propagated the supply-side creed. Wanniski's first political break came when he met Representative Jack Kemp.

Kemp and Wanniski got along very well. Before long, Representative Kemp was an ardent supporter of Laffer's theories. Kemp believed that the Republican Party needed to find ideas of its own rather than simply oppose whatever the Democrats proposed.

A key convert to the supply-side faith was Robert Bartley, editor for the *Wall Street Journal*. On 4 August 1976 a *Journal* editorial endorsed Jack Kemp's business tax-cut bill. In 1977 Kemp joined with Senator William Roth to advocate a full-blown supply-side tax-cut bill, which would create a 30 percent across-the-board reduction in marginal income tax rates. While the bill was endorsed by the Republican National Committee, it was opposed by many conservatives, who thought the first economic task in an era of high inflation and high unemployment was to cut the budget. In 1978 supply-side economics gained important, if tentative, support from both Martin Feldstein, a noted professor of economics at Harvard University, and Nobel prize-winner Milton Friedman, who supported the Kemp-Roth bill. Friedman viewed this as a way to force a reduction in government spending.[40] Before the 1980 election, Kemp met with Ronald Reagan to discuss the supply-side idea. At the time, Kemp was considering a run for the presidency on a supply-side platform. Reagan wanted Kemp out of the race; both men came out as partial winners. Reagan assured Kemp that he favored tax cuts, and Kemp agreed to stay out of the primaries.

Early in the presidential campaign Reagan sounded like a true believer. "In one early television commercial, he noted that the Kennedy Administration's tax cut had been an economic success, even the government gained $54 billion in unexpected revenue.... Mr. Reagan declared, 'if I become President, we're going to try that again.'"[41] While Reagan's vocal support of the supply-side idea waxed and waned, especially after George Bush referred to it as "voodoo economics," Reagan kept his promise and supported the Kemp-Roth tax cuts that became public law.

What can we learn from this case of agenda setting? First, there was a problem. The problem was "stagflation": high inflation with high unemployment. This problem was not supposed to exist if the Keynesian prescription of increasing aggregate demand, which would create lower levels of unemployment, was to work. Thus the "conventional wisdom" was not working. Second, from the periphery comes the idea of supply-side economics. Schon argues that most new "'ideas in good currency' will come from the periphery since most people in power in disciplines like economics, are committed to the conventional wisdom."[42] It is not in their interest to support ideas that challenge the existing paradigm of their field. Third, in supply-side economics we see an idea coupled with an interest. Washington, New York, and other centers of government, finance, and the media are filled with policy entrepreneurs like Wanniski and Laffer. They are relatively helpless until they have their idea accepted and adopted by someone who commands a forum such as the *Wall Street Journal* or an arena such as the U.S. Congress. Fourth, this entry is made easier if there are sponsors to aid this transition. The conservative movement developed a powerful and richly funded network of think tanks such as Heritage, American Enterprise Institute, and Cato, in addition to training programs, journals, and organizations of right-wing propaganda.[43] The conservative's goal is to increase the probability that if ideas obey a law of limited numbers, and only a few ideas can possibly be attended to, the ones that survive will be ideas of the right rather than the left. Fifth, adoption is aided if the idea flows with, rather than against, the Zeitgeist or spirit of the times. The tax revolt of the 1970s provided a promising climate for an idea that argued economic growth was driven by lowering marginal tax rates. Sixth, an idea needs a powerful champion. Ronald Reagan became that champion. Ideologically Reagan was in favor of less government and lower taxes. Supply-side economics gave him the theory he needed to make a sharp break with past practice. "No president, no matter how willful and committed, can retain the confidence of his advisors and allies, to say nothing of the public more generally, unless his policies are consistent with at least some minimally acceptable policy doctrine."[44]

What occurred with supply-side economics was the creation of a policy community that grew up outside universities, held an important forum in the editorial pages of the *Wall Street Journal* and such neoconservative publications as the *Public Interest,* and gained access to the arena of government through Jack Kemp and a few other congressional offices and committee staffs. It is through the efforts of these policy entrepreneurs that the entire focus of the national policy debate has changed from an overriding concern with redistribution to an almost exclusive concentration on economic growth.[45] In this guise, supply-side economics is now the "conventional wisdom."

THE GREENHOUSE EFFECT

"There is considerable debate whether the hot temperatures during the summers of 1988 and 1989 signal that greenhouse warming is already occurring. There is no question, however, that as a topic on the political agenda, greenhouse has arrived."[46]

The theory of global warming and the attempt to validate it empirically go back at least 100 years. Svante Arrhenius in the late 1880s employed measurements of infrared radiation to calculate the possible effects of carbon dioxide on the Earth's temperatures. He concluded that average global temperatures would rise as much as nine degrees Fahrenheit if the amount of carbon dioxide in the air doubled from preindustrial levels. This "hothouse" theory had been explored nearly a century before by Jean-Baptiste-Joseph Fourier, who speculated that carbon dioxide, a by-product of fossil-fuel combustion, trapped solar infrared radiation, and similar to a greenhouse, heated the Earth's lower atmosphere. Several scientists intermittently considered the effects of carbon dioxide on the atmosphere, but little attention was given to the greenhouse concept until the late 1950s.

G.S. Callender, a British physicist, speculated in 1930 that rising carbon dioxide levels could account for warmer temperatures in North America. Several scientists also argued that the ocean would compensate for man's excess carbon dioxide production—heightened by the Industrial Revolution—by capturing excess carbon dioxide in its vast waters. It was not until 1957, with a publication by Roger Revelle and Hans Suess in *Tellus*, that a "concept of limits" was applied to the ocean's capacity to cope with excess carbon dioxide.

Revelle and Suess, both scientists at the Scripps Institute of Oceanography, argued that the ocean had a limited threshold for capturing excess carbon dioxide. "They found that the conventional wisdom was wrong: the upper layer of the oceans, where the air and sea meet ... would absorb *less than half* of the excess carbon dioxide produced by man."[47] Revelle and Suess claimed that humans were carrying out a "large scale geophysical experiment," of which no one knew the results.[48] With this scientific predication, the greenhouse effect, as an issue, was born. Born also was the career of Roger Revelle as an advocacy scientist: "The significant discovery he made in 1957 with H.E. Suess initiated a commitment to gaining attention to global warming that continues to the present."[49]

As with supply-side economics, the idea of global warming resulted from a theory not supported by the accumulated empirical research or the conventional wisdom in the scientific world. The idea, however, was based on some evidence, and it was an idea that had been familiar to scientists for many years. What was new was the role the scientist played as an advocate: writing not for the scientific community but for the world of public policy.

The research of Revelle and Suess spurred Scripps to hire Charles Keeling and to set up two monitoring stations, one at the South Pole and one in

Mauna Loa, Hawaii, to measure accurately carbon dioxide levels. Keeling's first readings were taken in 1958 and showed a 315 parts per million (ppm) of carbon dioxide that year. Subsequent readings showed annual increases, initially as small as 7/10 ppm. These annual increases have more than doubled since 1958.

Keeling's scientific measurements created a flurry of activity and a great deal of concern. The results were startling, in part, because the world's population has tripled in this century, creating a greater use of fossil fuels and an increase in carbon dioxide production, and in part because four-fifths of the industrial growth we have seen has occurred since 1950, indicating that these early, low figures will lead to a rapid and deleterious increase in future levels.

This wave of concern started by Revelle and Suess led to the design of complex computer models that could map the entire globe. Concern was no longer focused on levels of carbon dioxide but was turned to other "greenhouse gases" as well as methane, ozone, nitrous oxide, and chlorofluorocarbons. Perhaps the best-known model is that designed by James Hansen of NASA'S Goddard Institute of Space Studies.

Hansen and his model made headlines in June 1988 when he testified before the Senate Committee on Energy and Natural Resources that the warming trend apparent in that hot, dry summer was not just cyclical but was more probably the result of the greenhouse effect. Hansen was the first scientist to throw traditional scientific caution to the wind and claim that there was a 1 percent chance that "the temperature increases seen in the last few years were accidental, and that we now lived in the greenhouse world."[50] His testimony made headlines in three prominent newspapers: the *New York Times,* the *Los Angeles Times,* and the *Washington Post.* It sparked national attention, much of which was negative, to the effects of greenhouse gases on the atmosphere. Part of the dismay with Hansen's testimony lay in the fact that many scientists felt so bold a stance was premature. These scientists argued that not enough information existed to confirm conclusively that the greenhouse effect had begun. In addition, some of the press coverage was sparked because parts of Hansen's testimony had been altered during the congressional hearing by the Office of Management and Budget, and concern over these changes elicited a number of accusations. Thus, this hearing in June 1988 marks the placement of the greenhouse effect on the public agenda and the birth of an idea whose time had come.

The issue of the greenhouse effect had a long gestation period, from the late 1950s to the late 1980s. Thirty years is a long time for an issue to exist and still be viable. One likely reason is that while the greenhouse effect fit well with the Zeitgeist of the environmental 1960s and 1970s, it was overwhelmed by the eco-doom predictions of the period. Being poisoned by pesticides was a much more proximate end than the gradual global warming the scientists predicted.

In addition, policy entrepreneurs, during this long gestation period, kept the issue alive. Revelle and other advocacy scientists interested in this issue held meetings of the AAAS, spoke and wrote about the problem, and continued to conduct research on the issue.[51] When a new concern with the environment was presented to them in the form of a political "window of opportunity," the issue of global warming had the potential to gain agenda status. The ingredients were there to bring the greenhouse effect to the public agenda: it was a new peripheral idea, the Zeitgeist had changed, there existed policy entrepreneurs, and Mother Nature provided two hot summers.

As with supply-side economics, the greenhouse issue was moved onto the public agenda when it joined with an interest. Just as Representative Jack Kemp joined forces with Laffer and Wanniski, Senator Albert Gore joined forces with "greenhouse scientists," and the issue was spurred to the legislative agenda. "While still a member of the House of Representatives in 1981, Gore came to the rescue of an AAAS interdisciplinary proposal for research on global climate change."[52] In 1988 Gore, a young senator and presidential candidate, used the greenhouse issue as one element of his strategy. He needed an issue to differentiate him from the number of contenders in the Democratic primary. Along with other legislators, he introduced legislation on global warming during the long hot summer of 1988.

When Congress holds hearings, they are covered by the media, as they are a regular press "beat." In this sense regular beats constitute a vital connection to legislative agendas. For an issue such as the greenhouse effect, the dissemination of information was aided by the fact that, in the 1970s, "science" became a regular beat of most major newspapers. In the 1980s this information began regularly infiltrating front pages. The *New York Times,* for example, pioneered this effort with their "Science Tuesday" feature. As further evidence, it is becoming common occurrence for an article to appear in a newspaper, or a story to air on television, that focuses on an interesting article that appeared "that day" in such journals as the *New England Journal of Medicine* or *Nature.* Writers who cover this beat attend scientific conferences, interview leading scientists, and apprise themselves of the specifics of an issue by monitoring scientific journals in the field. This heightened coverage has drastically reduced the gestation period required for scientific issues to move onto the public agenda. More dramatic have been the recent "science by press conference," such as the University of Utah's press conference held on "cold fusion," which occurred *before* the journal article was in print.

Child Abuse

Child abuse has been a sad feature of the human condition for a very long time. It was not recognized as a social problem in the United States until the nineteenth century. Three different reform movements called attention to children who were delinquent, beaten, or neglected. These movements included the campaign for juvenile courts, the "house of refuge" movement, and the founding of the Society for the Prevention of Cruelty to Children, a spinoff of the Society for the Prevention of Cruelty to Animals.[53] "In each case the primary objective was not to save children from abusive parents, but to save society from future delinquents.... Thus, it was children, not their abusive guardians, who felt the weight of the moral crusade. They, not their parents, were institutionalized."[54]

What gave currency to the idea of child abuse, which as Barbara Nelson points out was not a new social problem, but a newly recognized one, was the framing of the issue in medical terms.[55] The discovery of child abuse can be attributed to the medical field of pediatric radiology. In 1946 Dr. John Coffey, a pediatric radiologist, noted the cause of long-bone fractures in children as being of "unspecific origin." Eleven years later, Coffey made a specific connection between these fractures of "unspecific origin" and the "misconduct and deliberate injury" of children.[56]

The point at which child abuse became a newly recognized and newly defined issue occurred in 1962 with the publication of "The Battered Child Syndrome" in the *Journal of the American Medical Association*. The labeling of abuse as a medical syndrome was endorsed in an editorial that accompanied the article.[57] Although no data on incidence were presented in the article, the editorial that accompanied it stated that it was likely to be a more frequent cause of death than leukemia, cystic fibrosis, and muscular dystrophy. As the issue gained agenda status, "official after official and article after article repeated the comparison as though it were fact ... [which] shows how powerful a credible source can be in defining the extent of a social problem, even when that source offers no figures whatsoever."[58]

Once the syndrome had been recognized as a medical problem, it was unconditionally accepted. No one argued the case for the abusers. Articles began to appear in the popular press almost as soon as the "Battered Child Syndrome" appeared. *Time, Newsweek, Life,* the *Saturday Evening Post, Good Housekeeping,* and the *New Republic* all published articles, often written in sensational terms, that served to bring the issue to the attention of a much larger audience. The problem was now real in the sense that medical professionals, social workers, and the public perceived it as such. As the issue further diffused, a series of television shows aired featuring child abuse as an issue the characters in the show confronted. Shows such as ABC's "Ben Casey, M.D.," NBC's "Dr. Kildare," and CBS's "The

Nurses" featured scripts that treated the problem of child abuse, giving further coverage to the issue.[59]

As might be expected, the government responded quickly to the problem. It was hard to make a case against it. "Once alerted to the problem, the U.S. Children's Bureau and other organizations drafted model child abuse reporting laws which were rapidly passed by all state legislatures."[60] As the laws were passed the issue was framed in a narrow, medical manner. Race and class were treated equally. Any mention of poverty or discrimination as contributing to the conditions leading to child abuse was omitted.[61] This point is illustrated by the hearings held in 1973 by Senator Walter F. Mondale (D-Minn.) on his Child Abuse Prevention Act. In a way this was similar to Albert Gore's insisting that there could be no winners, only losers, with the advent of the greenhouse effect. Both Mondale and Gore were attempting to frame the issue in a convergent fashion, where all parties would agree that its effect would be equally and universally harmful.[62]

Child abuse was an issue that Mondale was "staking out" as his own in preparation for an anticipated presidential race in 1976. The hearings he held illustrated two things: (1) that child abuse had arrived on the public agenda, and (2) that child abuse fit the American conception of a social problem that was individually rooted, described as an illness, occurred universally, and was solvable.[63] "Any more elaborate view, especially one which focused on injustice as a source of social problems, threatened to scuttle [Mondale's] ... efforts to move this small piece of categorical legislation through Congress," notes Nelson. "With able maneuvering, Mondale's approach prevailed, and on January 31, 1974, President Richard M. Nixon signed the Child Abuse Prevention Act (CAPITA) into law."[64]

This public law authorized Congress to spend $86 million over three and a half years on research and demonstration grants as well as for discretionary social service grants to the states. As Nelson points out: "Eighty-six million dollars for child abuse, a problem which did not even warrant an entry in the *Reader's Guide to Periodical Literature* in 1968!"[65] This legislation continued to be reauthorized until, like so many other social programs, it fell victim to President Ronald Reagan's budget cuts.

Child abuse illustrates several points. First is the key role that framing an issue plays to get it on the agenda. By medicalizing child abuse, those who championed legislation made the issue appear universal and treatable. Second, the case illustrates the interactive relationship between a professional community and the media. Once "The Battered Child Syndrome" appeared, the media paid attention to research reports and articles in scholarly journals that previously would have attracted little attention outside a narrowly defined group of doctors and social workers. At this point the issue became an item on the medical beat of the media. This interaction continued long after the law was passed and the research funded by the Child Abuse Prevention Act was released. The issue stayed on the agenda longer than Anthony Downs's "issue attention cycle" would predict. This in part reflects the Children's Bureau's desire to keep the issue alive. Fueled by funding goals, the findings on child abuse continue to flow to the media from the Children's Bureau and its funded researchers.

Similar to supply-side economics and the greenhouse effect, the child abuse issue was coupled with an interest. Walter Mondale was the "interest" for child abuse. A distinction must be made, however. Mondale ratified the child abuse issue by supporting *federal* legislation, but by the time Congress acted, eleven of the fifty states had already established child abuse reporting systems. The issue had already been on the public agenda for ten years. Congressional action was slow to follow the states' lead. This longer shelf life may be attributed to particular characteristics of issues that diffuse intergovernmentally.

As with supply-side economics and the greenhouse effect, data on child abuse was a relatively minor factor in the issue's rise to the formal agenda. "No one actually knows the extent of child abuse and neglect, or whether their incidence is increasing or decreasing," notes Nelson.[66] The actual numbers were less important than the vivid descriptions evoked by the issue itself.

Finally, an important distinction between this case and the previous ones can be made. No one chose sides either "for" or "against" child abuse. It was, in Cook and Skogan's terms, a "convergent issue," an issue with only one side. In contrast to abortion, which they would term a "divergent" issue, where both sides feel so strongly about the problem that it creates polarity and a "no-win situation" for politicians, opposition to stopping child abuse was not heard.[67]

DRUNKEN DRIVING

During the late 1970s opposition began forming to the perceived lenient treatment of drunken drivers by police and the courts. This began as a local issue with citizen groups forming in a number of cities. These groups usually formed after a drunk driver killed or severely injured someone and received lenient treatment by a judge. The rise of these early groups can be described as a local response to a specific problem. This local interest soon fanned out across the nation.

In 1980, Candy Lightner formed the first chapter of Mothers Against Drunk Driving (MADD). This occurred after her daughter was killed by a chronic drunken driver. "Since then more than 400 local groups have started nationwide and have directed the efforts of thousands of volunteers toward reducing the amount of drinking and driving in their communities."⁶⁸ In less than ten years a powerful grassroots social movement had emerged in communities all across the United States. "In alliance with others, including state agencies, law enforcement officials, and insurance companies, they have worked to bring about changes in citizen attitudes toward drinking and driving, shifts in law enforcement patterns directed toward drunk drivers, legislative and administrative changes focused on the control and punishment of drunk drivers."⁶⁹

What accounted for the rapid ascent of opposition to drunken driving as an issue on the public agenda? As with almost all issues, multiple factors can be cited to explain its emergence as an agenda item. First, like child abuse, there was no opposition. It is hard to imagine supporters of drinking while intoxicated. Second, the most vociferous opposition came from those most directly affected. Those mobilizing the issue at the local level were the families and friends who had lost a child, wife, or husband to an intoxicated driver. "Activists in the movement typically refer to the surviving relatives of persons killed in alcohol related crashes as victims. The movement is predominantly led by such victims and consists primarily of a victim membership," notes McCarthy et al.⁷⁰

The manner in which an issue is framed serves to shape the way society will deal with it. Drunk driving is an example of an issue once found to be socially "acceptable" but later redefined as a social problem. People have been driving while intoxicated since the invention of the automobile. Initially, the response to the drunk driver who killed or injured someone was tempered by the knowledge that it could happen to anyone. Only recently has the problem been sharpened and redefined. The idea of the "killer drunk" and the construction of "victims" or those who had lost a loved one to a drunken driver was a concept the National Safety Council and other interested groups created.⁷¹ Through their efforts, the idea that drunken drivers were responsible for their own actions came to be shared opinion. The policy implication was that measures had to be taken to protect society from these drunks, just as the public must be protected from drug pushers and murderers.

In some ways this construct was similar to another "valence" issue, child abuse. As with child abuse, it was hard for anyone to make the case for drunk driving. Both issues were medically portrayed, one as a "syndrome" and the other as a "disease," but differed in their treatments of the perpetrator. With drunken driving, a practice that was common to all classes, its social definition was narrowed so that opposition focused on a villain: the "killer drunk." Unlike the issue of child abuse, groups focused on an enemy.

Those responsible for this changed social definition included an active professional community. This community centered on the National Safety

Council and the newly created National Highway Transportation Safety Administration. These agencies published a guide that served as an organizational template for such groups as MADD, lowering organizational costs for these groups.[72] As these groups developed, growing from the ranks of the "victims," they became the foot soldiers in the fight against drunken driving. They lobbied for stricter enforcement at state and local levels, monitored judges they suspected of being too lenient, and became adept at using local and national media.

At state and local levels these citizens' groups have close linkages to state and local government agencies and receive their support. We have been to meetings with police where instructions were handed out on how to get the attention of the local media and how to lobby the state legislature for funding programs that would pay off-duty police to enforce traffic laws strictly in areas and at times when people who have been drinking are likely to be on the road.

What we have seen in regard to this issue's emergence as an agenda item is that a changing definition of the problem by a professional community and organizational encouragement and advice helped mobilize a movement of "victims" in the late 1970s through the mid-1980s, a movement that spread all across the United States. Between 1978 and 1985, 424 groups were formed.[73] During this same period, media attention to this issue also grew. The interactive effect of a professional community, a valence issue with sharp definition, people with grievances, government agencies' offering support, and the media all jointly explain how this issue came to its place on the public agenda.

COMPARABLE WORTH

Women working full-time earn about 30 percent less than working males. At the same time, almost three-quarters of all full-time working women are in occupations dominated by women, such as nurses, secretaries, and teachers. It is also a fact that when an occupation is dominated by women, the job will pay less than an occupation dominated by men. "This is the essential argument for comparable worth: as the proportion of women or minorities in an occupation goes up, wages go down."[74]

Because so many men are in different occupations from women, the Federal Equal Pay Act of 1963, guaranteeing equal pay for equal work, has not ended the wage gap between the sexes.[75] This has led to a two-tiered labor market where jobs in male-dominated occupations pay better than jobs in female-dominated occupations. This pattern seems to exist "because it embodies deeply ingrained beliefs (which many workers share) about masculine and feminine interests and skills ... [and] traditional patterns of family life," notes Kaminer.[76] While the nature of this dual labor market is not in doubt, the causes of it are. "Do women choose less demanding, lower-paying jobs than men because of some kind of natural preference for domesticity ... or the failure of men to assume equal responsibility for child rearing?"[77]

The issue of comparable worth sprang from the Zeitgeist of "liberation" and "equality" that came to dominate the 1960s. This worked in tandem with the development of a self-conscious feminist movement in the United States. "The founding of the National Organization of Women (NOW) in 1966 brought together professional women, political activists, and members of the UAW Women's Bureau."[78]

With 1967 came the emergence of the women's liberation movement, which appealed to a younger and more radical clientele than did NOW. The initial demands that both NOW and women's liberationists made was for equal opportunity in hiring, the end of "men only" and "women only" want-ads in newspapers, and affirmative action in hiring and promotion.[79] This effort was reasonably successful in attaining its aims with the movement itself culminating in the passage of the Equal Rights Amendment by Congress in 1972. As the movement battled for ratification of the ERA by the states over the next decade, the focus of its demands shifted from the individualistic concept of justice in the early period of the struggle for women's rights and toward a collective concept. This was when comparable worth became a rallying cry for the women's movement. The demand was for pay equity between workers in an occupation dominated by women and another occupation, which had a similar level of skill requirements, dominated by men. The question asked was, What caused wages to be higher in the latter than the former? If the pay differential could not be justified on the basis of objective requirements, then the differential was caused by sexual discrimination and was not a true wage differential based on skill.

Underlying the issue of comparable worth were major demographic changes in American society: divorce rates skyrocketed, labor force participation by women increased; and the majority of American families no longer fit the nuclear, male-supported model.[80] As in so many other cases, interests combined with the Zeitgeist to propel an issue onto the public agenda.

"Feminization of poverty" was the term coined by researchers to describe the growing number of women and children who were unable to achieve even a minimal standard of living.[81] With large numbers of women concerned about the problems of earning a living wage, individual solutions such as equal opportunity and affirmative action were no longer compelling. What comparable worth offered was the hope of altering the occupational structure of the whole society so that the wage rate would actually reflect the worth of the work and not be biased by the male-created social definition of the job. "Comparable worth was one attempt to reach a broader constituency and shift the ground of the debate towards a policy that would be effective and successful."[82]

No policy community pushed for a redefinition of the problem, as was true in drunk driving and child abuse. This issue was dealt with and defined more in terms of an "issue network" that was both loosely coupled and diffused widely across a range of organizations. "A skilled and knowledgeable network of women in government at national, state, and local levels increasingly lent their support to efforts to resolve a number of demands made in the name of women. A shared agenda emerged from this politically powerful coalition as it debated the problems of working women in union halls, working women's organizations, professional associations, government agencies, and courtrooms."[83]

The issue has been tested in the courts, but the results are inconclusive. The Supreme Court held that women had the right to attempt to prove that lower wages were being paid for comparable jobs, but declined to endorse wage disparities among the sexes as prima facie evidence of this sex discrimination. State legislatures have been more hospitable venues for the issue of comparable worth than the federal courts.[84] "Since the state of Washington undertook the first comparable worth study in 1974, twenty states have made compensatory payments to state employees."[85]

Comparable worth is still an alive issue, but it has passed through part of the issue attention cycle without achieving clear resolution. The problem of pay inequity remains, though a powerful movement to resolve it does not. One reason for this lack of resolution is the use of the courts and the almost exclusive focus on pay differences at the state government level. Government workers rarely elicit empathy, and they particularly did not fare well during the conservative, Reagan-dominated 1980s. Their litigation strategies are by nature remote from the everyday experience of the working woman.

What did not occur in any of the states or at the national level was any attempt to require comparable worth in the private sector. The mere possibility of this plus the growing discussion of the issue in the media turned comparable worth into a "divergent voice" issue.[86] Issues of this type cause people and interest groups to square off, and politicians see no clear advantage to getting in the middle of the very acrimonious debate. In this case comparable worth became a Democratic Party issue at a time when Republican fortunes were high. The Republicans controlled the White House and through it such agencies as the Civil Rights Commission and the Equal Employment Opportunity Commission. They also controlled the Senate for part of this period. Comparable worth seemed like a leftover issue from the civil rights era at a time when the Zeitgeist had shifted dramatically in the opposite direction.

The signal that comparable worth was an issue whose time had *been* as signaled by the 1985 decision by the Civil Rights Commission to reject comparable worth as a remedy for sex bias in the workplace. Also in 1985 came the reversal of the first victory in the battle for comparable worth, as the Washington state court of appeals overturned the earlier comparable worth case.[87]

In retrospect, comparable worth's journey through the agenda-setting process can be seen as an issue that missed its "window of opportunity." The issue seemed better suited for an earlier time. And even though the comparable worth problem became worse during the late 1970s and early 1980s, the spirit of the times had turned against it. Economic growth and opposition to government interference in the marketplace replaced equity and justice as ideas that moved citizens to action. Comparable worth also had the misfortune to become a partisan issue at a time when its partisans (Democrats) were weak. In addition, it was an issue that had many ports of entry, but no champion. It was debated in Congress and state legislatures and was heard in the courts, but never coupled with a powerful interest. Comparable worth perhaps proves the contention of Mancur Olson that the few often defeat the many as they are able to overcome the high costs of organizing.[88]

Agenda-Setting Factors

AN ANALYSIS OF THE FIVE CASES

What we have learned from these five cases in agenda setting allows us to construct a model that moves beyond the stage of verbal constructs to one whose dimensions can be reasonably well specified and whose expected relationships can be empirically tested. Based on the cases and the literature reviewed, certain factors reappear with some regularity. The way in which the factor affects the issue is consistent if not uniform in its impact. In some cases, not all the factors are operative, but there are at least plausible explanations for why they are not. These nonoperative factors may explain why the issue dropped off the public agenda.

FRAMING THE ISSUE

The way the issue is framed is critically important to the success of the issue on the public agenda. In the case of child abuse the issue was framed in terms of "the battered child syndrome." This medicalized the issue, suggesting that it could happen to anyone, like a disease, and that it was treatable. It became a medical issue rather than a problem caused by the pathology of poverty and confined to the lower class. Opposition to drunken driving diffused rapidly because it took a problem that every drinker confronts and defined it in terms of a villain: the "killer drunk." Here it allowed drinkers as well as nondrinkers to believe that the problem was with a specific type of drinker who became lethal when operating a car. Supply-side economics as an issue was framed, not as a redefined problem, but as a new idea for solving a problem that the conventional wisdom, Keynesian economics, could not solve: stagflation. It thus illustrates the power of an idea in good currency in confronting the conventional wisdom. The greenhouse effect is still in its infancy and hence is currently being defined. Hot summers have been attributed to it, but so have cold winters and other climatic variations. Albert Gore tried to define it as a valence issue by asserting that there would be no winners from the greenhouse effect. One reason it may still be on the agenda is its as yet undefined frame. Comparable worth seems to be going nowhere because it is not clearly framed. Is the discrepancy between men's and women's salaries the result of structural discrimination or women's career choices?

A clearly framed issue is one that succinctly states what the problem is in plausible terms and embodies an easily understood solution. Child abuse, opposition to drunk driving, and supply-side economics all were clearly framed issues. Also, child abuse and opposition to drunken driving were "valence" issues, where a uniform response was generally elicited from those involved in the agenda-setting process. Supply-side economics did not elicit a uniform response, but came to be defined in partisan terms.[89] The Democrats opposed it, and a powerful Republican president supported it. The greenhouse effect and comparable worth are, according to this definition, issues that are not well framed.

Factors That Influence Agenda Success

COUPLING

Coupling is a factor that has a positive impact on the relative success of an issue in the agenda-setting process. Coupling occurs when the idea joins with an interest. In the case of supply-side economics, both the *Wall Street Journal*'s editor and Jack Kemp, and later Ronald Reagan, coupled with the issue. This crucial coupling allowed supply-side economics to be taken seriously as an issue during both a presidential campaign and in the legislative process. The greenhouse effect has coupled with the fortunes of Albert Gore. Unfortunately for the issue, Gore, unlike Reagan, did not become president. Coupling occurred with child abuse when Walter Mondale adopted it as an issue when he was considering running for president in 1973. This case, like drunken driving, is different in that the issue was dealt with by many states before the federal government got involved. State involvement is important in giving an issue legitimacy prior to federal action as the states are often viewed as laboratories of democracy. Comparable worth was dealt with at the state level before it became a federal issue. The state record was mixed. Some states, like Washington, took it seriously; many others did not. Its success in the federal courts was mixed and by the time the issue was considered at the national level, a hostile president and agency heads were in place to deflect the issue from the public agenda.

A POLICY COMMUNITY

A policy community consists of a set of "interested parties" that revolve around issues in an area of professional or policy relevance. The community can be tightly knit, as in medicine, or loosely knit, as is the case in women's issues. The fact remains that a professional community can serve as the incubator for an issue. It can emerge as the consensus of the policy community and be submitted to the outside world as the solution to a problem that the community has defined, such as child abuse. There are factors within most policy communities, so an issue can also arise from opposition to the conventional wisdom in a policy community, as with supply-side economics. The fact that this type of issue has something to debunk is no less important than the policy community's imprimatur. The greenhouse effect comes out of the policy community of science. Its problem is that it is so poorly framed that its meaning is unclear, and the policy community of science has a much higher standard of proof than many other policy communities. Opposition to drunk driving did not emerge from a policy community but from community action. As the issue gained attention in the popular media, it was aided by the highway safety and law enforcement communities. Comparable worth had the misfortune to emerge at a time when the women's movement was splintering. The ERA was being attacked by conservative women and thus comparable worth never had strong and united support from women, who are, at best, a very loosely organized community.

POLICY ENTREPRENEURS

Policy entrepreneurs have played key roles in several of our cases: Edward Laffer and Jude Wanniski with supply-side economics; Roger Revelle with the greenhouse effect; and Candy Lightner, who formed Mothers Against Drunk Driving. In each case their role in formulating the issue and getting it onto the public agenda is similar to the role ascribed to the entrepreneur in the private sector who has a vision and seeks to implement it against great odds and in the process overcomes entrenched interests and hostile competitors. Child abuse did not have one policy entrepreneur. It also occurred in the pre-Ralph Nader period when policy entrepreneurship was not as well established and the media were not so attuned to it. Child abuse had an incubation period of some seventeen years before the medical community announced it to the world in 1963. The period between discovery and proposals for solving a problem have been drastically shortened. Comparable worth again is the outlier; it had no policy entrepreneur and is the least successful of the issues that have been through the issue attention cycle.

Policy Windows

Thus far, much has been made about the spirit of the times: the Zeitgeist. Kingdon recognized this in his book on agenda setting. An idea's success will have as much to do with how well it fits the general notion of what society needs at any point in time. Ideas have their best chance of success if they can be launched during a favorable policy window. Child abuse moved on to the agenda at least partly because it fit so well with the spirit of the Kennedy era, which held that all problems were solvable if enough effort, intelligence, and money were applied to solving them. Ideas often travel in packs because they are a response to the sentiment of the age.

If equality and justice were the hallmarks of the 1960s, it is no surprise that comparable worth fared so badly in the era of the rebirth of free enterprise and opposition to government interference in the marketplace. Supply-side economics, in contrast, was perfect for this era. The greenhouse effect fits well with our current concern for the environment. To date, this issue does not have a powerful champion and remains unframed. Drunk driving had a favorable policy window. It was a proposal that appealed to an era in which there was little sympathy for drug use, and alcohol was increasingly viewed as a drug. It also was medicalized as the "killer drunk" syndrome. This was also the era that favored local over federal solutions to problems, and clearly this was an issue defined and first acted on in cities and states. The actors were citizens, not bureaucrats seeking to expand their own turf.

Events

Some issues are created or driven by events. The strength of this factor can vary greatly. With supply-side economics, this did not really come into play. What you had instead was a period when the performance of the economy did not respond to applications of the conventional wisdom. Two hot summers in a row helped the emergence of the greenhouse effect on the public agenda. There was no one event for child abuse, but there was a long period of gestation within a professional community before the issue emerged. Many singular events played a role in the emergence of opposition to drunk driving. While people have been killed by drunk drivers since the automobile's earliest days, deaths caused by drunk drivers in the late 1980s helped trigger its emergence as an issue. Why these deaths helped activate collective action at that time and not earlier must be explained by other factors. Comparable worth had no specific triggering event to aid in its emergence onto the public agenda.

SPONSORS

Schon argues that ideas obey a law of limited numbers.[90] If only a few ideas in good currency can become agenda items, then, all other things being equal, ideas whose diffusion costs are subsidized stand a better chance of becoming agenda items. Sponsors can come in a variety of guises. A political party can include an issue in its platform, as the Republican Party did with supply-side economics. Likewise, television can help sponsor an issue like opposition to drunk driving with a docudrama on the policy entrepreneur most associated with the issue, Candy Lightner. Child abuse was, in a sense, sponsored by the American Medical Association with the editorial that accompanied the article on the "battered child syndrome." Global warming was underwritten by the Scripps Institute after the initial findings of Revelle and Suess. Comparable worth was an issue sponsored by the National Organization for Women.

None of the issues included in this chapter illustrate the real power of sponsored ideas in good currency. There are a rich array of think tanks, foundations, and national associations that have very clear interests and seek out those whose ideas are consistent with the sponsor's values. The tobacco industry has for years sponsored research on smoking that looks at factors other than cigarettes as causal agents in the development of cancer. The Manhattan Institute, a right-wing think tank, supported Charles Murray, an avid supply-sider, during the year he was writing *Losing Ground*. This turned out to be the book most often cited in justifying Reagan's cutback on domestic spending. The book's thesis was that social programs created the pathology of the underclass, rather than poverty and lack of access to jobs and education. Sponsored policy is a very important and little understood element of agenda setting.

STRATEGY

Strategy in regard to the agenda-setting process is intentional action on the part of policy entrepreneurs and their supporters to seek to get the policy on the agenda. The best illustration would be Cobb, Ross, and Ross's three models of agenda setting. These "models" are in reality strategies. Some items get on the agenda through "outside access." That is, citizens bring issues to the government. It is the citizens, usually through mass action, who force government to respond. Civil rights and environmental protection are two successful issues that emerged on the public agenda in this manner. Homelessness and the Equal Rights Amendment are unsuccessful examples. The second way issues get on the agenda is termed the "mobilization model." That is, people in government, in alliance with a policy community, seek to create the appearance of mass support for an issue. This seeming mass support makes it easier for legislators to support. In the "inside access" model, the policy is supported by those who are also the relevant decision makers. Policy is easy to adopt, but this strategy can create problems if there is a citizen outcry, as was true with the congressional pay raise issue. Policy entrepreneurs and the interests that support them may use all these strategies at different times in order to get their issue on the public agenda. To give just one example, consider opposition to drunk driving. It started out as an issue that was clearly following the outside access strategy. The people supporting it were "victims" who had lost a loved one to a "killer drunk." They were not part of the policymaking process. They were citizens with a problem and were bringing it to government. Later on, after the issue had gained legitimacy, the national traffic safety policy community, together with the police, served to mobilize support for drunk-driving groups in cities where they had not yet emerged; thus they followed a mobilization strategy to aid in the intergovernmental adoption of the issue.

AGENDA CHARACTERISTICS
In this chapter we adopt Barbara Nelson's convention of three agendas: the professional, the popular, and the public agenda. We hypothesize that each agenda has its own set of characteristics. We would expect professional agendas to be guarded by the notable persons in a field, so agendas consistent with the interests and values of the notables would have an easier route toward the field's professional agenda. The professional agenda is the domain of the policy community, and in many of these domains one would expect to find a dominant paradigm that defines the way the policy community should address the problems and matters within the purview of the community. If one added a time dimension, it would be interesting to look at the relation between policy communities and agenda items. We have assumed that the former creates the latter. There are some instances, particularly during the Great Society years, when legislation was passed wholesale, and agenda items such as poverty and crime created policy communities from scattered sets of interests.[91]

The popular agenda consists of all the ideas, problems, and proposals competing for the public's attention at a point in time. Who proposes them will affect their success; where they were proposed and how many similar proposals are floated at the same time will affect agenda success. If a well-known figure, such as Daniel Patrick Moynihan, senator from New York and well-known policy intellectual, makes a proposal, it is almost guaranteed space in leading newspapers, periodicals like *Atlantic Monthly, Public Interest,* and the *New Republic,* and perhaps in interviews on issue-oriented television shows like "Meet the Press." In granting immediate access to the popular agenda, the press has a lower threshold for coverage if the person proposing the idea has "standing." There is a fine line between having "standing" and being known as a media hound who wants to comment on every issue. Politicians who do this are in danger of being labeled "media sluts," according to the *New Republic*.[92]

There is a high end and a low end to the popular agenda. We have been discussing the high end. The low end consists of the mass media. Daily newspapers, popular newsmagazines such as *Time,* television news and "infotainment" are influential in the setting of the agenda. We would include television "disease of the month" movies and innovations such as ABC's segment on the evening news, "The American Agenda." The strength of the influence will vary by the issue being considered. Drunk driving had more impact on the low end of the popular agenda and supply-side economics on the high end.

Success on the public agenda is not defined in column inches. The venue of the public agenda is some level of government, either federal, state, or local. It is defined by what powerful interests are pushing the issue through the legislative process and is judged by whether the idea in good currency is granted standing as a public issue, with legislators debating it, holding hearings on it, and perhaps ultimately crafting it into public law. The characteristics of the public agenda are defined by the characteristics of the legislative process. The policy density (existing legislation) in the issue's domain may slow the agenda item's progress, as there will probably be more vested interests in the status quo. Earlier we discussed the role of gatekeepers in agenda setting. While there are now many gatekeepers in Congress, giving those pushing an idea a number of different ports of entry to the legislative process, state legislatures may by quite different. They may have only one port of entry and that one guarded by a powerful majority leader or Speaker of the House.

Issue Characteristics

Issue characteristics are the aspects of the issue that aid or impede its ability to gain agenda status. The characteristics of the issue are related to how the issue can be framed. Supply-side economics is an issue that is very difficult to personalize. Child abuse and drunk driving both leave "victims," either the person abused or the families of the person killed by the drunk driver. These issues can be identified with by people who have not experienced either child abuse or a collision with a drunk driver because they could happen to anyone. For that reason, issues that can be personalized are more likely to diffuse in the electronic media either at or even before they diffuse in the print media.

Some issues, such as supply-side economics, do not appear to have any way of being personalized. We suspect that Ronald Reagan was able to bring this home to the public by ignoring the theory and selling it to the public as a tax cut. A tax cut is a proposal that almost anyone can identify with, even if the theory behind it cannot be personalized. Another way of understanding this is to study whether ideas diffuse differently based on whether they are visual and visceral (drunk driving and child abuse) or cerebral and remote (supply-side economics and the greenhouse effect). The latter would seem to be more amenable to presentation in the print media and the former in the electronic media.

What follows is a list of issue characteristics that might affect the agenda success of an issue.

1. *The issue is dramatic.* It has consequences for large numbers of people, and those consequences can be vividly portrayed by the media.
2. *The issue is driven by demographics.* Large increases in the numbers of the young or the elderly or veterans will serve to push an issue onto the public agenda. Likewise, it is very difficult, as children's advocates found in the 1980s, to swim against the rising tide of elderly demands that issues that affect them be attended to.
3. *The issue is driven by an increase in the problem.* If drug use is increasing, then this should aid those seeking increased resources for this issue. Sometimes it is not even an absolute increase in the problem. President Bush admitted that drug use has been declining since 1981, but the number of hard-core users was increasing (which is certainly to be expected if casual use is down).
4. *The issue has no credible opposition.* There are no spokespersons for "killer drunks" or for child abusers. Issues with a clear villain should be easier to get on the agenda and addressed by a legislative body because there is no credible opposition. Tobacco is a villain in the media, but it is a villain protected by a powerful and diversified industry and a coterie of senators and representatives from tobacco-growing states. Thus, issues like curbing smoking can have a difficult time if the opposition defines the issue as "freedom of choice" or protecting the jobs in growing and manufacturing tobacco.
5. *Issues can be driven by public opinion.* Begging the question of whether public opinion reflects the media, or vice versa, politicians

and policy entrepreneurs can exploit the fact that public opinion polls show that the public feels that an issue is important and should be addressed by government. Poll results showing that the public wants increased domestic spending on the environment, education, and the nation's infrastructure have been seized on by politicians frustrated by defense expenditures and the deficit serving as a sea anchor for domestic proposals.

6. *Issues can be changed by the length of time they are on the agenda.* This can be seen in the number of categories or classifications of an issue in bibliographic materials. As the number of categories for an idea in good currency increases, this differentiation is a sign of its power. As more and more stories appear, it becomes apparent that there are different aspects and nuances to the idea that need to be differentiated from the main heading. Thus, child abuse at some point in time added a subcategory of child sexual abuse.

MEDIA CHARACTERISTICS

How the media treat an issue plays a large role in agenda success. For example, do different issues have different placement patterns in the newspaper (back page or front page, editorial or op-ed page, inside page)? One would think that issues that consistently appeared on the front page would have the greatest chance of agenda success. Another media characteristic would be whether or not the issue was covered by an existing beat. If an issue is part of an existing beat, one would expect that it would have greater agenda success than an issue that was not. Coverage itself increases the probability of subsequent coverage. The media watch one another. A story in the *New York Times* will be covered by "NBC Nightly News." An article in the *Atlantic* will lead to a story in the *Wall Street Journal*.

AGENDA SUCCESS

Throughout this list of factors that influence agenda success, we have left the meaning of "success" undefined. It is clearly the dependent variable if we construct and test a model of agenda setting. Most would assume that agenda setting means that an issue became a public law at some level of government. We have a less restricted meaning. We follow Cobb, Ross, and Ross in defining agenda success as placing an issue on the formal agenda for serious consideration by decision makers.[93] While clearly an issue that becomes a public law has achieved agenda success, we do not restrict our definition to public law.

A second measure of success under this definition would be whether or not legislative action was taken. Were hearings held? Was the issue defeated in committee? Was it bound over for consideration to the next session of the legislature? All these actions are examples of whether the issue was a serious item on the public agenda.

This set of factors concludes the initial phase of our research on agenda setting. We are in the process of constructing an agenda-setting model based on these factors. The detailed specification and operationalization of our complete model is the ultimate goal of this research effort.

Notes

1. Charles H. Levine, "Where Policy Comes From: Ideas, Innovations, and Agenda Choices," *Public Administration Review* 45 (January/February 1985): 255–58.
2. Ibid., 255.
3. Ibid., 256.
4. Roger W. Cobb and Charles W. Elder, *Participation in American Politics: The Dynamics of Agenda-Building* (Boston: Allyn and Bacon, 1972).
5. Ibid. The analysis that follows is a summary of pp. 82–93.
6. Roger Cobb, Jennie Keith-Ross, and Marc Howard Ross, "Agenda-Building as a Comparative Political Process," *American Political Science Review* 70 (March 1976): 126–38.
7. Barbara J. Nelson, *Making an Issue of Child Abuse: Political Agenda Setting for Social Problems* (Chicago: University of Chicago Press, 1984), 21.
8. Ibid.; and Jack L. Walker, "The Diffusion of Knowledge, Policy Communities and Agenda Setting: The Relationship between Knowledge and Power," in *New Strategic Perspectives on Social Policy,* ed. John Tropman et al., 75–96 (London: Pergamon, 1981).
9. Donald A. Schon, *Beyond the Stable State* (New York: Norton, 1971).
10. Andrew H. Van de Ven, "Central Problems in the Management of Innovation," *Management Science* 32 (May 1986): 592.
11. Ibid., 593.
12. Schon, *Beyond the Stable State,* 142.
13. Van de Ven, "Management of Innovation," 593.
14. Anthony Downs, "Up and Down with Ecology: The Issue Attention Cycle," *Public Interest* 28 (1972): 38–50.
15. Schon, *Beyond the Stable State,* 129.
16. Guy B. Peters and Brian Hogwood, "In Search of the Issue-Attention Cycle," *Journal of Politics* 47 (1985): 238–53.
17. Jack L. Walker, "Setting the Agenda in the U.S. Senate: A Theory of Problem Selection," *British Journal of Political Science* 7 (October 1977): 430–31.
18. John W. Kingdon, *Agendas, Alternatives, and Public Policies* (Boston: Little, Brown, 1984).
19. Michael Cohen, James March, and Johan Olsen, "A Garbage Can Model of Organizational Change," *Administrative Science Quarterly* 17 (March 1972): 1–25.

20. Edward O. Laumann and David Knoke, *The Organizational State: Social Choice in National Policy Domains* (Madison: University of Wisconsin Press, 1987).

21. Charles Price, "Attack of the Radio Talk-Show Hosts," *California Journal*, September 1989, 365–69.

22. Fay Lomax Cook, "Crime and the Elderly: The Emergence of a Policy Issue," in *Reactions to Crime*, ed. Dan A. Lewis, 123–47 (Beverly Hills: Sage, 1981).

23. Nelson, *Making an Issue of Child Abuse*, 27.

24. Ibid.

25. For a review of this literature on social problems, see Joseph W. Schneider, "Social Problem Theory: The Constructionist View," *Annual Review of Sociology* 11 (1985): 209–29. Recent works in this tradition include Joel Best, ed., *Images of Issues: Typifying Contemporary Social Problems* (New York: Aldine de Gruyter, 1989), and Malcolm Spector and John I. Kitsuse, *Constructing Social Problems* (New York: Aldine de Gruyter, 1987).

26. Nelson, *Making an Issue of Child Abuse*, 12–31.

27. Ibid., 25.

28. Ibid.

29. Ibid.

30. Stephen Hilgartner and Charles L. Bosk, "The Rise and Fall of Social Problems: A Public Arenas Model," *American Journal of Sociology* 94 (July 1988): 53–78.

31. Christopher J. Bosso, "Setting the Agenda: Mass Media and the Discovery of Famine in Ethiopia," in *Manipulating Public Opinion*, ed. Michael Margolis and Gary Mauser, 153–74 (Chicago: Dorsey, 1989).

32. David C. Colby and Timothy Cook, "Social Movements and Sickness on the Air: Agenda Control and Television News on AIDS," paper presented at the American Political Science Association annual meeting, Chicago, 1987.

33. Hilgartner and Bosk, "Rise and Fall of Social Problems," 54.

34. Ibid., 55.

35. Ibid., 54–55.

36. William H. Sewell, Jr., "Toward a Theory of Structure: Duality, Agency and Transformation," University of Michigan, Sociology Department. Paper read at the Social Organization Seminar, University of Arizona, 19 September 1989, 4.

37. Fay Lomax Cook and Wesley G. Skogan, "Agenda-Setting: Convergent and Divergent Voice Models of the Rise and Fall of Policy Issues," Northwestern University, unpublished paper, June 1989, 1.

38. Peters and Hogwood, "In Search of the Issue Attention Cycle," 238–53.

39. Robert W. Merry and Kenneth H. Bacon, "Supply-Side Economics and How It Grew from a Theory to a Presidential Program," *Wall Street Journal*, 18 February 1981.

40. Paul Blustein, "Supply-Side Theories Become Public Policy with Unusual Speed," *Wall Street Journal*, 8 October 1981.

41. Ibid.

42. Schon, *Beyond the Stable State*, 128.

43. See Sidney Blumenthal, *The Rise of Counter-Establishment* (New York:

Harper & Row, 1986), 166–210. (See for an account of how the institutions of the right played a role in supply-side economics diffusion and adoption in law.)

44. Paul E. Peterson, "The New Politics of Deficits," in *The New Direction in American Politics*, ed. John E. Chubb and Paul Peterson, 365–97 (Washington, D.C.: Brookings Institution, 1985).

45. Jonathan Rauch, "Where's That Dragon?" *National Journal*, 11 July 1987, 1768–72.

46. Helen Ingram and Carole Mintzer, "How Atmospheric Research Changed the Political Climate," unpublished paper, University of Arizona, 1989, 1.

47. Bill McKibben, "End of Nature," *New Yorker*, September 1989, 52.

48. Ibid.

49. Ingram and Mintzer, "Atmospheric Research," 3.

50. McKibben, "End of Nature," 58.

51. Ingram and Mintzer, "Atmospheric Research," 3.

52. Ibid., 6.

53. Stephen J. Pfohl, "The Discovery of Child Abuse," *Social Problems* 24, 3 (1977): 311.

54. Ibid.

55. Nelson, *Making an Issue of Child Abuse*, x.

56. Pfohl, "Discovery of Child Abuse," 315.

57. C.H. Kempe, F.N. Silverman, B.F. Steele, W. Droegemuller, and H.K. Silver, "The Battered Child Syndrome," *Journal of the American Medical Association* 181 (July 1962): 17–24.

58. Nelson, *Making an Issue of Child Abuse*, 16.

59. Pfohl, "Discovery of Child Abuse," 320.

60. Nelson, *Making an Issue of Child Abuse*, 13–14.

61. Ibid., 15.

62. Ingram and Mintzer, "Atmospheric Research," 7.

63. Ibid., 2.

64. Ibid.

65. Ibid.

66. Ibid., 15.

67. Cook and Skogan, "Agenda-Setting."

68. John D. McCarthy, Mark Wolfson, David P. Baker, and Elaine Mosakowski, "The Founding of Social Movement Organizations: Local Citizens' Groups Opposing Drunken Driving," in *Ecological Models of Organizations*, ed. Glenn R. Carroll (Cambridge, Mass.: Ballinger, 1988), 71.

69. Ibid., 72.

70. Ibid., 73.

71. Joseph Gusfield, *The Culture of Public Problems: Drinking, Driving and the Symbolic Order* (Chicago: University of Chicago Press, 1981).

72. McCarthy et al., "Social Movement Organizations," 74.

73. Ibid., 78.

74. Wendy Kaminer, "Men Drive Trucks; Women Type," *New York Times Book Review*, 30 July 1989.

75. Ibid.

76. Ibid.

77. Ibid.
78. Sara M. Evans and Barbara J. Nelson, *Wage Justice: Comparable Worth and the Paradox of Technocratic Reform* (Chicago: University of Chicago Press, 1989), 29.
79. Ibid.
80. Ibid.
81. Ibid., 30–31.
82. Ibid., 31.
83. Ibid., 32.
84. Kaminer, "Men Drive Trucks."
85. Ibid.
86. Cook and Skogan, "Agenda-Setting."
87. Evans and Nelson, *Wage Justice*, 41.
88. Mancur Olson, Jr., *The Logic of Collective Action* (New York; Schocken Books, 1968).
89. Cook and Skogan, "Agenda-Setting."
90. Schon, *Beyond the Stable State*, 123.
91. For an elaboration of this argument, see H. Brinton Milward and Ronald A. Francisco, "Subsystem Politics and Corporatism in the United States," *Policy and Politics* 11 (1983): 273–93.
92. Jacob Weisberg, "Bright Lights, Spin City," *New Republic*, 26 February 1990, 16–17.
93. Cobb, Ross, and Ross, "Agenda-Building," 137.

4

Political Power and Policy Subsystems in American Politics

JAMES A. THURBER

American federal government policymaking takes place in a wide variety of settings ranging from fairly open and public systems involving a large number of actors to relatively closed systems with few participants. The location of decision making in government, the scope of an issue, the nature of a policy, and the number of participants involved in a decision all have an impact on the characteristics of a policymaking system.[1] The type of policy being considered affects the politics of the decision-making system handling it. Schattschneider put it succinctly: "New policies create new politics."[2]

Circumstances may develop that are beyond the immediate control of American decision makers. The Organization of Petroleum Exporting Countries (OPEC) oil embargo in 1973, the decline of communism and breakup of the former Soviet Union, droughts and floods in the United States, the Exxon Valdez oil spill, and the Three Mile Island nuclear power plant accident all changed the type of policymaking system that routinely handles these energy, foreign policy, water, and environmental policies.

Policymaking is responsive to the nature of the issues being considered. New problems create new policies, which in turn create new politics. Major problems that affect large numbers of people attract the attention of a wide range of policy makers. Minor issues affecting limited numbers of people involve few decision makers.

American public policy results primarily from the activities of thousands of actors in hundreds of decision-making systems organized around discrete programs and issues. These decision-making systems operate within constitutional, electoral, and political party structures of the wider American political system and in effect make it work. Interested individuals, businesses, and groups cluster naturally around congressional committees and executive branch agencies whose decisions affect them either positively or negatively. An explanation of the organization and behavior of these decision makers is essential to an understanding of political power and public policymaking in the United States. The nature of American policymaking elicits several basic questions about policymaking systems and democracy: Are policymaking systems "irresponsible" elements in society? Do they have an "interest group" bias? Who is left out and who is in on the decisions? What kinds of issues never appear on the government agenda because of system bias? Can American democracy afford the luxury of our form of policymaking systems dominating and often clogging our legislative, regulatory, and judicial processes? Is our system of decision making inherently elitist or is it democratic?

A Typology of Policymaking Systems

In answering the questions posed above, it is a useful analytic tool to think of policymaking processes as falling into specific kinds of systems. One way to think of them is as a continuum ranging from *macro policy systems,* or "high politics" (general policy decisions with major political effects involving broad public interests, visibility, divisiveness, extensive media coverage, and many participants), to *policy subsystems* (dominant, competitive to disintegrated), to *micro policy systems* (narrowly focused decision making involving a very small, and often closed group of decision makers).[3] Policy issues may move up or down the decision-making continuum from micro politics to subsystems to macro policymaking systems. Policy subsystems

TABLE 4.1
A TYPOLOGY OF POLICYMAKING SYSTEMS

Policymaking system	Visibility of decision	Scope of conflict	Level of conflict	Number of participants
Macro policy systems	High	Wide	High	Many
Policy subsystems	Low	Narrow	Low	Few
Micro policy systems	"Invisible"	Very narrow	Low and personalized	Few

NOTE: These are the characteristics for the most common policy subsystems, that is, dominant subsystems.

tend to dominate the political landscape in American public policymaking. Policy subsystems are such a common organizational form of American public policymaking that they have been referred to by a variety of titles such as subgovernments, iron triangles, cozy little triangles, intermediary politics, policy whirlpools, power networks, power clusters, power triads, or policy coalitions. I use policy subsystems in place of these concepts as a term that captures the dynamic nature of these decision-making systems. Table 4.1 outlines a typology showing how policy subsystems fit between macro and micro politics.

Macro Policy Systems

Macro policy systems, or "high politics," make major decisions that may change policies or the power structure surrounding a major policy area. These systems often include presidents, congressional leaders, the mass media, the general public, the Supreme Court, or leaders of broad-based groups in society. The issues considered in macro policymaking systems may include major policies such as negotiations over final passage of the federal budget, macro economic policy, cutbacks in the defense budget, or cuts in the capital gains tax. Macro policy systems also include highly controversial, often emotion-packed issues that are narrowly focused with heavy media coverage and widespread public concern, such as the freedom of choice/anti-abortion issue, changes in social security benefits, or major tax increases. These issues have as common elements high visibility, extensive news coverage, "gangs" of high-level public officials, divisiveness, potential for extended controversy, and salience in the electoral arena. Macro policy systems often develop in response to crises resulting from an uncontrollable domestic or international social, economic, or political event such as the breakup of the Soviet Union and eastern Europe as a communist bloc. The reaction to external major social, economic, and political events often centralizes power, taking control away from policy subsystems. The subsystems are seen as obstacles to resolving conflict, but subsystem experts are relied on for policy options and expertise. Macro political decision making brings new and higher-level decision makers into the policy process and produces new policies unobtainable through subsystem decision making.

Often macro decision-making systems form because an issue cannot be resolved at lower levels of government. They evolve from competitive system to disintegrated subsystems to macro political decision making. Extended controversy, competition, and deadlock often push issues into the White House, onto national television news, and into the macro political realm. The annual battle over the budget starts from dominant subsystems considering programs, moves to competitive subsystems attempting to hold on to their "fair share" of federal dollars, and then breaks down into disintegrated subsystem politics and into the view of the nation, macro political negotiations.

The transformation from policy subsystems to macro politics can be an annual process such as consideration of the budget or it can be dramatic or prolonged. An example of dramatic change is the energy crisis stemming from the cutoff of OPEC oil in 1973–74. Before this event, oil politics was controlled by producers of petroleum products. The OPEC cutoff pushed energy policy and its many well-organized and closed subsystems out of congressional subcommittees and administrative agencies and onto television, the front page of newspapers, and into national electoral politics. Charles O. Jones characterizes the dramatic expansion of the oil crisis into macro politics, or "sloppy large hexagons," as follows:

> Those cozy little triangles which had come to characterize the development of energy politics had become sloppy large hexagons. Demands by environmentalists and public interest groups to participate in decision making, involvement by leadership at the highest levels in response to crisis, and the international aspects of recent energy problems have all dramatically expanded the energy policy population ... the expansion is up, out, and over —*up* in public and private institutional hierarchies (e.g., the involvement of presidents of companies and countries, rather than just low-level bureaucrats, and of congressional party leaders rather than just subcommittees); *out* to groups that declared an interest in energy policies ..., and *over* to decision making processes in other nations or groups of nations.[4]

A prolonged and incremental transformation of routine politics to macro politics often results less from a single event than from cumulative incidents coupled with a growing public awareness of the gravity of an issue. One of the best examples is the increase in illegal drug use over the past three decades.

MICRO POLICY SYSTEMS

Micro policy systems, at the other end of the policymaking spectrum, involve attempts by a relatively hidden elite to influence government policy. The impact of the policy being influenced is often of limited interest to the general public. Micro policy decision making can be focused on areas of such technical complexity that it is removed from the daily living of most Americans and excluded from all but a few relevant subsystem actors. Micro policies seldom appear in election campaign rhetoric; most constituents are unaware or uninterested in them. Micro policy systems are characterized by limited participation, limited access, and limited communication aside from those decision makers with the inside technical knowledge to understand the issues or political actors who want a favor and those in government who can grant it. Success is measured by micro political actors as their ability to control the process and, above all, by their ability to stay out of the news. Micro politics are often described in the popular media as corrupt, closed, elite decision-making systems linked to vested economic interests. Because of the secrecy, there is a potential for abuse but no certainty of it. The apparent intervention by five U.S. senators in the late 1980s in the regulation of the failing Lincoln First Savings and Loan Association and the involvement in Department of Defense weapons procurement contracts by members of Congress and their staffs are two examples of micro politics or, as some critics call it, micro management. The American news media often describe public policymaking using a micro political framework even when it is not applicable. Micro political conceptions of policymaking detract from a more complex and realistic description of routine federal government decision making: macro policy systems and the three kinds of policy subsystems. Micro policy systems obviously have an impact on public policy, but often it is not as lasting or significant an influence as policy subsystems or macro policy systems, which are more democratic and representative modes of decision making.

The Policy Subsystem Model

Two predominant images of the policy process are *iron triangles,* relatively closed policy arenas emphasizing stable relations among a limited number of participants, and *issue networks,* which are fragmented, open, and extraordinarily complex systems not well suited to resolving conflicts or reaching decisions quickly. The iron-triangle metaphor linking executive bureaus and agencies, congressional committees, and interest-group clienteles, sometimes referred to as *power triads* or *cozy triangles,* is used to describe a fixed, closed, and autonomous system for making policy. Hugh Heclo rejects the iron-triangle metaphor and replaces it with the idea of open issue networks that have disaggregated power and have many participants flowing in and out of decision making.[5] Both iron triangles and issue networks are useful but incomplete metaphors. They are only part of the picture. A more inclusive term is *policy subsystem.*

Several political scientists have used the idea of policy subsystems, but few have gone beyond a general conception. J. Leiper Freeman introduced the idea with his phrase "web of relationships in the subsystem."[6] Grant McConnell followed with a comparable term, "sub-government."[7] Theodore Lowi argued that policymaking had been coopted by status-quo interest groups; and he referred to a triad of decision making (for example, in the case of agriculture): "The politics within each system is built upon a triangular trading pattern including the central agency, a congressional committee or subcommittee and the local district farm committee ... each side of the triangle complements and supports the other two."[8]

David Mayhew describes policy subsystems from the congressional viewpoint as "Congressmen protect[ing] clientele systems—alliances of agencies, hill committees, and clienteles—against the incursions of presidents and cabinet secretaries."[9]

Pluralist and interest-group theories of politics fit closely with the subsystem approach. Pluralists argue that groups make demands on government to foster their legitimate interests and that government has perceived its proper role as the promoter of these interests in society.[10] The public interest is defined by the aggregation of special interests with their sponsors in Congress and the bureaucracy. Pluralists further argue that new policies are enacted, new agencies created (or old ones expanded or reorganized), new congressional committees or subcommittees added (or jurisdictions expanded) to promote the interest of powerful competing groups in society, as interest groups in society gain sufficient power to "own" some "turf" in Congress and the executive branch.[11]

Interest groups often gain political power when their policy subsystem receives a structural "promotion." The elevation of the Veterans Administration to presidential cabinet status under President Ronald Reagan was a high-level promotion for veterans' groups and the congressional Veterans Affairs Committees. Similarly, President Jimmy Carter created the U.S. Department of Education in his first year in office after making a public commitment to the National Education Association and other educators during his bid for the Democratic presidential nomination, something that the broad coalition of elementary, secondary, and higher education interests had sought for at least two decades.[12] Lineberry argues that the creation or expansion of jurisdiction is common to policy subsystems:

> When a group becomes strong enough, it gets a part of the government, its own piece of the action. The measure of an interest group's strength is how many "shares" of the government it controls. "Little" interests, such as the fisheries or tobacco growers, may have only an agency or two within a cabinet department and only a subcommittee of Congress. "Big" interests, such as business and labor, have whole cabinet departments upon whose support they can rely. But whatever the nature of the subgovernment, interest group liberalism is a pluralism without competition, a system of government where interest groups capture shares of the government and where the regulators are often drawn from the regulated.[13]

Specifying a General Model of Policy Subsystems

Policy subsystems can be characterized by networks of actors, the substantive policy domain with which they are concerned, and various modes of decision making. They are organized to make focused demands on policymakers and to influence specific programs, not to win elections or form governments. Most public problems considered by subsystems are addressed without being fully considered in the electoral arena, often with only a cursory nod from presidents, political parties, congressional leaders, or top executive branch administrators. Thousands of clientele-oriented subsystems, expressing many points of view, form the web of American public policy dominating the workload of congressional committees and subcommittees, interest groups, and executive branch agencies. Political power in each policy area is wielded by actors who often serve their own private interests. This has been called *multiple elitism* or *plural elitism,* but such terms do not acknowledge the democratic and open nature of subsystem politics.

Subsystems are decentralized power structures with predictable informal communication patterns among participants who come primarily from interest groups, members and staffs of congressional committees and subcommittees, bureau and agency personnel in the executive branch, and other policy specialists from universities, state and local governments, and specialized media (e.g. newsletters and professional journals). Washington lawyers, functioning as lobbyists, also play a key role in the structure of subsystem representation.[14] Presidential advisers from the Executive Office of the President, especially the Office of Management and Budget, can also become involved in subsystems. These participants have varying roles in moving issues onto the public agenda, developing and passing legislation, making rules and regulations, preparing and passing budgets, administering and implementing programs, and evaluating and changing them.

Subsystems and Functional Representation

Subsystems are dynamic and evolve because of a society's need to divide decision-making tasks and promote the development of knowledge to solve public problems. As this natural progression of dividing labor and developing expertise continues, the general electorate is frequently excluded from decision making, especially when it comes to highly technical and complex issues. Most people find government programs irrelevant unless they have an impact on their daily lives. Subsystem actors develop policy expertise and continuing relationships with one another in arenas of direct interest to themselves. Because they understand the issue, they have considerable independence in the development, implementation, and evaluation of policy under the subsystem's jurisdiction.

American politics is organized around thousands of subsystems, functionally oriented decision-making systems, sometimes in conflict, often in cooperation. Functions in society such as education, transportation, health-delivery systems, and environmental protection are represented primarily by specialists in those fields both within and outside of government. Subsystems are a form of *functional representation* (the representation of societal functions through governmental institutions) stemming from the division of labor and development of expertise and specialization in society. Functional specialists or persons with expertise and technical competence with regard to an issue or program dominate the subsystem. Functional specialists come from interest groups, academia, Congress, the executive agency, state and local governments, think tanks, and the other subsystem organizations that bring specialized knowledge to public-sector decision making.

Functional representation generally has a greater influence on routine policymaking than on highly controversial issues or "high politics." Policy embroiled in controversy attracts the attention and involvement of presidents, congressional leaders, political parties, the media and the general public, but the political system cannot handle very many highly controversial issues at one time. Most public policymaking is not electorally conflictual but routine. Consequently, the functional representation inherent in policy subsystems is more pervasive and influential than the formal and more commonly understood forms of representation based on geographic territory (U.S. Senate) and population (U.S. House of Representatives). Presidents discover quickly that it is difficult to establish a central core of authority over functional specialists and the policy subsystems. They cannot simply order that something be done and expect it to change. Passing a law in Congress does not automatically guarantee its implementation either. Power and authority in the bureaucracy is usually decentralized and housed in policy subsystems around the functions for which each agency has responsibility.

Any major public *policy arena* consists of a complex set of semiautonomous *subsystems* organized around *programs* or narrow issues such as titles within major legislative acts or specific regulations promulgated and administered by an administrative agency. Some programs are distributive, others regulatory, and others redistributive. Federal education policy, for example, generally perceived to be distributive, is divided into clusters such as higher education policy, primary education policy, secondary education policy, vocational education policy, and so forth. Within each of these education policy clusters are dozens of federal programs and thus dozens of policy subsystems.

Political Parties and Subsystems

The relationship of policy subsystems to political party organization within and outside government can be close or distant and can even supplant a party on a particular issue. When policy subsystems work through or become identified with political parties, the alliance is often both tentative and temporary because party members in this country share only some of the values of their fellow members from subsystem interest groups. More often, subsystems cut across party lines; they are nonpartisan. Subsystems in highly technical areas are most likely to be nonpartisan; for example, the allocation of funds for biomedical research to the National Institutes for Health is neither a Democratic nor a Republican issue. Such subsystems may help to democratize parties or even nation-states.

Subsystems as Open Communication Networks

Freedom of speech, assembly, and press allows for a free flow of information among subsystem actors. The open sharing of information among subsystem actors is the primary method of issue resolution for the subsystem.[15] Access to trustworthy and timely information about an issue or policy also helps determine the strength of subsystems. The better the quality and greater variety of information and the more diverse the sources of knowledge subsystem actors have, the more power they possess. Using specialized knowledge, they can anticipate and respond to policy events affecting their interests more effectively than can nonsubsystem actors.

Subsystem actors usually build coalitions, bargain, and compromise with one another in their quest to resolve an issue of public policy. The norm of reciprocity is widely practiced among subsystem actors. They share information, power, and influence over a program or public policy issue. Cooperation, friendly legislative oversight, and "cozy" program evaluation, often hidden from public view, are common to policy subsystems. Conflict is generally kept within well-defined boundaries, at a low to middle level within the executive branch and within subcommittees and their staffs in Congress. Surprises among subsystem actors are not appreciated, and the sharing of information and knowledge is rewarded.

Solutions to issues facing subsystem actors are seldom arrived at by the ideal of an abstract rational actor who systematically scans all alternatives and selects one that maximizes utility. The process of decision making is full of ambiguities at every stage in the policy process. Basic uncertainties occur in identification of a public problem, definition of goals and objectives the actors want to achieve, the strategy to be taken to solve the problem, and the criteria to be used to determine success. Despite these challenges, subsystem routines dispose actors toward a stock set of solutions that can be applied to a wide range of problems.[16]

SUBSYSTEM CONFLICT AND VISIBILITY

A small number of people participate in the subsystem, and dispute resolution tends to move toward equilibrium among the most powerful actors. The number of critical actors with jurisdiction over an issue often number fewer than 100 people. Professional careers are built around the issues and programs dominated by subsystems. People often move between interest groups, agencies, and Congress, building expertise and a reputation for knowledge about a subsystem and its programs.

A major characteristic of subsystem politics is its low level of visibility to the public and lack of involvement by the electorate. Policy subsystems evolve in such a way that important actors are hidden to the general public and nonsubsystem players. Since policy subsystems are organized around single issues or programs, they are rarely perceived to be important to a large constituency in the general public. Subsystems become naturally closed and out of the public eye because it is the most "efficient" way to make decisions about complicated and highly technical issues. Television and the general news media rarely focus on subsystem politics, and that is the way subsystem actors like it. Most highly visible political actors and institutions in American politics are not included in policy subsystems.

How many persons and what interests they represent in a subsystem depend primarily on the issues addressed, but in all cases, participants are drawn from a finite sphere of potential system members. There are approximately 1,300 federal government programs according to the Congressional Budget Office.[17] The exact number of policies within these programs and subprograms and thus the number of policy subsystems that exist is difficult to state authoritatively, but it easily exceeds 2,000. Nevertheless, the key players in the relationships among interest groups, congressional committees, agencies, and others amount to a few thousand out of potential millions of elected and appointed political actors. There are 2.9 million civilian employees in the federal government, but fewer than 3,000 managers with around 10,000 key subordinates who play a critical role in subsystem decision making.[18]

Approximately 75 percent of the bureau leaders (General Schedule levels 16–18 and the Senior Executive Service) are career federal executives.[19] In 1993 there were 284 committees and subcommittees in Congress with approximately 31,000 staff associated with Congress.[20] The staffs of House and Senate standing committees, key actors in subsystem politics, number slightly more than 3,000. Personal staffs to senators and house members number around 11,500. Finally, it is estimated that over 80,000 lobbyists and staff are connected with Washington-based interest groups and associations.[21]

"Mapping" the framework of a policy subsystem or determining who the key decision makers are in any issue arena is critical to understanding public policymaking. The number of subsystem participants can range from a few dozen to hundreds, even thousands, depending on competition within a subsystem, visibility of the issue, complexity and scope of the policy being considered, and involvement of the news media, presidents, and the general public.

The Importance of "Political Turf"

Jurisdiction over an issue or program, or "political turf," defines who will be involved in the resolution of conflict and the nature of the policymaking process in that arena. Control of political turf is considered essential to the survival of policy subsystems. Powerful subsystems are usually successful in thwarting challenges to their authority and in keeping conflict within their own jurisdiction.

Administrative agencies and congressional committees and subcommittees all have jurisdictional claims. Knowledge of the policy preferences of the primary actors who have authority to deal with an issue is often enough to predict what the public policy will be for a public problem. Graham Allison argues: "Where you stand depends on where you sit."[22] Those actors with responsibility for a program, whether they are from interest groups, the Hill, or the executive branch, organize themselves so that they do not expose the subsystem to threats from outside adversaries. Generally, bureaucrats, committee and subcommittee chairs, and interest-group leaders rigorously defend their jurisdiction to make decisions about a program. Policymaking is often affected by jurisdictional battles. The importance of struggles over jurisdiction was expressed by a manager in the U.S. Department of Transportation when discussing the internecine battles between highway and urban transit advocates:

> You had to sit down people from the Highway Administration and the Urban Mass Transit Administration to negotiate the regulations. They wouldn't talk to each other for two months. They'd sit across the table from each other and scream at each other. The highway people didn't care one iota about UMTA's problems, the UMTA people didn't care one iota about the highway people's problems. It took eight months before they got out of the regulations.[23]

Sometimes several agencies or congressional committees exercise joint or sequential jurisdiction over a program, which can lead to increased conflict and competition. Often more than a single coalition of interest groups has a stake in the outcome of a specific issue. This increases the potential for conflict and, when taken to the extreme, can foster the disintegration of the policy subsystem. Jurisdictional disputes can also lead to stalemate, as occurred during the battles between the congressional energy and environmental committees over consideration of the opening of Arctic wilderness for oil exploration.

SUBSYSTEMS AND THE ADMINISTRATIVE SECTOR OF GOVERNMENT

Policy subsystems have their locus of power at a low to middle level within the executive branch. Power often resides with experts in the bureau or agency handling a specific program, rather than at top management levels. Presidents and their appointees and members of Congress come and go, but the key functional specialists survive elections, reorganizations, cutbacks, and new policy directives. If political appointees do not learn how to work with policy subsystems, they find it difficult to achieve their objectives. In higher education policy, for example, the principal administrative actors include a complex matrix of middle-level managers of the Department of Education (DOE) programs (the Fund for the Improvement of Postsecondary Education, Student Financial Assistance, Higher Education Programs, Higher Education Program Services, and International Education) and independent agencies such as the National Endowment for the Arts, the Endowment for the Humanities, the National Science Foundation, and other agencies with programs that are of interest to postsecondary educational institutions.[24] This network of executive branch actors is linked to its counterparts in states, in Congress, and among dozens of interest groups.

Each program and issue in postsecondary education is handled by different bureaucrats and political appointees. If you want to know about student loans for postsecondary education, the Office of Student Financial Assistance "owns the turf" within the Office of Postsecondary Education. If you are interested in federal policy on foreign study, the Office of International Education has responsibility within DOE, but the U.S. Information Agency and the Department of State share this jurisdiction. These programs have networks of key administrators and small staffs that are the functional specialists in student financial aid and international education. Maybe twenty to thirty people are well known by the other actors in these subsystems. They play an essential role in generating new ideas and legislation, promulgating rules and regulations, and administering existing programs within their jurisdiction. These administrative actors have their administrative counterparts in state government and in colleges and universities. They know each other well and communicate regularly through national associations, newsletters, on the telephone, and, of course, in person in D.C. and in the states. They push their own agendas, bargain, compromise, keep one another informed, and generally try to help each other.

It is difficult for presidents, secretaries, undersecretaries, or even assistant secretaries for the Office of Postsecondary Education to keep up with all the issues and participants of higher education policy subsystems. Even when presidential appointees and top civil servants are experts in education, they often become "captured" by their agencies and the clients they serve. Thus the top political appointees, because of their unfamiliarity with the subject, have much less power than is suggested by their titles, or if they are already experts when appointed, they often exercise their power in agreement with the agency specialists.

Executive branch functional specialists can have substantial autonomy in the formation and implementation of public policy. They often initiate legislative proposals that help set the agenda for the authorization-appropriating process in Congress. They draft legislation and help congressional committees build support with members and interest groups. They forge relationships with interest groups and congressional committees to shape legislation and the flow of information essential to the policy process.

In addition to the federal government program managers, state and local administrative units with responsibility for a federal program are often part of the policy subsystem. State and local public officials are well represented through their respective national associations.[25] These officials communicate most effectively through special committees in "peak" associations such as the National Association of Counties, the National Governor's Conference, the National Conference of State Legislatures, the Council of State Governments, the International City Management Association, the National League of Cities, the U.S. Conference of Mayors, the so-called seven pigs (public interest groups). Each peak association has developed expert committees and staff on a variety of topics that are a critical part of domestic policy subsystems.

Congress and Subsystems

The work of Congress is the work of committees and subcommittees. Power in Congress is decentralized and specialized in 295 committee and subcommittees, giving access to interest groups and administrators through members of Congress and staff assigned to committees and subcommittees. Congressional committees have their formal responsibilities defined by the rules of the House and Senate and by precedent. Members of Congress seek committee assignments that will help them get reelected and help them focus on programs and issues that are of direct interest to them and their constituents. Once a committee assignment is made, senators and representatives become deeply immersed in the policy subsystems within the jurisdiction of their assignment.

Congressmen and their staffs quickly become functional specialists (if they were not before coming to Congress) in the several well-defined program areas under the jurisdiction of their committees and subcommittees. Most of the work of Congress is handled by specialists on subcommittees; thus it is easy for members to become specialists responsive to their counterparts from interest groups and agencies. The subsystem fosters a norm of "mutual noninterference" that reduces the number of battles over jurisdiction. The insulation of committees also insulates the subsystem.

Members supplement committee assignments by joining special congressional caucuses (e.g., the Steel Caucus, Travel Caucus, Mushroom Caucus, and Black Caucus) that are closely tied to interest groups outside Congress. Caucuses help shape the policymaking process in Congress and serve as contact points for liaison officers in the executive branch. Political action committees (PACs) raise funds for election campaigns and play a key role in "buying access" to members by interest groups. The total number of PACs has grown rapidly from 600 in 1974 to more than 4,000 in 1989 with most of their contributions going to incumbents regardless of political party. PACs reward members of Congress on committees and subcommittees and help reelect them to the subsystem most relevant to interest groups.

Senators and representatives practice a division of labor and allow "experts," their colleagues and staff members on the appropriate committees and subcommittees that have jurisdiction over an issue, to make the major decisions about a program. A common exception to the division of labor norm is when an issue is perceived to involve their state or district directly. Another exception is when an issue is a major electoral issue and is perceived to be of national importance. Members, whether or not they are on committees with jurisdiction over these macro issues, are actively involved in proposing solutions (e.g., solutions to the budget deficit, cuts in military spending, and cuts in income and social security taxes).

As a result of the reforms of the 1970s that decentralized congressional power (especially in the House), subcommittee chairmen and their immediate professional staff play an important role in policy subsystems. Committees and subcommittees are centers of subsystem policymaking by setting the agenda for initial consideration of new legislation, old programs and recurring issues; they have resources to oversee and evaluate the administration of programs; they have close contacts with interest groups, bureaus, and experts on an issue or program; and they have formal jurisdiction over an issue at the first, and often most important, stage of the legislative process. Legislators understand the connection between reelection and committee assignments. They are primarily motivated to get reelected, to satisfy their constituents, and to pass good legislation. Subsystem politics fits those incentives nicely. Congressmen realize that a strong relationship between their subcommittee, relevant executive agencies, and interest groups can help them get reelected, serve constituents, and achieve good public policy.

Other important actors are the approximately 31,000 congressional staff: the personal staffs of senators and representatives, professional staffs of the subcommittees and committees (by far the most important congressional staff in the subsystem), and the program and policy specialists in other congressional work groups (e.g., the Congressional Budget Office, the Congressional Research Service, the General Accounting Office, and the Office of Technology Assessment). Each group has policy experts that assist the members, subcommittees, and committees in the development of new laws and the evaluation of old ones. They offer policy options, analyses and information for members. This bureaucracy of staffers has an independent power base in the policy process. Hill staffers build prominence through expertise and through the simple fact that they have more time to focus on the issues facing a policy subsystem than do Senate and House members. Committee staffs are especially important at hearings, markup, and report stages of subsystem policymaking. The committee agenda is largely set by the staffs. They draft legislation, arrange for hearings and witnesses, write amendments and floor speeches, and negotiate agreements among interested parties (interest groups, legislators, and executive branch officials) behind the scenes. Their expertise, access to powerful members, and concentration on subsystem politics make them very powerful in the policy process.

In conclusion, congressional committees dominate subsystem agendas in the House and Senate. Their decisions largely determine which policies will be considered in the House and Senate. They link subsystem actors during the legislative process and contribute to the fragmented, but representative nature of the subsystems.

Subsystems and the "Revolving Door"
Participants in policy subsystems have predictable career patterns. Congressmen and congressional staff often move to the executive branch or to interest groups to work in the same substantive areas they worked in during their tenure on the Hill. Executive branch officials often move to congressional staff assignments or to the private sector related to their bureau and agency work. Interest-group representatives and others from the private sector move in and out of governmental institutions, working on common substantive interests. This regularized movement of personnel around policy subsystems is so extensive that it has been called "incest groups." Each actor is in a series of exchange operations that depend on and receive benefits.

When new presidents take office, they often appoint experts from pressure groups or from the Hill to key positions in bureaus and agencies in the executive branch. Presidents Carter and Reagan campaigned against the bureaucracy and called for a new cadre of managers in Washington, D.C., during their election campaigns; but after appointing a few insiders from Georgia and California, respectively, they turned to the pool of functional specialists in Washington, D.C., to run their governments. It is not surprising that experienced Hill staffers are attractive appointees to a new administration. They have well-established linkages to their subsystems; and they bring with them knowledge and established communication networks.

A Typology of Subsystems

Although they are the predominant type of policymaking system in American politics, policy subsystems vary over time and according to the policy being considered. I suggest a simple typology to help delineate the dynamic nature of policymaking.

Subsystems are dynamic and can vary from *dominant* to *competitive* to *disintegrated*. Although the most common state of a policy subsystem is closed, static, and dominant over a particular program, competition and even policy disintegration occurs in any policy area from time to time.

Subsystems, like the policy process itself, are not static. They can range from dominant subsystems that are stable, with well-defined jurisdiction, low political visibility, narrow conflict, and few participants to competitive and disintegrated subsystems with instability, overlapping or fragmented jurisdictions with many players and extensive political conflict. The nature of subsystems is related to the type of policy, issue, and event facing the actors in the subsystem.

DOMINANT POLICY SUBSYSTEMS

Dominant policy subsystems are relatively stable communication and decision-making clusters with a small number of participants who significantly influence and often control government programs or issues. They are "relatively well-bounded," "differentiated from their environment," and "relatively complex."[26] Within a specific policy area, a few actors tend to be better organized and dominate the more passive interests. Dominant policy subsystems are usually structured around distributive policies such as tax deductions for home mortgages, Elementary and Secondary Education Act benefits, federal highway funds, water projects, veterans' benefits, and a variety of subsidies for business and industry. There is a flow of information and knowledge that follows well-worn and enduring channels among mutually trusted actors sharing common interests and broadly shared policy preferences. The actors, including executive branch officials, legislators, businessmen, lobbyists, representatives of the specialized media, policy specialists in universities and think tanks communicate with one another, are relatively unseen and unknown to the general public. Decisions are made in dominant subsystems without regard to their overall impact on the political system. They are uncoordinated and decentralized.

Dominant subsystems exhibit relatively stable relations because the actors strive to reduce uncertainty, information costs, and opportunistic behaviors of the subsystem members by creating relatively stable channels of communication and well-established norms of the game. The norm of the dominant subsystem is cooperation, bargaining, and compromise. Subsystem actors develop an esprit de corps that flows across ideological and partisan lines. There is a high degree of mutually rewarding logrolling. There is a narrow scope of policy conflict usually at a middle or lower level within government institutions. Dominant subsystems are naturally resistant to pressure from outside powerful actors such as presidents, high-level executive branch officials, congressional committees that do not have formal jurisdiction over their subsystem issues, and interest groups that are not regular participants in the subsystem. Unless the general print and broadcast news media are considered useful to the cause of the subsystem, the key actors try to exclude reporters. Dominant subsystems work to thwart challenges to their authority over issues and programs within their jurisdiction, usually with great success.

Subsystem players try to limit conflict within the boundaries of their subsystems. Outside challenges to dominant policy subsystems usually do not pose a major threat. When new issues and policy problems are presented, the automatic response is to attempt to control the scope and level of competition, keeping it within the subsystem jurisdiction. Therefore, access to the decision process is often closed. An important norm of dominant policy subsystems is reciprocity. Dominant subsystems help private-sector producers through government action, whether this is new legislation, helpful regulations, or funding programs that the subsystem's clients want. Dominant subsystems are often organized in well-defined hierarchies with centrally located actors who mediate communication and decision making among more peripherally located actors. Alternatively, they may be structured in a wheel of relationships that is more diffuse. The structure of this type of dominant subsystem lacks hierarchy and centralized coordinating actors.

COMPETITIVE POLICY SUBSYSTEMS

A second type of policy subsystem, *competitive,* is distinguished by how the decisions are made. Coalitions of actors are in a constant state of competition. Government actors may have an independent power to initiate new policies, but this may lead to challenges and conflict. Although the communication network is limited within each competing network of policy actors, the systems are more complex and open than in dominant subsystems. The political structure of the subsystem may shift dramatically from event to event and issue to issue. Peak associations and top governmental officials often must play a mediating role in the conflict between supporters and opponents of a particular policy preference. Government subsystem actors may initiate ways to reduce conflict, such as negotiated rulemaking, organizing short-term ad hoc groups of decision makers, or by using policy coordinating mechanisms such as the congressional budget committees.

Hugh Heclo's conception of "issue networks" fits the description of competitive policy subsystems. His description of many actors who move in and out of decision-making networks is a central tendency of competitive subsystems: "Issues networks ... comprise a large number of participants with quite variable degrees of mutual commitment or of dependence on others in the environment.... Rather than groups united in dominance over a program, no one, as far as one can tell, is in control of the policies and issues."[27]

Relationships among the actors in competitive policy subsystems are often unstable for a short period, until the various factions are structured into competing clusters or there is general agreement among the key actors and the subsystem evolves into a dominant state. Competition may evolve through a redefinition of the scope and level of issue conflict among the actors inside an existing subsystem or by attacks from the outside by other actors. For example, in the view of Cigler and Loomis, "increased representation often leads to heightened levels of competition within a given policy subsystem, particularly as budget demands redefine more and more policies as redistributive."[28]

The policy being considered by a competitive subsystem is often defined as redistributive or regulatory. When redistributive policy conflict cannot be resolved within a single subsystem, other actors and subsystems often join the battle and resort to open conflict. Multiple referral of legislation is a sign of a competitive subsystem. For example, in 1992, the long-awaited major energy bill was referred to nine committees in the House of Representatives, causing delay and policy deadlock. The multiple referral of the energy bill and competition surrounding many of its provisions eventually caused further delay and deadlock in the conference committee with the Senate. Often, when new legislation is needed from competitive subsystems, approval from the larger political system is needed. This creates competition, conflict, and new policy players. Nevertheless, approval is usually forthcoming, and the system generally defers to the experts with the policy jurisdiction, but the challenge and heightened visibility creates short-term conflict and permeability within and among subsystems.

Andrew S. McFarland designates regulatory negotiation as a "power triad," but the actors do not form a tight coalition; they conflict.[29] Regulatory negotiation with government actors mediating between two triadic participants is increasingly common but has much more bounded conflict than most competitive decision-making systems. For example, although labor, business, and the government have a continuing battle over the regulations to protect the health and safety of American workers, the decision-making system has not designated a static formal relationship between the three sectors. Occupational health and safety policy is competitive and complex; it includes not only the agency charged with regulating in that area but also government agencies or departments such as the Department of Health and Human Services, congressional committees and subcommittees, the courts, specialized media, public-interest groups, the Office of Management and Budget's Office of Information and Regulatory Affairs, and a variety of experts from the university and health communities. Competition and decision making is formally organized by the Occupational Safety and Health Administration (OSHA), which has the responsibility to regulate the health and safety of the workplace for most American laborers. Labor unions, health and safety experts, medical researchers, and workers lobby for a safer workplace, and businesses and their associations conflict with OSHA and those pushing for a safer workplace. The OSHA relationships are far from a competitive power triad but are a complex, fluctuating subsystem.

Challenges to an existing dominant subsystem are rare and usually short lived, since it is to the advantage of most subsystem actors to minimize the costs of competition. Above all, the players try to keep final decisions out of the view of the public and the media. Competition is costly and unpredictable, and widespread publicity about a subsystem battle increases uncertainty. Most subsystem actors want to control the policy outcomes, even though they might not win all they desire. Generally, competitive subsystems are short lived, but competition can be institutionalized, such as the conflict between industry and environmentalists over clean air policy. A competitive subsystem tends to undermine dominant subsystems and micro politics, but tends to remain bounded. The supporters and opponents of a policy are well known to one another, such as those involved in the rewrite of the 1990 Clean Air Act. Competition often results from external events that have an impact on a subsystem or challenges to an existing subsystem power base. Competition generates new interaction patterns and eventually a new dominating coalition. There is often confrontation over policy jurisdiction or the right to decide and always a contest over the substance of a program or policy. Competitive policy subsystems have more participants than dominant subsystems do, but numbers are still limited to knowledgeable insiders from two or more subsystems. The general public, congressional leadership, and high-level executive branch personnel can be involved but usually they are not.

THE CLEAN AIR ACT AND THE NATURE OF COMPETITIVE SUBSYSTEMS. An excellent example of an institutionalized competitive subsystem that experienced intense sustained conflict between industry and environmentalists occurred over the Clean Air Act from 1977 to 1990. The Clean Air Act of 1963 and amendments in 1977 gave the federal government a role in airpollution abatement that acts almost like a national zoning law. The battle in 1990 pitted industrialists against environmentalists, which put powerful competing pressures on members of Congress.

The Clean Air Act probably has a greater impact on industry than any federal statute except the tax code. Nearly every congressional district has polluting industry targeted by the clean air legislation. Most districts also have well-organized environmentalists pushing for the elimination of toxic emissions. Industry predicted financial disaster and a loss of jobs if the most far-reaching proposals advocated by environmentalists were written into the new Clean Air Act. Environmentalists predicted dire health and environmental consequences for the continuation of acid rain, polluting motor fuels, and airborne toxic emissions. Most members of Congress try to protect the economic well-being of their districts by protecting jobs, and some members of Congress see it as their duty to protect petrochemical plants, automobile factories, local utilities, and coal jobs. Others represent districts with serious problems of air pollution and acid rain.

In the volatile and highly visible battle over clean air legislation, Republican President George Bush coalesced with such arch Democrats as Senator Robert S. Byrd, representing high-sulfur coal interests in West Virginia and chair of the powerful Senate Appropriations Committee, and Congressman John R. Dingell, chair of the Energy and Commerce Committee representing the automobile industry located primarily in Dingell's Michigan district. Congressman Henry Waxman from Los Angeles (an area with serious air pollution), and chair of the Subcommittee on Health and Environment of Dingell's Energy and Commerce Committee, and Senator George J. Mitchell from Maine (a state receiving regular doses of acid rain from the industrial Midwest), the Senate Democratic Majority Leader, were two key players representing the pro-environmental position. For years, Congress has been divided into warring camps, with northeasterners and environmentalists on one side and utility and high-sulfur coal interests on the other. Issues of acid rain, alternative fuels (ethanol and methanol), acceptable levels of urban smog and carbon monoxide, tailpipe emission standards, requirements to build more clean-fuel automobiles, reduction in chlorofluorocarbons that deplete the stratospheric ozone, and cutbacks on cancer-causing air toxins are all related to the fight over jobs and clean air.

The inability to reconcile the clashing industrial and environmental interests in the rewrite of the Clean Air Act tied up Congress for over a decade. If most congressional behavior can be explained by the single, central fact that members want to be reelected, then it is understandable how this competitive subsystem caused delay and deadlock.[30]

DISINTEGRATED POLICY SUBSYSTEMS

Although rare, disintegrated policy subsystems can develop in at least one of several ways. Intense, prolonged competition over a policy can push it into a disintegrated, and at times macro political, mode of decision making. The annual battle over the federal budget is an example of this. A congressional reorganization like the reorganization of the U.S. Senate committee system in 1976–77 can redefine jurisdiction and break up an old dominant subsystem. Changes in bureaucratic boundaries such as President Reagan's attack on the Economic Development Administration can disintegrate an old subsystem for some time. The scope of conflict in disintegrated policy subsystems is extensive, often leading to permanent jurisdictional change or a subsystem's demise. The level of conflict and visibility of policymaking is prominent within the executive branch and Congress, forcing issues to the attention of congressional leaders, departmental secretaries, and even presidents, and into the headlines of the mass media. Disintegrated policy subsystems have large numbers of participants at high levels of government and engage the interested public not usually focused on subsystem politics. There is no central core of authority over the issues under consideration in disintegrated subsystems; therefore it is difficult or impossible to come to quick, rational closure in the decision-making process. Totally disintegrated policy subsystems permit policy change by placing an issue at a higher level of decision making in government, by changing the jurisdiction over an issue, or by adding new actors to the subsystems through elections or reorganization.

THE DYNAMICS OF SUBSYSTEM CHANGE

Policy subsystems behave like organisms, adapting to new conditions, evolving into new structures, languishing into extinction, and regenerating into new and viable political forces. Subsystems can be challenged by "outsiders" or by new actors trying to encroach on an established policy territory. Competition can also occur between two or more subsystems. Competition among subsystems and among new actors may lead temporarily to total disintegration of an existing subsystem, into a state of disintegration, or into macro politics. Some sort of disruptive event may expand the interest, conflict, and the number of participants in an area and cause a subsystem to change.

SUBSYSTEM CHANGE AND THE ENERGY CRISIS. An example of the transformation of a dominant subsystem into a disintegrated one is the recent history regarding the pricing and distribution of refined petroleum products in the United States.

Conflict over oil policy in the United States came quickly in 1973 when the OPEC nations cut off oil exports to the United States. This caused shortages in heating oil, gasoline, and jet fuel, and an increase in price for all petroleum products. Before the cutoff of foreign oil, there was a classic closed, dominant policy subsystem over import quotas, oil depletion allowance, pricing and distribution, and other key petroleum public policies. The old politics of energy before the crisis was a classic example of subsystem politics dominated by the primary economic interests associated with the exploration, production, and distribution of oil, producer state interests, and their associations such as the American Petroleum Institute (an association consisting of almost all the petroleum companies in the United States); the Interior Committees of Congress and the tax committees (House Ways and Means and Senate Finance), and the Department of Interior's Division of Oil and Gas (DOG). A key player, the former president of the American Petroleum Institute (API), Frank N. Ikard, a former member of the House Ways and Means Committee, and his staff had extensive experience in the oil industry and in government. This was a well-established network of influential oil subsystem actors using their expertise and access to pursue narrow economic goals.

The oil subsystem of API, the Interior Committees, Finance, Ways and Means, and DOG was closed, autonomous, and rarely challenged. It was dominated by tax and oil experts freely moving information and their careers through a "revolving door" from private sector to public sector and back. Little public concern was expressed from nonenergy specialists until there was a dramatic change in the nature of the policy conflict caused by the 1973 energy crisis. The old dominant subsystem "controlling" oil policy changed dramatically when Americans quickly discovered the energy crisis in the long lines at gas stations and in increased prices for heating oil, airline tickets, and almost all consumer products. The general population entered the world of energy policy when they became concerned with the cost and shortages of oil. This led to direct challenges and ultimately to the disintegration of the old closed decision-making core of authority over oil policy. And it spread to other energy decision-making systems. Consumer-oriented interest groups were invigorated and challenged the dominant position of the oil and gas producers and their friends in government. There was a proliferation of new congressional subcommittees and intense jurisdictional conflicts over the issue. Members and congressional committees wanted to be part of the energy policymaking action because their constituents expected their congressmen to have an answer to the energy crisis. A new Department of Energy was created; a dozen subcommittees claiming energy jurisdiction sprouted in the House and Senate; and as many new energy-consumer and producer-oriented interest groups were established shortly after 1973. OPEC's cutoff of oil fractured the hegemony of the dominant oil policy subsystem into dozens of policy positions. It was difficult to set energy policy priorities and legislate an end to the crisis. The old subsystem was faced with intense competition and ultimately disintegration, pushing the energy issue eventually into the macro political realm.

The increased political competition was all sound and fury. There was no long-term, rational energy policy in the United States. No one dominated the open, dynamic, and complex set of subsystems surrounding energy policy. There were no longer groupings of semi-autonomous, dominant subsystems in control of every aspect of energy policy. Charles O. Jones describes the expanded participation in energy policy as follows: "[energy policy participation] has expanded *up* institutional hierarchies, out to citizen groups, *over* the other nations, and *across* from one resource subsystem to others."[31]

The disintegrated energy policy systems of the mid-1970s slowly evolved into several dominant subsystems structured around oil, natural gas, nuclear power, hydroelectric power, and other sources of energy in the 1980s and 1990s. Under the Reagan and Bush administrations, as other issues pushed energy issues off the macro political agenda, the old energy dominant policy subsystem revived and reassembled itself without great fanfare, agreeing on the deregulation of oil pricing and tax expenditures for oil exploration. In conclusion, the post-1973 energy crisis between oil producers and consumers thrust the energy issue into turbulence, disintegration, and ultimately macro politics from 1973 to 1979. But energy policymaking quickly contracted into a world dominated by producer interest groups, subcommittees in Congress, and relevant executive agencies in the 1990s.

Changing the scope of conflict, increasing the level of conflict, changing key personnel, reorganizing jurisdiction over an issue, and using the regulatory process of administrative agencies and the courts are several important methods of changing the power of policy subsystems.

The *scope of conflict* and the *level of conflict,* as argued by E.E. Schattschneider, are two primary factors that influence the nature of politics and the power of the policy subsystems.[32] The successful resolution of a policy or issue conflict within a policy subsystem is essential to the survival of a subsystem. If the actors in a subsystem cannot quickly and successfully resolve conflict on their own turf, "outsiders" from other committees, agencies, bureaus, groups, and the media or the general public will take the issue away from them. These new actors in the decision-making system increase their influence and the probability of a policy change as the amount of internal subsystem conflict increases and becomes uncontrolled. Thus a primary motivation of the actors in policy subsystems is to control the *scope* and *level* of conflict associated with the programs and issues within the jurisdiction of the subsystem. Subsystems tend to be closed and naturally resistant to externally generated forces of change.

Although long-lasting competitive policy subsystems are rare, they often lead to significant policy changes. An example of challenge to a dominant subsystem and a major change in policy is the history of the passage of the Airline Deregulation Act of 1978. For years, airline regulation was made in a dominant subsystem made up of the Civil Aeronautics Board (CAB), the regulated airline industry, airline labor groups, specialized media covering the airlines, and the congressional aviation subcommittees. From 1938 to the mid-1970s, Congress generally followed the lead of the airline industry and the CAB for the regulation of routes and rates of air passenger and air freight carriers. In 1975 a direct challenge to the airline regulation policy subsystem was made by Senator Edward M. Kennedy. He held a round of oversight hearings on the CAB through his Senate Judiciary Subcommittee on Antitrust and Monopoly. These hearings immediately expanded the focus on airline regulation by providing a valuable public forum for those outside the established subsystem. Many expressed displeasure over airline regulation and the CAB. Kennedy also challenged President Ford to reform much sooner and more vigorously than desired. After some prodding, Ford endorsed airline deregulation as a major part of his regulatory reform efforts. Ford also appointed a new reform-minded chairman of the CAB, John Robson, a new actor in the subsystem. The result of Kennedy's challenge as an outsider to the commercial aviation subsystem, and Ford's response was a redirection of CAB policy.

During the same period, a new chairman of the Senate Commerce Committee's Subcommittee on Aviation, Senator Howard W. Cannon, was concerned about Senator Kennedy's challenge to his jurisdiction over airline regulation. The infusion of new players and the competition among Ford, Cannon, and Kennedy over airline deregulation shattered the "holy alliance" of the CAB, airline unions, airline companies, and congressional subcommittees. The issue of airline regulation was highly volatile and competitive for a short period until the major actors compromised and endorsed the reform and a new coalition that favored deregulation was created.

Conclusion

In conclusion, how do we evaluate policy subsystems as a theory and as a way of making political decisions? The concept of policy subsystems is simple but joins a variety of theories of decision making and the American political process. Drawing from the literature on sociological network analysis, pluralism, corporatism, power triads, plural elitism, traditional legal-descriptive analysis, behavioralism, and rational choice, the theory of interest groups and policy subsystems can further our knowledge of how the policymaking process works in American politics.

Several concluding observations can be made about a theory of policy subsystems. Policy subsystems seem to describe routine policymaking accurately, but they are not static. They evolve and adapt to events and changing conditions. Dominant subsystems are the mode of distributive policymaking, but dedistributive (in times of scarcity), redistributive and regulatory policy may range from competitive to disintegrated to macro modes of decision making.

In summary, several basic propositions help specify a general model of policy subsystems in American politics:

1. American public policymaking is generally structured around specific programs and issues.
2. The relations among subsystem players are the basic determinants of public policy in each substantive program area.
3. Interest groups (public and private groups) organize to put pressure on policymakers in their arena of interest.
4. Countervailing groups organize to oppose the interests of interest groups.
5. Policy subsystem actors have significant influence over public policy within well-defined jurisdictions.
6. Subsystem actors lose power when an issue becomes highly visible and evolves into macro politics.
7. Subsystems provide stability for existing equilibria among interests.
8. Subsystems provide predictable access and opportunity for influence primarily to well-organized interests.
9. Subsystems provide some access and representation to interests that do not dominate a particular issue area.

10. Substantial changes in the balances among interests served by subsystems can be expected to occur only through macro-political intervention that modifies the rules and roles operating in the systems.
11. Subsystem actors generally adopt the norm of reciprocity; government actors subsidize interest-group actors, and interest-group actors assist government actors.
12. There is an interdependence among levels of government and between government and the private sector surrounding most policy subsystems.

The relationship between the scope and level of policy conflict and the influence of policy subsystems can be summarized in the following added hypotheses:

13. The wider the scope of conflict, the higher the level of conflict.
14. The wider the scope of policy conflict, the less the influence of policy subsystems over policy outcomes.
15. The higher the level of conflict, the less the influence of policy subsystems over policy outcomes.
16. Subsystems are unstable when resources are scarce and uncertainty surrounds the program.

Whether subsystems are good or bad is an issue that goes back to the roots of our democracy. The framers of the Constitution thought that by providing for elections and by delegating power to elected representatives they would prevent policymaking from falling into the hands of the "irresponsible" elements in society. James Madison warned of the dangers of faction, and contemporary critics of American democracy complain of interest-group liberalism, an upper-class bias in pluralism, exponential growth in political action committees, penetration of vested economic interest groups in the legislative and regulatory process, and the failure of the system to protect the "public interest." Do subsystems contribute to the "granting of preferences to a few favored interests" or check the power of large governmental and economic power bases? Policy subsystems allow for representation of a wide variety of interests, but there are no guarantees about fairness of outcome in our system; there are only guarantees of fairness of the rules of the decision-making game.

Acknowledgment

This chapter was written in honor of Charles H. Levine, distinguished scholar-teacher, generous colleague, and reliable friend. From the first time I met Charlie and became his friend as a fellow graduate student at Indiana University in 1966 to his death at the age of forty-nine, he was a constant source of inspiration and candid reviewer of my scholarship. This chapter continues the dialogue that Charlie and I had about policy subsystems and the key role played by Congress in the policy process. We coauthored a chapter entitled "Reagan and the Intergovernmental Lobby: Iron Triangles, Cozy Subsystems, and Political Conflict," in *Interest Group Politics,* 2d ed., ed. Allan J. Cigler and Burdette A. Loomis (Washington, D.C.: CQ Press, 1986) that made public our ongoing discussion of policy subsystem theory. Following his last recommendation about my work on subsystems, I have described a more elaborate model that focuses on the dynamic nature of policymaking, something that I am sure Charlie would have appreciated. Part of this argument appears in the third edition of *Interest Group Politics* (1991).

Notes

1. See Theodore J. Lowi, *The End of Liberalism,* 2d ed. (New York: Norton, 1979).

2. E.E. Schattschneider, *The Semi-Sovereign People* (New York: Holt, Rinehart and Winston, 1960).

3. Charles O. Jones describes three kinds of policymaking systems that predominate in American politics: cozy little connections or micro politics, cozy little triangles or intermediary politics, and sloppy large hexagons or macro politics. See Jones, *The United States Congress: People, Place, and Policy* (Homewood, Ill.: Dorsey, 1982), 362. Also see Emmette S. Redford's useful typology of micro politics, subsystem, or intermediary politics, and macro politics in *Democracy in the Administrative State* (New York: Oxford University Press, 1969), 84. John W. Kingdon argues that a *visible cluster* made up of actors such as the president and prominent members of Congress has more effect on the policy agenda than the *hidden cluster* that includes specialists in the bureaucracy and professional communities. See Kingdon, *Agendas, Alternatives, and Public Policies* (Boston: Little, Brown, 1984).

4. Jones, *United States Congress,* 353.

5. Hugh Heclo, "Issue Networks and the Executive Establishment," in *The New American Political System,* ed. A. King (Washington, D.C.: American Enterprise Institute, 1978). For an excellent critique of the concepts iron triangles, issue networks, and corporatism, see A. Grant Jordan, "Iron Triangles, Woolly Corporatism, and Elastic Nets: Images of the Policy Process," *Journal of Public Policy* 1, pt. 1 (February 1981): 95–123.

6. J. Leiper Freeman, *The Political Process* (New York: Random House, 1965).

7. Grant McConnell, *Private Power and American Democracy* (New York: Knopf, 1966). Also see Grant McConnell, "The Public Values of the Private As-

sociation," in *Voluntary Associations,* ed. J. Roland Pennock and John W. Chapman, 147–60 (New York: Atherton Press, 1969).

8. Theodore J. Lowi, "How Farmers Get What They Want," *Reporter,* 21 May 1964, 35. Also see Lowi, *End of Liberalism.*

9. David Mayhew, *The Electoral Connection* (New Haven: Yale University Press, 1974), 128. Also see Roger Davidson, "Breaking Up Those 'Cozy Triangles': An Impossible Dream?" in *Legislative Reform and Public Policy,* ed. S. Welch and J.G. Peters (New York: Praeger, 1977).

10. See the pluralist arguments of Robert A. Dahl, *Who Governs?* (New Haven: Yale University Press, 1961), and Nelson W. Polsby, *Community Power and Political Theory* (New Haven: Yale University Press, 1963). Also see Robert A. Dahl, *Dilemmas of Pluralist Democracy: Autonomy vs. Control* (New Haven: Yale University Press, 1982).

11. Lowi, *End of Liberalism,* 36–39. For a refutation of this point, see Dahl, *Dilemmas of Pluralist Democracy.*

12. The close relationship of education groups to the Democratic Party during the Carter campaign proved helpful in the creation of the Department of Education; however, it also proved to be a hindrance during the Reagan presidency as Reagan attempted to dismantle the Department.

13. Robert Lineberry, *American Public Policy* (New York: Harper & Row, 1977), 38.

14. See John P. Heinz et al., "Inner Circles or Hollow Cores? Elite Networks in National Policy Systems," *Journal of Politics* 52 (May 1990): 356–90.

15. See Edward O. Laumann and David Knoke, "Policy Networks of the Organizational State: Collective Action in the National Energy and Health Domains," in *Networks of Power: Organizational Actors at the National, Corporate, and Community Levels,* ed. Robert Perrucci and Harry R. Potter (New York: Aldine de Gruyter, 1989).

16. James G. March and Johan P. Olsen, *Ambiguity and Choice in Organizations* (Bergen: Universitetsforlaget, 1976).

17. Interview with staff from Office of the Director, Congressional Budget Office, November 1989.

18. Three million civilian employees include 811,000 U.S. Postal Service employees. See Congressional Budget Office, *Federal Civilian Employment* (Washington, D.C.: Government Printing Office, 1987). Also see U.S. Office of Personnel Management, *Civilian Employment of the Federal Government* (Washington, D.C.: Government Printing Office, 1984). The number of civilian employees on 1 January 1963 was 2.5 million; on 1 January 1973, 2.8 million; and on 1 January 1990, 3 million.

19. Unpublished memo, Office of Personnel Management, Fall 1989.

20. Norman J. Ornstein et al., *Vital Statistics on Congress, 1989–1990 ed.* (Washington, D.C.: CQ Press, 1990). Also see *Federal Civilian Employment,* 27.

21. Burdette Loomis and Allan Cigler, eds., *Interest Group Politics,* 2d ed. (Washington, D.C.: CQ Press, 1986), 6.

22. Graham T. Allison, *Essence of Decision* (Boston: Little, Brown, 1971), 176.

23. Kingdon, *Agendas, Alternatives, and Public Policies.*

24. See Lawrence E. Gladieux and Thomas R. Wolanin, *Congress and the*

Colleges (Lexington, Mass.: Lexington Books, 1976) for an analysis of higher education subsystems.

25. Charles H. Levine and James A. Thurber, "Reagan and the Intergovernmental Lobby: Iron Triangles, Cozy Subsystems, and Political Conflict," in Cigler and Loomis, *Interest Group Politics,* 202–20.

26. These definitional criteria come from Nelson W. Polsby, "The Institutionalization of the U.S. House of Representatives," *American Political Science Review* 62 (1968): 145.

27. Heclo, "Issue Networks and the Executive Establishment," 102.

28. Allan J. Cigler and Burdette A. Loomis, "Moving On: Interests, Power, and Politics in the 1980s," in Cigler and Loomis, *Interest Group Politics,* 306.

29. Andrew S. MacFarland, "Groups without Government: The Politics of Mediation," in Cigler and Loomis, *Interest Group Politics,* 289–301.

30. See David R. Mayhew, *Congress: The Electoral Connection* (New Haven: Yale University Press, 1974).

31. Charles O. Jones, "American Politics and the Organization of Energy Decision Making," *Annual Review of Energy* 4 (1979): 105.

32. Schattschneider, *Semi-Sovereign People,* chaps. 1 and 4.

5

Explaining the Growth and Contraction of Municipal Services

IRENE S. RUBIN AND BERNARD H. ROSS

The period from the end of World War II until the early 1970s was characterized by economic stability and public-sector growth. Political theories of the public sector that were written during this period, such as incrementalism and public choice theory, assumed that such growth was inevitable. They suggested a variety of causes for this growth, including the inappropriate public-sector assumption of private-sector functions paired with excessive public demand for services, and bureaucrats who, to forward their own careers and push their own programs, continually pushed up budget estimates. The inability of budget reviewers to examine requests in detail contributed to rules of thumb that allowed continuous slow growth.

The years from 1974 to about 1984 saw recession, inflation, and a decline in federal aid to cities. Many industrial cities in the Northeast and Midwest suffered declining economic bases. When taxes began to grow more quickly than incomes, tax protests became widespread. After California's Proposition 13 and Massachusetts' Proposition 2½, politicians sometimes took action to reduce or reform taxes to head off more stringent tax controls they assumed to be in the wings. As cities wrestled with cutbacks, existing theories that postulated a deterministic and continual expansion of the public sector fell short, and new ones began to emerge that emphasized alternation of growth and contraction, the role of the banks in precipitating a shift from growth and extensive borrowing to loss of credit and cutback, and focused attention on who benefited from growth and who benefited (relatively speaking) from contraction.[1]

Much of that early literature focused on the experiences of New York City, which was tottering on the brink of bankruptcy in the mid-1970s. While some academics were building theories to explain what they saw, politicians often chose to simply blame New York for its own problems, claiming that the city had been too liberal to the poor and too poorly managed. Charles Levine's pathbreaking essay "Organizational Decline and Cutback Management," published in 1978,[2] argued that fiscal stress was neither epiphenomenal nor something that happened only to poorly managed organizations. Instead, fiscal stress was likely to occur to many public organizations during their lifetimes. Their political support could erode, their missions could be fulfilled, or they might face a declining economy and eroding tax base.

The focus of Levine's work shifted from the sources of fiscal stress to the responses to and consequences of fiscal stress. These responses included increased efficiency, load shedding, contracting of services, and citizen coproduction. The political consequences often included a reduction in autonomy of local governments and visibly increased business control over finances. These results, and the early focus on New York City in the literature, suggested the possibility of alternating periods of greater social consciousness and increased spending with more conservative business dominance intentionally reducing the scope of government services and reducing taxes, returning public-sector functions to the private sector. Partly because of Levine's focus on cutback management, which has a kind of timelessness (use cutback techniques whenever fiscal stress hits), and partly because some scholars who picked up the cutback themes put them in the context of organizational life cycles, the historical implications of Levine's work were never developed. The political theories of the postwar period had not prepared scholars to look for periods of alternating growth and decline. The massive popular tax protests took political scientists somewhat by surprise; they observed and theorized about them, but did not initially look for similar periods of tax protest and cutback in earlier periods. Nevertheless, the recent period of cutback is best understood in historical context. This chapter is an attempt to explore some of the themes of Charles Levine's work in historical context.

This examination shows initially the relative explanatory power of models that assume continuous governmental growth compared to those that suggest alternation of growth and periods of stability or decline. Then we look at whether cities shed functions and privatize, or whether they merely pare back expenses during periods of stable or declining expenditures. Last, we examine the question, to the extent that the historical record suggests alternation of periods of expansion and contraction in the scope of municipal services, whether alternation is best characterized as an alternation between classes, with the poor dominating the periods of expansion and the rich dominating the periods of contraction.

Has the Expansion of Municipal Expenditures Been Continuous?

No matter which author one looks at, which series of data, or which time period, the evidence is clear that the rate of growth of municipal spending has been erratic. Alan Anderson notes, for example, that in 1902 per capita municipal expenditures were $12. By 1927, they were up to $49. For the next twenty years, they stayed under $50, but after World War II, there was another great expansion. By 1971, per capita expenditures were $364.[3] The Advisory Commission on Intergovernmental Relations (ACIR) provides a series for local government expenditures, about a third of which are cities, from 1929 to the middle 1980s. The figures are in 1972 constant dollars, and so differ a bit from Anderson's figures, but the same trends are plain. The per capita spending in 1929 for local governments was $138. The figure dropped to $116 in 1949, and then increased to a peak in 1976 of $288 per capita. Then spending per capita declined again, to a low of $264 per capita in 1981. From 1982 to 1984, per capita spending increased again, to $299.[4] Viewed as a percentage of GNP, local spending was 5.3 percent in 1929, 5.4 percent in 1939, dropping to 3.5 percent in 1949, increasing to 4.8 percent in 1976, decreasing to 4 percent in 1981, and then increasing to about 4.3 percent for the next few years.[5] Histories of individual cities suggest that there was slow growth in municipal revenues after the Civil War until the beginning of the Progressive era around 1900, then rapid growth until about the beginning of World War I, and reductions in expenditures, often sharply, during the early years of the Great Depression.[6] There was a stabilization in spending until about the early 1950s and then a surge that lasted until the middle 1970s.

No matter what part of the time series one looks at, sharp differences appear in the level of expenditure growth from one period to the next. Growth was not continuous; it stopped, started, accelerated, retreated, did everything but dance. This suggests there was nothing automatic about the rate of growth of municipal spending. Alternation between growth and stabilization or cutback seems to be more descriptive than continuing growth. The model of continuous growth assumes a willingness, even an eagerness, on the part of governments to assume new functions. The historical record suggests that cities in particular resisted assuming new functions, even in the face of rather extreme provocation by private monopolies.

For many years, cities resisted the sometimes extreme provocation of the street railways and opted for franchises or regulation rather than municipal ownership. Only after street railways ceased to be profitable, and ridership was depressed as a result of the increased popularity of the automobile, did most cities begin to take over their private companies. Often this did not happen until the federal government became involved and covered the capital costs of system development. Cities became involved with private railroads, often as investors, but seldom owned or ran their own railroads. Later, they divested themselves of this level of involvement.

Of three major utilities—water, gas, and electricity—cities, often after many years of delay and private-sector failures with disastrous consequences, took over and developed their own water systems. Less often, they took over electricity production and later largely returned this function to the private sector. Cities seldom took over gasworks.

E.W. Bemis, an advocate of municipal ownership, suggested three reasons why cities did not take over private gasworks. The first had to do with timing. The municipal ownership movement was just getting under way when electricity was beginning to light city streets. When the private sector was leery of making the technical investments in electricity, cities created their own plants to light the streets. Having done that, there was little incentive to take over gas plants in order to light the streets. Bemis's argument here suggests that cities got into production when the private sector was unable to produce something the city needed and that cities were not generally interested at that time in taking functions from the private sector to sell to citizens in general. They were not competing with the private sector.

The second reason that Bemis gives is that gas companies came earlier than electric companies and were often able to gain very-long-term franchises with favorable terms to themselves if the city wished to purchase them. Cities made better deals for themselves later, but in this early period, the utilities outwitted the cities. The consequences were that it would have been extremely expensive for cities to buy out the gas company franchises. This argument suggests a continuing sensitivity on the part of city officials to the level of taxation, the rates they could charge, and the possible profitability of enterprises they undertook.

The third reason that Bemis offers for cities' reluctance to take over gasworks is that compared to electricity, it was disproportionately expensive to extend gas pipes to cities with less than 10,000 population. That is, if a small city had a choice between spending large amounts of capital to buy an electric plant or a gas plant, it made more sense economically to buy the electric plant than the gas plant.

In short, the historical record does not support a model of continuous growth, not only because expenditures per capita expanded at times and fell back at other times, but also because cities never seemed eager to assume new functions, even during the heyday of the municipal ownership movement, at the height of the period of abusive monopolistic private corporations. They generally searched for other, cheaper techniques to control their problems, often settling for state regulation of rates rather than municipal ownership.

The Decision to Privatize

Part of the argument made for continuous public-sector growth is that once a function is performed by the public sector, it is rarely returned to the private sector. Functions may be cut back or reorganized, but they are seldom terminated. The current period of privatization represents a bold refutation of the continuous growth thesis, but there have been earlier periods of privatization as well.

Cities took up functions when the private sector had developed monopolies and put price pressure on the citizens in vital areas; when the private sector could not provide the capital necessary for municipal growth, either because of high risk or perceived low profitability; when it was no longer profitable for the private sector to continue the service; or when the quality of private-sector services was abysmally low. When those conditions changed, cities generally abandoned the functions they had assumed.

The history of the municipal assumption and abandonment of electricity production is important because it illustrates that cities were generally not interested in expansion of functions for its own sake. Cities were involved in the early stages of development of the electric industry. The first lights were arc lights suitable only for large areas. Cities adopted them to light streets and bridges. The limited market and experimental nature of the early efforts were not attractive to private capital.[7] As incandescent bulbs became common and markets for the sale of electricity larger, companies became more interested. As technology improved, private companies were able to build bigger plants and deliver electricity more economically over a wider area. Although many cities were forced to develop or protect an entire watershed to provide clean water, in electricity, cities stayed mainly within their own boundaries, which meant they were producing in uneconomically small amounts.

As one industry association described it, "many cities, having tried municipal ownership of their electric generating plants shut them down after a trial period and now purchase power for the operation of their distribution systems. Others have disposed of their system entirely, depending on companies to supply them with better and less costly services than they could furnish themselves."[8] Most of the cities that continued to provide their own electricity were small and apparently were unable to attract private producers. In 1928, only forty-four cities with more than 10,000 population had their own capacity to produce and distribute electricity.[9] The response of the cities to the consolidation of the electric companies and the enlargement of their networks was twofold: on the one hand, large cities in the private network dropped their own production capacity; and on the other, small cities away from the distribution networks began to produce their own electricity.

During the Great Depression of the 1930s there was some resurgence of municipal interest in the production as well as distribution of electricity. This interest was fed by the effects of private consolidation and the ineffectiveness of public regulation, by the lack of capital in the private sector for additional acquisitions, and by the declining revenues of cities resulting from tax delinquencies and property tax reductions and the desire to gain revenues in an acceptable way and control the need for tax increases. In addition, federal funds became available for loans for self-funding projects. Later, federal hydroelectric projects made it cheap and easy for nearby cities to purchase publicly produced electricity and resell it.

The era of the depression witnessed a resurgence of municipal electric plants, but the number of new production facilities in the 1930s and 1940s did not equal the number of abandonments in the 1920s. More than 600 municipal plants were privatized in the 1920s, while only about 200 new ones were created from 1934 to 1945, of which only about half had generating capacity.[10] From the end of World War II until the early 1980s, the balance between public and private production has remained fairly constant, with few new entrances or exits.[11]

The history of municipal ownership of electricity not only illustrates the reversibility of location of functions, and hence the lack of built-in deterministic factors pushing public-sector growth, but also brings into question the meaning of municipal ownership. On the one hand, there was a tendency to try to offset big business when the privates consolidated and gained monopoly control; but on the other hand, the purpose of the expansion during the depression was to keep property taxes down and find another source of municipal revenues when the tax base was weak. This function remains dominant today.[12]

The history of electricity production in cities suggests the possibility that the expansion of municipal functions that took place was not socialist in intent, but a way of keeping taxes down. Despite the public ownership movement, the Great Depression of the 1930s was not a period of expansion of municipal services, but one of divestment of functions. Summarizing the effect of the depression on municipal scope, one author argued:

The number and nature of the activities performed by local governments increased continuously over a long period of years. The trend is now reversed. Many public services are being abandoned. Few new activities are being added. Municipal activities of a service nature, such as garbage collection, are being frequently financed through monthly or quarterly charges the same as water or other utility services. School terms have been shortened, curriculums simplified, and extracurricular activities abolished. Citizens must now determine how much government they wish to pay for, what services they wish to go without, and the things they wish to have done by private individuals instead of by government.[13]

Following the Great Depression and World War II, cities experienced a long period of growth. From the early 1950s to the middle 1970s, state and local spending increased at a rate faster than the economy. But this growth period was followed by much slower growth in the economy and a leveling out of the growth rate for cities. Two major recessions, in 1974–75 and 1982–83, added to financial problems and encouraged cities to find alternative means of service delivery, particularly contracting with the private sector for services.

Studies of which services have been contracted for suggest that considerable thought has gone into finding the most efficient solutions. Small cities are likely to contract out for professional services, such as legal, architectural, or engineering services, that they do not have a year-round need for, and lack in house staff.[14] Cities of all sizes were likely to contract out for solid-waste collection.[15] One major study noted that cities were much more likely to contract out for services where there were multiple suppliers, and when the need was seasonal.[16] Since research has shown that in solid-waste pickup the private sector can often provide services, through contracting, more efficiently than the public sector,[17] the frequency of cities contracting in this area suggests a sensitivity on the part of public officials to efficiency and a lack of stubborn insistence on providing public services with public personnel. The finding that cities contracted more frequently in areas where there were multiple suppliers suggests a similar conclusion, since the benefits of cost savings from relying on the private sector are supposed to come from competition, not monopoly. Where competition keeps the costs down, cities rely more on the private sector. Finally, the finding that cities are more likely to contract out for seasonal employees also suggests a sensitivity to cost effectiveness and a positive aversion to adding unnecessary staff or staff that would be underutilized.

Recent studies suggest that privatization is not only continuing, but increasing. Refuse collection is now contracted in over 500 cities, up from 340 in the mid-1970s. Similar growth in the amount of contracting was found in data processing services and in emergency medical services. Other areas of growth appear to be security for schools, parks, and libraries; public health services; and school bus transportation.[18] The Privatization Council in New York estimates that about $100 billion of government services is now contracted out, compared with 1975 estimates by the Council of State Governments of $27 billion.[19]

To summarize, expansion of the range of municipal services has been reversible. Cities have been reluctant to take on new services, and having taken on particular services have sometimes dropped them when the conditions were favorable. Periods of tight budgets have encouraged privatization and its close cousin, contracting out. The services that have been either returned completely to the public sector or contracted have been those that have shown potentially the largest savings.

The assertions that government always grows and that government readily accepts new functions and never surrenders them are overstated and misleading. In view of the functions that have been contracted, and the clear goal of increased efficiency, the model of self-seeking bureaucrats always expanding government for their own ends does not seem applicable. In fact, the whole model of continuous governmental expansion seems a poor fit for the historical trends.

One could still argue, however, that the periods of growth represented a socialist expansion that was being curtailed by periods of business-dominated efficiency. The fact that public ownership of electricity was intended to keep taxes down during the depression raises the question of interpretation of municipal expansion of services more broadly. Who controlled and benefited from the periods of expansion and the periods of contraction?

Municipal Services for Whom?

An examination of the periods of growth and contraction from the point of view of who directed them and who benefited from them is easiest if divided into historical periods. The first period is the early 1800s to the Civil War. The second period is from the end of the Civil War to the middle 1890s, including a period of boom and one of cutback. The third period is the Progressive era from the late 1890s to about World War I. The next major period includes the Great Depression and World War II, from 1929 to 1945. The next important period for this analysis occurred after World War II, until the early 1970s. Then came the period of intense fiscal stress from the mid-1970s to the mid-1980s. There is always a risk in periodization, because different cities do similar things at somewhat different times, so the cutoff dates are only approximate and are intended to capture central tendencies of the period.

1800S TO THE CIVIL WAR: MERCHANT DOMINATION

From the early 1800s until about the time of the Civil War, cities actively carried out the functions desired by their commercial class. Before industrialization had transformed the cities and created the density and size we now associate with them, the cities were busy competing with one another to capture trade and agricultural products from the hinterlands.

In an economic order where the resources for fueling urban growth lay mainly outside the city in the nation's vast hinterland, the priority of urban political leaders invariably focused on enhancing the city's position as a marketplace. Consequently, authorizations of public money for market houses and detailed regulations for the operation of the town's public markets were among the earliest ordinances and greatest responsibilities of local government. Measures to protect the public against adulterated food, false measurements, and rigged prices were important matters to local officials.[20]

The merchant class that dominated the cities during this period used both city and state governments to invest aggressively in transportation to the hinterlands while limiting expenditures for almost all other services. The states were active in promoting canals during the earlier part of the period and then the cities themselves were active in promoting railroads. In many cases the cities spent their own money to buy shares of the proposed railroads. A few even built and ran their own railroads, to ensure the city's commercial dominance.

In one sense everyone in the city benefited from the economic growth that occurred when the projects were successful, but the merchants and some of the landowners along the tracks were by far the biggest promoters of urban expenditures for railroads and the biggest beneficiaries. The public sector provided the capital and took the risk, while the businessmen and landowners took a disproportionate share of the benefits. The costs to cities and state governments were enormous, and repayment of loans became a major portion of many city budgets for years thereafter. Many projects failed, and some cities defaulted on their loans. The public reaction was to curtail sharply the ability of cities and state governments to borrow, limits that were often written into constitutions.[21]

While the business community was willing to use the government to provide risk capital, it tried to constrain the growth of other services and limit their costs. Many services were maintained on a part time and volunteer basis, with little training or supervision. This level of services was inadequate for the growing cities, and services expanded during this period in response to obvious and clear emergencies, such as riots that police were unable to control, and fires that devastated large portions of the city. The fires were among the stimulants to improving the water systems because water was necessary for fighting fires.

The Post–Civil War Period to the Mid-1890s: Expansion and Contraction

The post–Civil War period was characterized by rapid urbanization, industrialization, and growth in both area and population. The total taxable wealth of the cities grew quickly, as did the need and sometimes the demand for more services. Increased density fostered the need for clean water supplies and disease controls; increased traffic and larger areas required some form of mass transit and improved streets; and police and fire protection needs grew with the population. The increased needs for services were not always directly translated into the budget, however. In fact, the post–Civil War period, especially from 1873 to the middle of the 1880s, was a period of dominance by business and wealthy elites, who sponsored low taxing and low spending policies. This was not uniformly the case, but it was a fairly widespread trend.

Historian Ernest Griffith described the era in terms of specific businesses dependent on the friendliness of city hall, which found ways to make their influence felt. "The 1870s opened with business groups in positions of power in all of the cities."[22] He lists specifically real estate interests, contractors, and utilities, including the railroads, as well as bankers, merchants, and manufacturers. Griffith describes the attitudes of business groups as shifting over the period from favoring low taxes to pride in modernization and willingness to spend more money to be the first or best.[23]

Griffith emphasized the importance of massive debt accumulated by many cities prior to 1870, and the effect of the recession of 1873 in strengthening the sentiment toward lower spending and financial solvency. He notes a per capita decline in debt outstanding between 1880 and 1890, which he attributes to debt limitations passed in response to the recession of the 1870s. Other authors downplay the role of the recession and emphasize different factors. Terrence McDonald supported Griffith's observation about the decreases in expenditure, but attributed the decreases to the efforts of the newly wealthy to insulate their wealth from municipal (and state) taxation. McDonald downplays the role of the recession for San Francisco because the city had a sufficiently diversified economy that recessions tended to hurt only one part of the economy.

McDonald argued for San Francisco that the level of debt had gotten out of hand well before the 1870s, amounting to 46 percent of the budget in 1860. This excessive amount of debt, combined with a sense that those building up the debt were rogues, stimulated a movement by business leaders to take over, clean up, and hold down spending. Part of the goal was to keep down taxes, in the belief that high taxation would drive away growth.[24] From 1860 to 1876, spending grew incrementally, but not as fast as the population; per capita revenues declined almost 7 percent.[25] From

1876 to 1882, the consensus among political elites solidified into a low-spending mold that brought the city's tax rate and expenditures to historic lows.[26] The Real Estate Protective Association was an active lobbyist for lower taxes and fewer capital projects.[27] By 1882, two political parties were vying for how much they could cut the budget, and the result was the dollar limit on taxes and further reductions on assessed valuation. These limits were effective for more than a decade. By the early 1890s, this consensus began to erode when neighborhoods and business groups began to demand municipal improvements.[28]

Existing data on other cities suggest that the period from 1870 to the middle 1880s was a period of retrenchment and cutback in other cities as well. Charles Huse described this period in the financial history of Boston as essentially one of retrenchment. He argued that the period of expanded expenditures from 1860 to 1873 "must be followed by long years of reaction."[29] He argued that the depression made it possible to reduce expenditures, not just delay capital projects.

Expenditures were lower in 1886 than in 1874.[30] Moreover, in 1885, a law was passed limiting the property tax to 2 percent of the assessed value of property. The city was curtailed at that time by both a borrowing limit and a tax limit, forcing the city to cut expenditures still further, despite the limited scale of activities during a general period of retrenchment.[31]

Griffith describes per capita reductions for Cambridge, Massachusetts, from 1875 to 1890, especially in spending for fire, schools, and debt outstanding, and from 1875 to 1885 for police, sewers, and streets.[32] Howard Stokes reported for Providence, Rhode Island, a period of tremendous growth in debt outstanding from 1865 to 1878, to which conservatives responded ultimately with a debt limit and a property tax limit in 1878. The debt and tax limits were passed by the state legislature, reportedly with support of city council members, who wanted to be relieved "from pressure to make improvements."[33] The impact was a dramatic reduction in both general outlays and per capita expenditures: outlays dropped from more than $5.6 million to a little more than $2.8 million from 1879 to 1880; per capita expenditures dropped from about $54 to about $27. It was about ten years before spending returned to the pre-1878 levels.[34] The mayor in 1881 explained this drastic drop in expenditures as the result of "great pressure upon the business community and the financial distress under which manufacturing interests were suffering."[35] Similar financial problems arose in Sacramento in 1863, New Orleans in 1870, Washington, D.C., in 1871, Mobile, Alabama, in 1873, and Memphis, Tennessee, in 1870.

The post–Civil War period of expanded debt and expenditure increase as well as the period of retrenchment that followed were directed by and for the business community, although not always for the same sectors of the business community. Often a change in attitudes by the business community was responsible for the shift from growth to contraction, and then from contraction back to growth. This dynamic is illustrated in the history of Houston, Texas.

The period of buildup of debt was directed by a commercial and civic elite in Houston, without much regard to how the debt would be funded, according to Harold Platt. This elite wanted improvements that would aid the city merchants economically, including harbor dredging, a public market, and street improvements in the downtown only. They hoped and assumed the resulting city growth would take care of the unfunded debt, but it did not, posing crisis after crisis of funding. Platt describes the period of the 1860s as one in which the property tax payers agreed to devote part of their income to the public sector, but "insisted that whoever ran city hall must accept their priorities and implement their plans without deviation."[36] This pattern of spending continued until the effects of the depression of 1873 became apparent and the city was near bankruptcy. A choice had to be made to pay either the bondholders or to maintain city services such as police and fire. The mayor tried to maintain services, allowing the city's reputation in the financial markets to decline, but the courts upheld the bondholders.[37] The city cut back on noncapital expenditures. As soon as the recession was over and the city economy and the taxpayers were better off, the demand for more capital projects to fund growth resumed. From 1877 to 1880, total outlays dropped, and per capita expenditures dropped from $6.71 to $5.25; the major cuts were in general expenditures, police, fire, and health. By 1887, the interest on debt had grown to 50 percent of the expenditures and the per capita outlays had increased from $.84 in 1877 to $4.48 in 1887, while general expenditures, police, fire, and health remained depressed.[38]

To summarize, existing studies of city finance and politics from the end of the Civil War to the early 1890s describe both the capital spending boom and the resulting low expenditure period that followed it as determined and directed by business elites. In fact, the reduction in spending was not simply the reaction of property owners struck for the first time with the costs of expensive public projects, but the result of the projects they themselves had asked for and presumably expected to pay for. The recession of the 1870s made it difficult to follow through on these growth plans, and there was a lull in major spending, often to restore the city's credit worthiness and eliminate the floating debt. The spending was pretty narrowly targeted to the benefit of the merchant and business elite; the neighborhoods were pointedly left out, and while spending on the poor was beginning, the dominant pattern was still that of the Dickensian poorhouse and workhouse.

THE PROGRESSIVE ERA: BUSINESS-DIRECTED EXPANSION

The next major spending period was the Progressive era, beginning in the 1900s. This period has been characterized as one including a broader range of interest groups, but it was in fact still dominated by the business agenda.[39] Even the municipal ownership movement, which dates from this time, had extensive business backing.

Martin Schiesl argues that the Progressive era agenda was dominated by business. He makes the distinction between the older businessmen who made accommodation to the city political machines and the younger ones in the newer industries who wanted more direct influence over municipal government and steady service delivery at low cost and high efficiency.

These businessmen acted indirectly in some big cities through the research bureaus that they supported. The first research bureau was located in New York City, but the idea spread throughout the country. They were business-funded research and policy shops, which formulated and pressed for a specific reform agenda. They did studies comparing the merits of various forms of government, and staff members sometimes acted as advisers to city government. The Rochester Bureau of Municipal Research was typical of these bureaus.

The Rochester Bureau was set up and financed entirely by the wealthy industrialist and inventor George Eastman, and supported solely by him until his death in 1932. He gathered about him ten other prominent men interested in civic affairs to form a board of trustees. Incorporated in 1915, it was accepted by the city government. It was an offspring of the New York Bureau and inherited its ideals, purposes, and methods. The Rochester Bureau played a role in the majority of important improvements in government operations over the next twenty years. It was a chief source of factual information, and it was especially important in bringing the city-manager form to Rochester. The bureau operated in a low-key and nonmilitant manner, offering both sides of issues, generally working through those in power, and never seeking a radical change in government, except possibly in the city manager campaign.[40]

These young activist businessmen operated directly in many smaller cities where they ran for office. They supported through business groups and chambers of commerce first the commission form and then the city-manager form, especially the at-large elections that helped them get elected, and the businesslike decision making that favored their preferred outcomes.

The reform movement itself was not particularly social, in the sense of providing services to the poor, serving the community or neighborhoods, or creating open space; it was characterized more by a business and growth agenda. Some individual reform mayors were open to the Progressive drive and were socially conscious and active. After the manager profession was created, some of the founders of the council-manager form and some of the practitioners too espoused more socially responsive goals of activism. There was thus some tension about goals, but the dominant thrust was to get better services without paying any more for them.

The political reformers focused on budget reform as a means of getting more services without paying more for them. Property holders, faced with higher tax bills, turned to reformers for the remedy to their problem: "they asked sympathetic officials to increase services and at the same time to reduce expenditures by stopping payments to the political machine."[41]

Many businessmen rallied around the commission form as a way of introducing businesslike government and getting themselves elected. The adoptions of the commission form suggested that it was most suited to places with old ethnic stock and above-average incomes.[42] These communities were dominated by a view of the public interest consisting of promoting economic growth. Government policies were directed toward the maintenance of an image of stability, honest administration, sound fiscal status, and cordiality toward business interests. What seemed to bring the commission form down was its budgeting inefficiency, because each commissioner was reluctant to cut any other commissioner's budget, so departmental requests came to drive the budget, and logrolling was the only form of coordination.

The structural reformers later came to support the council manager form. This reform differed from the commission form by centralizing much of the budget and managerial authority in a technically skilled manager. The reform was thus intended in part to solve the problems of the commission form, including lack of coordination, lack of budget control, and lack of expertise. Otherwise, the council-manager form kept many of the other features of the commission form, such as the at-large elections. Since the manager's position was at the pleasure of the council, the new form looked like it had a chief executive officer of a corporation. In the early discussions about the purpose of the city-manager form, there seems to have been a consensus that the manager should have some policy role in accordance with the business agenda. Again, there were important countercurrents, with proponents of the plan advocating programs to benefit the entire community.[43]

This is not to argue that there was no social program in the Progressive era, only that major pieces of the agenda were constructed by and for the business community, including the major spending projects. Major growth in school spending was business backed, for example. Some big spending projects that appeared socialistic were backed by business groups rather than socialists.

For example, the power companies in danger of being taken over by cities during this era (municipal ownership was a popular cry at this time) often accused the backers of municipal ownership of socialism. In fact, it was often a coalition of businessmen who wanted and advocated municipal ownership. It is easy to forget the excesses of the private power corporations from the distance of time, but during the Progressive era, from about 1895 to 1920, the utilities were often monopolistic, issued millions of dollars worth of watered stock, and raised prices beyond what the city officials felt was justified. The ineffectiveness of regulation led many people in frustration to offer municipal ownership as an alternative. In the case of electricity in particular, the possibility of cheap electricity was considered a boon to economic development and hence fit with the reformers' goals of appropriate public expenditure. In Los Angeles, the chamber of commerce was one of the major backers of public ownership of the electric companies;[44] other backers included the Merchants and Manufacturers Association and the Municipal League. None of these groups were in any sense socialist; they continued the business tradition of using the city to aid economic growth.

THE GREAT DEPRESSION AND WORLD WAR II: BUSINESS-LED RETRENCHMENT

The period of the Great Depression from 1929 through the 1930s is especially important in an analysis of the scope of city services and the question of expenditures for whom. World War II created a continuation of the stress and reduced municipal resources. The depression was particularly long and deep. Unemployment was widespread and suffering was obvious. It was difficult to blame the unfortunate for their own misery. What happened to city services at this time?

This period has often been characterized as one of government expansion, when social services were invented and became part of the budget, but very little expansion of these services occurred at the local level. Welfare was generally inadequate and was not developed through the city but was left for private relief agencies, which were soon overwhelmed. While some cities raised taxes to try to carry the burden, most found themselves facing massive tax delinquencies and cut their services and expenditures to meet reduced revenues. Some even cut their tax rates to provide some tax relief, exacerbating the problem. For the cities, the Great Depression was a period of cutback in services and spending, not expansion of budgets.

A series of papers by graduate students in urban history describes the depression in different cities in Texas.[45] The impact of the depression differed depending on the economy of the city before the depression. Generally, however, the municipal response was to cut back the budget and strive for budgetary balance, with little or no expansion of function. Some cities tried to maintain their capital projects to make jobs available, and some contributed to relief efforts, but most cities cut their budgets because of declining assessed valuations, increased tax delinquencies, and, often, reduced tax rates.

Turning first to the example of Houston,[46] "Houstonians, like policy makers in the Hoover administration and conservative businessmen everywhere, believed in retrenchment as a prerequisite for any solution to economic depression. Municipally-sponsored construction projects were desirable and acceptable, but balancing the city's budget came first."[47] Beginning in January 1930, the city government increased the number of building and improvement projects, but when the city tried to finance the projects, it required a tax increase, and the voters still had to approve a bond referendum. The mayor argued that the project would increase private business and stimulate the economy, and the resulting increased assessed valuations would prevent the need for more tax increases.

City bankers opposed the city's attempts to improve the local economy, sticking to a dogma of balanced budget and pay-as-you-go city government. The bankers threatened to cut off credit to the city if the budget was not balanced. The city was torn between a belief in frugality and a belief that the responsibility for stimulating the economy and providing relief was the city's. The bankers took over the situation by refusing further loans unless the city cut large amounts from its budget. The city was pressed on one side to provide more jobs to the unemployed and on the other side by taxpayers' associations to cut taxes, while bankers threatened to cut off loans if the budget was not cut.[48]

The city had to deal with fixed increases of expenditures, as well as declining revenues from tax delinquencies. Salaries were initially cut 10 percent and then another 5 percent; departmental budgets were cut by about $900,000, affecting thirty-two of thirty-five departments. The hospital and the sewer department escaped cuts. The fine arts museum lost 75 percent of its budget, and recreation was cut 60 percent.

The newspapers and bankers blamed the former profligacy of the city for the problem and did not see the banks as forcing cuts.[49] The bankers demanded a second round of cuts because of falling revenues. The city tried to fill the gap with a personal property tax, but that failed, so it then attempted a modest increase in the general property tax. Despite taxpayers' protests, the tax increase stood. "The bankers had a tight grip on the city's finances and the city, in turn, was forced to pull every bit of possible revenue out of its property holding citizens. This was retrenchment."[50] The second round of cuts involved a 5 percent reduction in salaries; many upper-echelon employees were let go; insurance policies on employees were cut in half; and donations to organizations such as the chamber of commerce and the National Guard were virtually eliminated. Half the streetlights were turned off. Expenditures in 1932 were reduced $1.5 million below the previous year.

To summarize, expenditures in Houston were cut back despite the need for increased welfare activities and capital projects that would put people to work. The bankers determined the city's policies, which put a balanced budget above other considerations.

The case of San Antonio is also instructive.[51] In response to declining tax receipts, San Antonio cut twenty policemen, sixty-two health department workers, and 250 street department workers. The telephone switchboards were eliminated at city hall and in the public health building. The city lost deposits of $509,000 when a local bank went under, almost 20 percent of the 1931–32 budget of $2.6 million. The result was loss of sixty parks workers and twenty employees from the office of the mayor, tax commissioner, and streets commissioner. Street department men were employed on an alternate-week basis. "With an announced deficit of $147,000, the city dropped unemployment relief efforts altogether."[52]

As assessed valuation dropped by $2 million, the city decided to raise the property tax rate, up 7 cents per $100 assessed. But taxes were increasingly difficult to collect. Pay for firemen was reduced by $50 per month. Police substations were eliminated, and fourteen city employees were discharged.[53] The banks reduced what they would loan to the city to less than one third, so the city had to cut its budget for 1933 by $1 million, compared to the previous year. Gone were the appropriations for city planning, public welfare, bands in the parks, and elections. Drastically cut were the public health department, (from $125,700 to $45,000) corporation court (from $20,000 to $8,000), contingencies (from $159,900 to $10,400), police (from $439,700 to $269,500), fire protection ($462,000 to $292,227), and street maintenance (down from $223,000 to $162,200). In 1929 there were 350 employees working on eighteen major street improvement projects; three years later there were 100 employees working on minor repairs and not one major project.[54]

By March 1933, the city cut its taxes by 19 cents, to 1.79 per $100 of assessed valuation. Total assessed valuation was down by 12 percent. The final 1932–33 budget, after the banks increased their loans a little, was $1,604,000, down 38 percent from the previous year. The tax delinquency problem kept getting worse, and the city actually missed a payday.[55]

"The municipal government consistently refused to appropriate funds for direct relief. The official reason given by the city commissioners was that the city charter prohibited the expenditure of public money for relief purposes. This reason, offered by the commissioners, was specious; every other major city in Texas technically 'violated' their charters in assisting materially the direct relief of the unemployed."[56] Other than minor expenditures, the city did not assume any responsibility for relief. The prevailing belief was that relief was the responsibility of social and charitable institutions. But they would have been strapped for funds anyway, since the charter precluded a diversion of funds from other purposes to relief. And the city was already at the limit of property taxes written into its charter, $1.25 per $100 of assessed value. The commissioners were not inclined to try to change the charter to increase taxes.

This kind of response to the depression was not exclusive to Texas or the South, as the following description of Chicago during the depression reveals.[57] The city was not well organized for the problems it was facing, with dozens of independent jurisdictions and a state government jealously guarding the city's purse strings. "By imposing hundreds of regulations pertaining to the minutiae of appropriations, rigidly defining the use of corporate funds, and scrupulously limiting debt and tax limits, the General Assembly carefully circumscribed the financial powers of the ailing metropolis. Thus hamstrung, the city increasingly failed to respond to demands thrust upon it by a depression that worsened with each year."[58]

The real estate system had collapsed, which was part of the problem. All tax collections had been suspended while reevaluation for greater equity was put in place, which was not complete until 1929, and many properties had reduced assessments as a result. The final 1928 figures were $400 million down over 1927. Intensified spending and reduced revenues created runaway debt at the beginning of the depression. Then, in 1929 a large number of property owners conducted a tax strike. These were mostly large property holders. Faced with dropping values and increased assessments, they sought delay until financial conditions improved; they won the early rounds, and the court did not side with the city until April 1932. Backlogs of tax payments increased from 20 percent in 1928 to 40 percent in 1929 and to 50 percent in 1930.[59]

The result was that the city could afford to do little with respect to welfare assistance and could not even afford to pay municipal workers. In 1929 the banks refused to accept any more tax anticipation notes, and the city was flat broke. Mayor Cermak tried to reduce spending; the corporate budget of 1932 was $50 million or so, down 20 percent from 1931; the 1931 budget was down $11 million from the previous year. The city became very dependent on federal aid.

When Mayor Kelly took over, he got the banks to accept new notes, got more state power to collect back taxes, and continued to cut the budget. He cut the corporate budget from $50,293,000 to $47,883,000 and focused most on the foundering school system to keep it open with major slashes in program and staff.

Explaining the Growth and Contraction of Municipal Services 123

The governor was not cooperative. He had promised to lower personal property taxes, and so when the city passed a new sales tax, it just about replaced the state-eliminated local taxes, incidentally making the local taxes more regressive. "The state would not jeopardize its balanced budget in order to supplement welfare spending."[60] This forced the city into alliance with the federal government; the city was later able to use these funds to bolster the machine and create patronage jobs.

Kelly "repeatedly maintained that the City of Chicago could not contribute any significant amount to the care of its indigent and unemployed." Social workers and the governor maintained that the city was spending too much money on graft, which had a high priority. "Kelly flatly refused to raise municipal taxes or trim patronage rolls, and he could get away with such intransigence because of federal largess."[61]

Mayor Kelly had the support of the business community throughout the depression.

> Mayor Kelly provided what the business community most coveted, a stable and unchanging environment in which investments might prosper. By keeping the city's finances in order, the mayor assured a reasonably profitable market for municipal bonds and tax anticipation warrants.... Kelly courted the favor of the city's silk stocking crowd by tailoring taxation to suit its needs—both by opposing a state income tax and by "adjusting" personal property assessments. While Chicago moguls might attack the New Deal or campaign on other ideological fronts, they accepted the local Democratic regime as consonant with their interests.[62]

In Chicago, both the banks and the major taxpayers played a key role. The city cut back expenditures and played little role in relief.

These reactions to the depression were repeated in city after city throughout the country. A series of articles in the city-managers' journal *Public Management* in 1934 and 1935 evaluated the impact of the depression on city functions across the country and concluded that the hue and cry everywhere was "the cost of government must be reduced."[63] City hall closely adhered "to a policy of low taxes and limited expenditures, while striving for a balanced budget."[64] The chamber of commerce advocated more business in government and less government in business.[65]

The attempt to limit increases and bring about reductions in the property tax was also widespread. Michigan (1932), West Virginia (1932), New Mexico (1933), Oklahoma (1933), and Ohio (1933)[66] passed or strengthened constitutional limitations on the overall rate of taxes on real estate. Indiana (1932) and Washington (1932) imposed such general restrictions statutorily. There were efforts to adopt such measures in nearly every state.

A hundred or more tax limits were introduced to state legislatures in the year 1934–35 alone.⁶⁷ By 1936, forty states had specific property tax limits on cities, although many of these predated the depression.⁶⁸ Thus the cities' capacity to raise additional revenues to provide either jobs or welfare was often constrained.

Some of the revenue constraints were not blanket limitations on rates but restrictions phrased in terms of the previous years' spending or revenues. Iowa in 1931 limited the budgets of all governmental units to 95 percent of the previous year, and a more drastic, similar law was passed in 1933.⁶⁹ In West Virginia, the 1933 levy was limited to 85 percent of the 1931 levy, exclusive of debt.⁷⁰

Who was pushing for these limitations? In Michigan, it was the farmers, the realtors, and those who had been speculating in real estate. The cities generally opposed the limitations. The farmers had been hit with declining economic circumstances, and their holdings in land kept their property taxes high; after trying first, unsuccessfully, to shift the burden of taxes on to some other form of taxation that would fall less heavily on them, they began to support property tax limits. In the cities, those with extensive real estate investments, especially those that had been bought on speculation, found that the decreasing prices for real estate were going to force them to sell at a loss unless they could get relief. They thus supported property tax limitations.⁷¹

The intention of property tax limitations was to reduce tax burdens and shrink the size of government. The benefits would typically fall on the relatively well-to-do. One author summarized the projected impact of proposed Illinois tax limitations on Chicago in the following terms: "The great mass of the actual residents of the city, comprising individuals of modest means, both renters and homeowners, would lose more than they gained by the operation of the limitation. The chief gainers would be the corporations, non-resident taxpayers, and resident property owners whose wealth placed them above the need for municipal social services."⁷²

A business ideology of low taxes, low spending, and balanced budgets dominated the political and financial responses of cities during the Great Depression. The focus of attention during World War II was on the war, and there was very little energy, creativity, or new money spent on municipal government during the war.

The Postwar Period: Business-Directed Expansion

Carl Abbott described a postwar reform movement in more than a dozen Sunbelt cities from 1945 to 1955.⁷³ The common element in the various efforts was the desire to replace small-time politics of city hall cronies with administrations of growth-oriented businessmen and bureaucrats. Their campaign platforms called for the modernization of outmoded municipal governments and the provision of adequate public services. The local businessmen who dominated these efforts had two goals: one was to mobilize public and private resources to provide the necessary physical facilities for business and commercial growth; the second was to manage the process of suburbanization to benefit the downtown businessmen. The list of desired projects included new docks, airports, highways, expanded water supply, and more electric power, but the key items were usually more office space and transportation for downtown business districts.[74] The business leadership was not single-mindedly for the business community, but promoting economic development was their primary goal.

For example, during this time, the city of San Antonio addressed massive drainage problems, built 1,000 miles of storm sewers, paved 2,000 miles of streets, bought 600 acres of parks, connected 10,000 homes to the water system, acquired and expanded the bus system, installed streetlights, and opened new libraries and fire stations. This was paid for with a long series of bonds, which were approved by the public. Transportation was a major priority, with $10.5 million for arterial roads and a controversial north expressway. By 1966, San Antonio boasted 98.3 miles of freeway in the city limits.[75]

Abbott argued that this reform movement was very similar to the business boosterism of earlier periods.

> Boosterism is primarily an ideology of businessmen oriented toward the local market and its basic urge is toward rapid population growth—more illnesses for the doctor, more litigation of the lawyer, more policies for the insurance agent, more customers for the retailer, more sodas for the soft drink bottler, and more subscribers and advertisers for the daily paper. In essence, only the rhetoric has changed over a century and a half.

The author described the later 1940s as an updated good government agenda from the Progressive era, stimulated by the possibilities of unprecedented growth. "Political coalitions led by eager businessmen and supported by professional administrators were consistently able to assist economic growth."[76] This business coalition furthered its aims using federal funds, especially for urban renewal. The goal was to assist private investment directly by assembling developable land at low cost and indirectly by providing necessary public facilities in downtown areas. In the urban renewal alliance, it was impossible to separate public and private interest, to untangle private real estate booms and surges of public construction, and to differentiate between the goals of bureaucrats and businessmen."[77] Urban renewal became a "tool in intercity rivalries for economic advantage.

Where nineteenth-century cities had competed to acquire the best railroad connections, those of the twentieth-century Sunbelt worked to provide the facilities for metropolitan activities of regional finance, public administration, business headquarters, and distribution and professional services."[78] The kinds of projects that cities built will sound familiar: a trade center, a convention-exhibition center with appended hotels, and a public university campus to train technical and managerial staff for the new white-collar enterprises. New sports arenas and stadiums were important to create the image of a "major league city."

This kind of business domination of local government to achieve growth was by no means limited to the South. The history of Pittsburgh after World War II sounds virtually identical, including many of the same projects such as massive office buildings and a new stadium. Describing the Pittsburgh experience, one author concluded that "the business and professional leadership of Pittsburgh, operating often through voluntary civic organizations, initiated and dominated the environmental reform tradition."[79] Environmental reform meant not only cleaning up air pollution but also reducing flooding and improving office space, making the city more generally attractive to live and work in. The foundation of the post–World War II renaissance of the city was the use of public powers, including those of the city, to preserve the economic vitality of the central business district and the competitive position of the Pittsburgh region.[80] "In essence, the Pittsburgh Renaissance represented a response to a crisis situation, one that precipitated a dramatic expansion of public enterprise and investment to serve corporate needs; it established a reverse welfare state."[81]

The role of business coalitions in supporting and developing urban renewal agendas was important and widespread. In many cities, the businesses most affected by the deterioration of the central business districts formed coalitions and drew up plans, consulted with city officials, and then presented their plans to the press. This pattern has been identified for San Francisco, Los Angeles, Philadelphia, Pittsburgh, and Boston. In other cities, the mayor took the lead and then drew in the business groups to support the plan. In either event, big businesses and government officials worked closely on the agenda, and the poor residents and marginal businesses were the ones hurt.[82]

THE YEARS OF CONTRACTION, EARLY 1970S THROUGH THE MID-1980S

The postwar boom lasted through the early 1970s. The years 1974 and 1975 saw deep recession, and another deep recession affected the 1982–83 period. The economy was generally not growing very quickly; inflation was periodically high; and cities, especially those in the so-called rust belt, de-

Explaining the Growth and Contraction of Municipal Services 127

pendent on heavy industry, experienced long-term declines in the number of jobs and the level of pay, as service industry replaced heavy industry. A drop in the price of oil and gas in the mid-1980s affected states that were taxing their resources heavily and had hitherto escaped financial problems. Texas and Louisiana were particularly hard hit. Not surprisingly, the middle 1970s, which were characterized by increases in taxes that exceeded increases in salaries, were marked by a new round of property tax limitations and an overall ideology of low taxes and low or controlled spending.

From 1970 to 1977, Minnesota imposed a limit on general revenues for cities, and New Mexico imposed a limit on expenditures for cities. Between 1978 and 1984, another six states imposed either general revenue or general expenditure limits for their cities. While some states had earlier imposed property tax limits, these general revenue and expenditure limits were new to this period. In addition, many states that did not have prior property tax limits added them during the 1970–84 period, and states that had some property tax controls added new ones during this time. Twenty-six states added new or expanded property tax limits applicable to cities during this period.[83]

Not only did the states limit taxes and spending for cities, but they also increased the amounts of tax breaks for the property tax. In 1988, thirty-two states plus the District of Columbia reported having some kind of circuit-breaker reductions in property taxes. These are normally intended to provide tax relief to the elderly poor or handicapped, but some states use them for all homeowners and renters. Of the thirty-two states and the District, twenty-eight passed their circuit breakers for the first time during the 1970–84 period. Forty-four states plus the District of Columbia use homestead exemptions. Homestead exemptions are normally reductions in the assessed valuations on which taxes are based. Often targeted for homeowners who live in their own homes, they are sometimes used for the elderly poor and handicapped, but they sometimes apply to all homeowners.[84] The circuit breakers were intended to increase the equity of the property tax, and protect the elderly and people on fixed incomes from losing their homes when inflation and increases in housing prices threatened to increase their tax burden beyond what these people could afford. The homestead exemptions were more of an attempt to respond to political pressure for broad tax limits by reducing the burdens of those most likely to campaign effectively for such limits.

The period from the early 1970s to the mid-1980s was one of contraction. Average property tax rates, which grew from 1.34 percent in 1958 to 1.98 percent in 1971, dropped to 1.26 percent in 1982, and then dropped further, to 1.21 percent in 1985, 1.16 percent in 1986, and 1.15 percent in 1987.[85] Local government employment grew faster than population from

1952 to 1978, but more slowly than population growth from 1979 to 1983.[86]

The overall economic downturn for many cities, which was accompanied by long periods of high unemployment, had the impact of increasing the power of the business community. Even relatively small cities developed economic development offices and spent hundreds of thousands of dollars to staff them. Those cities most in need were most likely to spend more money on incentives and infrastructure projects to lure businesses from other locations or try to convince existing businesses not to move out of the city.[87] Cities were not only giving up tax revenues through tax breaks for businesses, but also loaning money to risky businesses.

Often the threat that a major employer is going to leave a city is sufficient to motivate city officials to put together a package including tax breaks, planning and zoning exemptions, reduced land costs, facilities such as roads, parking and landscaping, and in some cases, unused buildings. Perhaps the best-known example of a city's efforts to retain a business at any cost was the Detroit–General Motors arrangement. Detroit, in an effort to keep a General Motors facility, demolished a residential neighborhood and then donated the land to GM. The cost of Detroit's contribution to GM is estimated at $350 million. Detroit pays $110 million annually on loans it obtained to keep the automotive giant in town. GM has never provided the full number of jobs it promised the city and now asked the city for additional tax abatements to upgrade some of the plant equipment. GM is even hinting it might leave the city if it is denied its request. Detroit had no option but to grant the abatement, since in the opinion of several analysts, if GM closes this plant before the year 2011, when Detroit will have paid off its loans, the city could go bankrupt.[88]

Detroit is not the only city caught in this kind of situation. New York provided more than $225 million in tax breaks to ensure that Chase Manhattan Bank would not move its 4,000 back-office workers to New Jersey.[89] Chicago was unsuccessful in negotiations to keep Sears, Roebuck from leaving the city; suburban Hoffman Estates offered a huge piece of free land to lure the headquarters out of Chicago, and the state government offered a range of incentives including new roads. Montgomery County, Maryland, is negotiating with the Marriott Corporation to ensure that their corporate headquarters will not be moved. In the latter instance, the governor has stepped in to add state incentives to the favorable resolution of the issue.

This period was also one of load shedding for cities. On the one hand, they often supported the regionalization of services so that they did not bear the entire financial responsibility for services that reach a whole county or metropolitan area. Such services included public transit, libraries, and colleges. Some cities privatized services as well, turning over zoos and museums to private, not-for-profits. As suggested earlier, they increasingly contracted out for selected services such as garbage pickup.

To summarize, the period was characterized by general contraction, tax limitations, and exemptions, many of which were not limited to the poor, and economic development efforts in the cities, where economic changes brought about the most poverty and unemployment. These economic development efforts may in some cities have benefited the poor and unemployed, but in many cases they seemed to be public-to-private transfers of wealth, without commensurate public benefit, and with tremendous outlays for each job produced. To some extent, without really trying, the business community increased its political clout and its ability to influence taxation and services. It benefited from the period of contraction. The simultaneous withdrawal of many of federal spending programs targeted to the poor or middle-income people made this period one of increased business dominance at the local level.

Conclusions

Municipal growth has not been continuous, and cities have intensely scrutinized the decision to locate a function in the public sector. When cities have added functions, the decision has historically been reversible, which casts doubt on the model of powerful bureaucrats always successfully expanding functions to serve their own desires for aggrandizement or pay. While some decisions about the location of functions in the public sector were made on ideological grounds—government is good and corporations are bad—the vast majority of such decisions were made on technical grounds and were altered when the environment changed those technical factors.

Cities have been characterized by alternating periods of expansion and stability or contraction of budgets and services. At first glance, it looks as if the periods of growth might have been working-class driven, while the periods of contraction were driven by banks and wealthy people fearful of being overtaxed. Expansion and contraction of the public sector looked like the result of a running battle between socialism and capitalism, where the outcomes shifted over time. But the historical record suggests that both the periods of expansion and the periods of contraction have been dominated by business agendas.

The growth periods were characterized by spending for business-related infrastructure and capital. These periods have often been characterized by boosterism and the desire to have the biggest and the best. Expensive symbols of big-league status, such as sports domes, have been on this list of projects, despite the fact that they almost uniformly end up in the red, with the public picking up the bill. Even the social agendas of the growth periods were business backed and perceived as for the benefit of the business community. The push for more public education was to create an educated labor force, and the municipal ownership of utilities was often for the purpose of maintaining favorable conditions for business.

The periods of contraction were directed by a different business ideology that called for tax and spending reductions and balanced budgets, at the expense of other city services and particularly at the expense of relief, public-sector job creation, or retraining.

This alternation in political belief and action on the part of the business community is somewhat puzzling. It would be clearer if there were distinct political alliances dominant in different periods, each with appropriate sets of beliefs. But the record suggests that some of the same actors switch sides. Banks and real estate interests in particular benefit from growth and from large amounts of borrowing, but when economic circumstances deteriorate, banks and real estate speculators may find their interests served better by lower real estate taxes, balanced budgets, lower borrowing, and a narrower scope of public services.

Alternation of points of view among similar interests over time makes more sense when one realizes that in the earlier days the costs of development were primarily borne by the well-to-do and the merchants themselves. When the costs of debt became excessive, they had a major incentive to reduce the size and cost of government. Since they were taxing themselves for their own projects, it is not surprising that they directed expenditures to projects they would benefit from. But in later periods, local taxation became more regressive; personal property taxes, never very successfully tapped, were eliminated, and cities gradually became more and more dependent on sales taxes. Spending for economic development and boosterism remains important, however, at the same time that services in other areas are being cut back or privatized. Since the well-to-do are paying less for economic development projects, they have less motivation to curtail them when borrowing or spending becomes excessive. This pattern is dependent on the widespread belief that economic development benefits everyone.

How periods of growth and contraction will occur in the future is unclear, as the previously existing mechanisms for alternation have been weakened. Ordinary folk want services for themselves, and want to keep taxes down, and politicians argue that they can achieve both only if they spend money for economic development, which promises to lower the taxes for everyone. Periods of recession, instead of becoming occasions for withdrawing government role in the expansion of the economy, become the excuse for spending the money of the relatively poor on businesses. Privatization and cutback coexist with boosterism. Cutback management may have become an ongoing activity.

Notes

1. See, for example, Martin Shefter, "New York City's Fiscal Crisis: The Politics of Inflation and Retrenchment," *Public Interest* 48 (Summer 1977): 95–127; Frances Fox Piven, "The Urban Crisis: Who Got What and Why," ed. R.A. Alcaly and D. Mermelstein, 131–44, in *The Fiscal Crisis of American Cities,* (New York: Vintage Press, 1977); C.R. Morris, *The Cost of Good Intentions* (New York: Norton, 1980); Alberta Sbragia, ed., *The Municipal Money Chase: The Politics of Local Government Finance* (Boulder, Colo.: Westview, 1983).

2. Charles H. Levine, "Organizational Decline and Cutback Management" *Public Administration Review* 38 (July/August 1978): 316–25.

3. Alan D. Anderson, *The Origin and Resolution of the Urban Crisis, Baltimore 1890–1930* (Baltimore: Johns Hopkins University Press, 1977), 9.

4. The ACIR has updated these figures to 1987, but in the process changed the years they used as sample years, the base year for the index from 1972 to 1982, and the deflator index from the CPI to the GNP implicit price deflator. The series are not quite comparable. Nevertheless, the trends are similar. For the more recent years, 1984 showed a slight dip in per capita spending, which then increased steadily in 1985, 1986, and 1987. See ACIR, *Significant Features of Fiscal Federalism, 1988* (Washington, D.C.: Government Printing Office, 1988), 2: 22–23.

5. ACIR, *Significant Features of Fiscal Federalism, 1984* (Washington, D.C.: Government Printing Office, 1985), 8.

6. Anderson, *Origin and Resolution of Urban Crisis,* 33, described the real growth in expenditures in Baltimore in percentage increase per year from 1860 to 1900 as .7 percent; from 1900 to 1915 as 4.5 percent, and from 1915 to 1930 as zero. The chapters in Robert Cotner, ed., *Texas Cities and the Great Depression,* miscellaneous papers 3 (Austin, Texas: Texas Memorial Museum, 1973), describe the typical budget cutting of the depression era. Clarence Ridley and Orin Nolting, eds., *What the Depression Has Done to Cities* (Chicago: ICMA, 1935), describes similar phenomena for cities throughout the country. The first essay in that book, by Carl Chatters, argued that operating expenditures were reduced 20–40 percent over the first three or four years of the depression. Terrence McDonald describes the phenomenon of constrained expenditures during the post–Civil War period of rapid economic growth, and the breakthrough in spending during the Progressive era for San Francisco, in his book *The Parameters of Urban Fiscal Policy: Socioeconomic Change and Political Culture in San Francisco, 1860–1906* (Berkeley: University of California Press, 1986).

7. National Electric Light Association, "Government (Political) Ownership and Operation of the Electric Light and Power Industry," NELA Publication 289-13, 1928, 14. This is generally an antimunicipal ownership tract put out by

the industry for its members, but its history of the industry seems sound, and is substantiated by less partial observers.

8. Ibid., 16.

9. Ibid.

10. David Schap, *Municipal Ownership in the Electric Utility Industry: A Centennial View,* (New York: Praeger, 1986), 54 and 82.

11. Ibid., 93.

12. Ruth Hoogland DeHoog and Bert Swanson found that in Florida the profits of electric utilities were used primarily by cities with weak tax bases to obtain revenues from tax exempt institutions, homeowners, and nonresidents. See "Tax and Spending Effects of Municipal Enterprises: The Case of Florida Electric Utilities," *Public Budgeting and Finance* 8 (Spring 1988): 48.

13. Carl Chatters, "Municipal Finance," in Ridley and Nolting, *What the Depression Has Done to Cities,* 1.

14. Pat Florestano and Stephen B. Gordon, "Public v. Private: Small Government Contracting with the Private Sector," *Public Administration Review* 40 (January/February 1980), 29–33.

15. Ibid. They found that the small cities contracted for solid-waste collection; Harry Hatry and Carl Valente found that larger cities did too, in their "Alternative Service Delivery Approaches Involving Increased Use of the Private Sector," *Municipal Yearbook* (Washington: ICMA, 1983), 199–217.

16. Hatry and Valente, "Alternative Service Delivery."

17. This argument is made convincingly by E.S. Savas, *Privatization: The Keys to Better Government* (Chatham, N.J.: Chatham House, 1987).

18. Robert W. Poole, Jr., and Philip E. Fixler, Jr., "Privatization of Public Sector Services in Practice: Experience and Potential," *Journal of Policy Analysis and Management* 6 (Summer 1987): 612–25.

19. Thomas Darr, "Pondering Privatization May Be Good for Your Government," *Governing,* November 1987, 42–50.

20. Paul Kantor, with Stephen David, *The Dependent City: The Changing Political Economy of Urban America,* (Glenview, Ill.: Scott, Foresman/Little, Brown, 1988), 45.

21. Ibid., 45–61.

22. Ernest Griffith, *A History of American City Government: The Conspicuous Failure, 1870 to 1900,* (New York: Praeger, 1974), 134.

23. Ibid., 159.

24. McDonald, *Parameters of Urban Fiscal Policy,* 137.

25. Ibid., 142.

26. Ibid., 143.

27. Ibid., 147.

28. Ibid., 159.

29. Charles Phillips Huse, *The Financial History of Boston, from May 1, 1822 to January 31, 1909* (Cambridge: Harvard University Press, 1916), 225.

30. Ibid., 226.

31. Ibid., 229.

32. Griffith, *History of American City Government,* 163.

33. Howard Kemble Stokes, *The Finances and Administration of Providence* (Baltimore: Johns Hopkins University Press, 1903), 247.

34. Ibid., 430. These figures are taken from his raw data, not from his text.

35. Ibid., 249.

36. Harold Platt, *City Building in the New South: The Growth of Public Services in Houston, Texas, 1830–1910* (Philadelphia: Temple University Press, 1983), 28.

37. Ibid., 51.

38. Ibid., 147.

39. Martin Schiesl, *The Politics of Efficiency: Municipal Administration and Reform in America, 1800–1920* (Berkeley: University of California Press, 1977).

40. Frederick Mosher et al., *City Manager Government in Seven Cities*, (Chicago: Public Administration Service, 1940), 11.

41. Ibid., 88.

42. Ibid., 136.

43. Ibid., chap. 9.

44. Nelson Van Valen, "Power Politics: The Struggle for Municipal Ownership of Electric Utilities in Los Angeles, 1905–1937," Ph.D. dissertation, Claremont Graduate School, 1964, 44–45.

45. Cotner, *Texas Cities and the Great Depression*.

46. William Montgomery, "The Depression in Houston, 1929–1933," in Cotner, *Texas Cities and the Great Depression*.

47. Ibid., 158.

48. Ibid., 160.

49. Ibid., 162.

50. Ibid., 163.

51. Mary Maverick McMillan Fisher, "San Antonio I: The Hoover Era," in Cotner, *Texas Cities and the Great Depression*, esp. 57–59.

52. Ibid., 57.

53. Ibid., 58.

54. Ibid.

55. Ibid., 59.

56. Lyndon Gayle Knippa, "San Antonio II: The Early New Deal," in Cotner, *Texas Cities and the Great Depression*, 89.

57. Roger Biles, *Big City Boss in Depression and in War: Mayor Edward J. Kelly of Chicago* (DeKalb, Ill.: Northern Illinois University Press, 1984).

58. Ibid., 21–22.

59. Ibid., 22.

60. Ibid., 26.

61. Ibid., 78.

62. Ibid., 46.

63. Ridley and Nolting, *What the Depression Has Done to Cities*.

64. Roger Biles, *Memphis in the Great Depression* (Knoxville: University of Tennessee Press, 1986), 67.

65. Ibid.

66. For a brief discussion of the Ohio tax limitation, see Herbert Nelson, "The Case for Tax Limitation," in *Property Tax Limitation Laws*, ed. Glen Leet and Robert Paige (Chicago: Public Administration Service, 1936), 6.

67. Rodney Mott and W.O. Suiter, "The Types and Extent of Existing Tax Limitations" in Leet and Paige, *Property Tax Limitation Laws*, 42.

68. Ibid., 44–45.

69. The 1933 reduction was 20 percent. See Carroll Wooddy, "Tax Limitation in Iowa" in Leet and Paige, *Property Tax Limitation Laws*, 54.

70. Mott and Suiter, "Existing Tax Limitations," 46.

71. Harold Smith, "Tax Limitation in Michigan," in Leet and Paige, *Property Tax Limitation Laws*, 64–65.

72. Clarence Heer "Who Benefits from Tax Limitations," in Leet and Paige, *Property Tax Limitation Laws*, 25.

73. Carl Abbott, *The New Urban America: Growth and Politics in Sunbelt Cities* (Chapel Hill: University of North Carolina Press, 1987).

74. Ibid., 124–25.

75. Ibid., 140–41.

76. Ibid., 145.

77. Ibid., 147.

78. Ibid.

79. Roy Lubove, *Twentieth-Century Pittsburgh: Government, Business, and Environmental Change*, (New York: Wiley, 1969), vii.

80. Ibid., 106.

81. Ibid.

82. Paul Kantor, *Dependent City*, 259.

83. ACIR, *Significant Features of Fiscal Federalism*, 1988 2: 102.

84. Ibid., 76.

85. ACIR, *Significant Features of Fiscal Federalism*, 1989 (Washington, D.C.: Government Printing Office, 1989), 72.

86. Ibid., 134.

87. Irene S. Rubin and Herbert J. Rubin, "The Poor (Cities) Pay More," *Urban Affairs Quarterly* 23 (September 1987): 37–62.

88. Robert Guskind, "Games Cities Play," *National Journal*, 18 March 1989, 634–40.

89. Ibid.

6

Managing Privatization: A New Challenge to Public Administration

Ronald C. Moe

One element in the appeal of privatization as a theory and as a political strategy is the belief that privatization, however defined, necessarily results in a substantial reduction in governmental involvement in the national economy and that this is a good thing. Less involvement means that the government, in this case the federal government, will not require the same degree of managerial authority and capacity. Thus, privatization has come to be associated in the minds of many not only with less government but with less effective government as well.

This chapter raises issue with both the explicit and implicit assumptions that inhere in this view of the purpose and consequences of privatization. While it is true that occasionally an entire activity or entity is transferred ("load shedding" or "divestment") to the private sector, thus truly "privatizing" the activity or entity, the typical privatization effort is not of this character. In popular parlance, privatization is considered to have occurred whenever the provision of a public good or service is assigned, usually by contract, to a third party. The assignment of public functions to third parties, while it may decrease the need for direct government employment, does not eliminate, or even substantially reduce, the requirements of government management, it simply changes the character of this management. Privatization, contrary to conventional wisdom, often results not in less but in new and more sophisticated demands being placed on public management, demands at present little recognized or appreciated by either privatization advocates or the public-sector management community itself.

The purpose of this discussion is to acquaint the reader with some dimensions of the public management of privatization. The working assumption behind this analysis is that the public and private sectors are fundamentally distinctive yet interdependent. The relationship is symbiotic, not adversarial, with the effectiveness and prosperity of the two sectors being positively linked.

Third-Party Government

In the United States, it has been a major political value since the founding of the Republic that officers and employees of the federal government should be held accountable for their actions to elected officials and through these officials to the public. This hierarchical model of administrative organization and accountability has remained the norm for two centuries and is supported by a system of constitutional requirements, statute law, and court decisions.

We distinguish in the United States between the public and private sectors, and this distinction is recognized in law. The federal government possesses the rights and immunities of the sovereign; organizations functioning in the private sector do not, or at least ought not, possess such rights and immunities. The public sector is governed by public law, the private sector largely by private law. Thus, officers of the United States, in performance of their duties, must adhere to the constitutional requirement of providing "due process" to their actions and decisions, a requirement not imposed on an officer of a private corporation. The assignment of functions between the public and private sectors must take into account the fundamental legal distinctions between the sectors.[1] All too often, however, the assignment process is based largely, if not solely, on economic factors.

In recent decades, two contradictory trends have emerged to influence the course of federal government management. The first is a reflection of the antigovernment bias prevalent throughout the political community generally; it takes the form of deliberately limiting the internal capacity of the federal government to perform its functions and responsibilities. This trend is most obvious in the arbitrary ceilings imposed by both the president and Congress on management expenditures, personnel, and compensation. The second trend, at odds with the first, is the continuing pressure to involve the federal government in more activities, such as the "bailout" of the savings and loan industry, environmental protection, hazardous waste cleanup, and AIDS research, activities that by their nature require substantial commitments of resources: managerial, financial, and personnel.

The principal means employed to bridge the gap between these two opposing trends has been to utilize the services of third parties. These third parties may be other governments, new quasi-governmental bodies of indeterminate legal status, instrumentalities, nonprofit organizations, or for-profit corporations.[2] Except in the case of utilizing the services of other governments, such as states and cities, the use of third parties is generally viewed as a form of privatization.

As the functions demanded of government have increased and become more complex, so the contracting process for these goods and services has become more complex and troublesome to the political leadership and the career management leadership of the country. Elected and appointed officials have found that while they can assign responsibility for producing goods and services to third parties, they are still held accountable by the public for the actual performance of the public function.[3]

Contracting Out: Where Are the Limits?

While governmental contracting for services is a practice of long standing, indeed one predating the formation of the Union, there has been a substantial increase both in the amount and kinds of activities being contracted for in recent decades. Scholars and journalists are beginning to write of the "shadow government"[4] and the "hollow government,"[5] terms referring to the decline in the capacity of the federal government to manage its own affairs and the increasing (and presumably undesirable) reliance upon third-party contractors. Although the term is not generally used in this context, these commentators are also questioning whether *privatization* has gone too far.

Promoters of privatization tend to emphasize economic affairs, almost to the exclusion of other criteria, in arguing whether a particular function should be performed by the public or the private sector. Not surprisingly, therefore, they generally find it difficult to locate many activities that should remain the sole prerogative of government or that should be performed by government managers or employees.[6]

The theoretical foundation for privatizing most public functions is furnished in large measure by the public choice school of economics. In essence, public choice theorists contend that the public and private sectors share much in common and that their behavior is largely explained in terms of economic incentives. Given what is alleged to be the monopolistic character of the public sector, the need for efficiency and cost effectiveness is largely absent from policy and administrative decisions of public sector managers. What is necessary, according to privatization promoters, is to alter the incentive system of public institutions and managers so that market competition can be brought to bear on both decisions and operations. The litany of their presentation is then to cite numerous instances where privatizing services, such as garbage collection and prisons, has led to "better operations" at less cost to the taxpayer.[7]

The contracting process is portrayed as a relatively simple, straightforward process in which a government agency seeks out would-be providers who submit competitive bids to provide the desired product or service at the least cost. The model presupposes the working of a relatively free and competitive market mechanism where there are a number of potential bidders, a presupposition frequently absent from real-life conditions.

Harold Seidman, in recent congressional testimony, observed

> The assumption that competition and market discipline are all that are required to produce optimal [governmental] performance is an illusion. When the government is contracting for intangibles such as policy analysis, management services and research and development, opportunity for competition among qualified suppliers is often limited or non-existent. Success or failure of the many companies whose principal—and sometimes only—customer is the U.S. Government depends more on their skill in manipulating the political system than in competing in the market place.[8]

At the federal government level, the policy governing the contracting-out process is to be found in Office of Management and Budget (OMB) Circulars A-76 (4 August 1983) and A-120 (4 January 1988). Circular A-76 "establishes federal policy regarding the performance of commercial activities" and then lists "examples" of activities considered commercial in character and thus likely candidates for being contracted out. The circular also states that certain functions are "inherently governmental in nature" and hence are not appropriate for the contracting process. Circular A-76 defines an "inherently governmental function" as

> a function which is so intimately related to the public interest as to mandate performance by Government employees. These functions include those activities which require either the exercise of discretion in applying Government authority or the use of value judgment in making decisions for the Government.[9]

OMB and a number of departments and agencies have promoted a relatively broad interpretation of what constitutes a "commercial" activity and, conversely, a relatively narrow definition of what constitutes an "inherently governmental function." This attitude has been reinforced by externally imposed limits placed on management and operations capabilities of departments and agencies. These limitations include such devices as budgetary restrictions, arbitrary administrative cost ceilings, personnel and compensation "caps." Program managers, faced with these externally imposed regulations and limitations, seek relief in order to accomplish their mandated mission, and this relief is generally provided through turning to third parties in contractual arrangements. Increasingly, decisions to rely on the contracting process have not been driven by theory but by the sheer absence of any other reasonable option.

Circular A-120 is designed to provide guidelines for the use of "advisory and assistance" services, better known as consulting. The circular identifies functions for which advisory and assistance services may not be utilized. The prohibited functions include "work of a policy, decision-making or managerial nature which is the direct responsibility of agency officials."[10]

While the guidelines may be helpful in a general way in determining the limits of contracting out, they require specific cases to give meaning to the general prohibition. For instance, can statutorily required auditing of the expenditures of public funds be contracted with a private party if the auditing process permits discretionary disposition of disputed monetary claims against the government? Or can the selection of candidates for participation in a federal program be assigned to a contractor?

In 1989, a Senate subcommittee requested the General Accounting Office (GAO) to investigate several specific contracts to determine if they involved the transfer of an "inherently governmental function" to a private party. One contract by the Department of Energy (DOE) called for the contractor to provide Hearings Officers to conduct hearings and Personnel Security Review Examiners to review findings concerning the eligibility of individuals for DOE security clearances. The GAO concluded that these functions are inherently governmental in nature and should be performed only by federal employees.[11]

What these instances illustrate is an important fact generally overlooked by those discussing privatization: there are fundamental distinctions between the governmental and private sectors, and these distinctions are based on legal principles, not economic theory. Ultimately there are limits to what public-sector services are *permitted* to be contracted out to private parties.

There are also limits, more subtle and less easily defined, as to what services *ought* to be contracted out. Services in support of management are a case in point. Agency libraries are sometimes put to contract, but from a public-sector management standpoint this is a questionable practice. Contemporary libraries are more than simply depositories for books, they are also critical data and information centers whose function is to support management. Private contractor personnel understandably have their primary loyalty, not to the head of the agency, but to the private firm that pays their check and seeks a profit. The agency head can have only an indirect impact on the management and priorities of the library and its personnel. Threats of canceling contracts is not a practical method of providing coherent managerial leadership. Thus, while libraries may not be legally considered an "inherently governmental function," it is probably correct to state that it is a function integral to the management requirements of a properly managed and accountable agency of government.

The notion that somehow privatization necessarily "shrinks" the size of government, as measured in financial terms, and that most functions of the federal government could be performed by private contractors simply misses the mark. Students of American politics today tend to confirm the view that it is not generally persons in the government who are seeking new government programs, new and better entitlement schemes, new forms of government guarantees against the risks of the marketplace, or new defense weapons systems; it is the private contractors and interest groups that have formed the largest and most effective lobbies for more interventionist, and less accountable, government.[12]

Changing Role of Public Management

Public management of third-party relationships is generally more complex and subtle than management relationships associated with the traditional hierarchical public sector. Even the strategic options available to public managers are substantially altered, as Don Kettl observes:

> The point is simple yet often overlooked. Third-party strategies are not self-executing and often replace one set of administrative problems with another. If directly administered government programs must deal with self-interested bureaucrats, third-party programs must deal with self-interested proxies, each seeking to maximize their own interest, sometimes at government's expense. Contracts must themselves be administered to insure high accountability and performance. The role of administrators is different, but it does not disappear.[13]

Indirect provision of services by third parties alters the management of the incentive structures of government.[14] Substantive program results, once the principal basis for judging managerial performance, are being gradually displaced by process managerial standards. Program managers tend to become "risk averse" as they find their political superiors are more interested in whether appropriated monies have been committed in a timely manner and contracts awarded in a politically acceptable mix, rather than in program results. Substantive program knowledge gradually erodes within agency management as managers are evaluated on how well they adhere to procedures rather than how well they are serving the mission of the agency.[15]

Many public managers are originally attracted to public service in general and an agency in particular because of the mission of the agency. Mission fulfillment, such as being involved in the management of the nation's space program in a "hands on" capacity, is an important attraction to public-sector management and helps compensate for comparatively low salaries. But privatization can often result in transferring important management decisions and even much policymaking to the private sector. Program managers see that the interesting work is being done by others, while they are left with accountability to political leaders for the program and with the routine tasks of contract management.

Harold Seidman and Robert Gilmour contend that the reduction in federal agency responsibilities for direct provision of services has resulted in the emergence of a new type of career executive.

> Administration through third-parties has converted the roles of senior career executives to those of grant and contract administrators, paymasters and regulation writers and enforcers. Emphasis has inevitably shifted from delivering services and evaluating results to complying with rules and regulations.[16]

Assume for the moment that an activity is selected for assignment to third parties with public-sector managers retaining residual authority. What are some of the changes likely to be encountered as management is shifted from a command to a negotiations mode?

The most important change is that contract writing becomes a critical tool of public management. In a hierarchical organization, managers can accept a general program objective and make incremental corrections in operations as the program evolves. They can interact directly with field personnel. In a contract relationship, the public manager must negotiate with private managers, thus making subsequent incremental corrections more difficult. Public-sector management in a privatized environment must be heavily front-end loaded. That is, a premium is placed on planning, on anticipating problems in advance, and on being able to correct these problems within the contract-writing process. Contract writing, now principally viewed as a technical task performed by mid-level managers, must become one of the principal tools of the new public management.

Congress and the president have both found the contracting process a convenient tool on which to attach certain social objectives that would have difficulty being accepted on their own merits in the legislative process. As a result, private contractors often find themselves required to implement certain political objectives as a condition for obtaining a contract. Perhaps in seeking to maximize the contracting-out process, we are governmentalizing the private sector more than we are privatizing the public sector.

The potential dangers of mixing governmental powers with privately owned corporations is most evident in the financial area. Government-sponsored enterprises (GSEs), such as the Federal National Mortgage Association ("Fannie Mae"), partake of the best of both the private and public worlds. They are able to pursue private profit under private management, yet are shielded from major financial risk because their obligations are implicitly guaranteed by the federal government. We have yet to develop an effective theory or practice of public management of these GSEs.[17] Privatizers themselves tend to be ambiguous about GSEs and contribute little to the management dialogue.

It is critical to the management of third-party contracts that the agency itself retain the capacity to produce the goods, perform the research, or deliver the services. Only by keeping this capacity will the necessary in-house capability be assured, not only to replace the contractor, if necessary, but also to permit the qualitative evaluation of the product, findings, or service from the contractor. If this is not done, the evaluation process may become simply an auditing process providing information on how well the procedures have been followed for expending funds in a legal manner.

The introduction of market-oriented thinking has already profoundly affected public-sector financial strategies and management. Market mechanisms, such as user fees, are being imposed in a number of areas, and this has important implications for public management.[18] User fees tend to shift the burden of paying for certain activities from the general public to the specific beneficiaries. User fees also tend to discourage the indiscriminate or overuse of certain resources.

This shift of costs from the general treasury to the beneficiary has implications for agency management because political power tends to be related to the source of agency financing. If there is a shift away from financing through appropriations toward user financing, the ability of Congress and central management agencies to supervise the agencies decreases. From a congressional and presidential perspective, therefore, user fees are not simply a convenient and politically neutral form of financing, but a major political decision. Indeed, privatization has already been a major contributing force in disaggregating the organization of the executive branch and in weakening the president's managerial capacity.[19]

The Costs of Government Disinvestment

Privatization, properly understood and managed, is a valuable option for the provision of public goods and services. In the United States we have utilized the private sector to a greater extent than any other nation. But there are limits to the legality and utility of privatization. When privatization is improperly used, it is costly not only to the capacity of government to perform its mission but costly to the private economy as well.

In 1989, a new secretary of energy, James D. Watkins, was shocked to find out how little capacity for supervision and oversight was available internally for managing the vast array of departmental programs and responsibilities and how dependent the DOE had become on private contractors. He found, and was dismayed, that his congressional testimony was drafted by a contractor. He found contractors were supervising other contractors. Arbitrary personnel ceilings, inadequate compensation, and OMB pressure had denuded the department of its managerial capacity and institutional memory. The department itself noted its workforce is 16,000 versus a contract force of well over 100,000. A recent Senate report on the DOE concluded:

> DOE relies on private workforce to perform virtually all basic governmental functions. It relies on contractors in the preparation of most important plans and policies, the development of budgets and budget documents, and the drafting of reports to Congress and Congressional testimony. It relies on contractors to monitor arms control negotiations, help prepare decisions on the export of nuclear technology, and conduct hearings and initial appeals in challenges to security clearance disputes.... DOE top management does not have the basic information it needs to understand the dimensions of its reliance on a contractor workforce. Available data indicate that the private workforce may approach or even exceed the number of federal employees in offices responsible for highly sensitive activities.[20]

The situation found in the Department of Energy is replicated throughout the federal government. The Securities and Exchange Commission, for lack of attorneys, is unable to bring necessary suits to maintain the integrity of private securities markets.[21] The Food and Drug Administration, its personnel severely reduced, is unable to conduct all the testing required by law.[22] The navy, forced to rely on private contractors to run some of its ships, now is criticized by its own inspector general for assigning sensitive governmental functions to private parties.[23] Finally, the Internal Revenue Service (IRS), unable to attract or retain auditors and underfunded for systems development, is rapidly becoming antiquated.[24]

Speaking to the latter point, the IRS, once the envy of the world, has been permitted to decline to the point where the comptroller general, Charles Bowsher, estimates that $87 billion in taxes were not paid. Antiquated systems are extremely costly. "But better systems alone won't solve the IRS's problems," states the comptroller general; "the agency must also invest in people. The IRS must attract top graduates in accounting, legal and computer fields ... a task that is increasingly difficult as federal pay in these jobs lags behind the private sector more every year. While all government agencies face problems in competing for qualified people, the need is especially acute at IRS."[25]

Disinvestment in governmental institutions is costly in monetary terms, but it is also costly in terms of supervising the vast "indirect workforce" so as to protect the public interest. This so-called indirect workforce of contractors, consultants, grantees, and others is estimated to be as high as 8 million.[26] Much of this bureaucracy is a product of efforts to assign as many functions as possible to the private sector. Privatization, instead of being short-changed by the federal government, as frequently charged by privatization advocates, in many areas and agencies may well have gone beyond what is sensible or legal.

Deregulation, like privatization, is a concept and term subject to many definitions and interpretations. It is generally conceded that deregulation, which resulted in eliminating price controls, restrictive market entry requirements, and restraints on competition, has been beneficial to the economy and the consumer. In many instances, however, deregulation was interpreted as simply less governmental regulatory capacity in fields where government regulation is necessary to ensure honest transactions, the safety and soundness of financial institutions, and the interests of the general public as against private interests. Thus it is estimated that cuts made in the budgets of key regulatory agencies during the 1980s will cost the economy tens of billions in the 1990s. Comptroller General Charles Bowsher in November 1989 observed: "When you look at what happened in the S&L crisis and look at the situation at HUD and things like that, if we had adequate financial reporting, if we had the right number of auditors to go out and check on this, we would have saved billions of dollars. In other words, we have been penny-wise and really pound-foolish here."[27]

Disinvestment in the capacity of government to perform the functions citizens expect of their government is a high-risk strategy where the negative consequences tend to be cumulative and difficult to reverse. The antigovernment bias of most public choice theorists and privatization advocates is both misdirected and unnecessary. Regulation is not bad per se; there is useful and appropriate regulation just as there is costly and inappropriate regulation. The challenge is to decide where regulation and oversight is useful and appropriate and then to assure that the government is provided authority and resources sufficient to perform its function effectively.

Similarly, the answer to the problem of unwise assignment of governmental functions to private parties is not to launch an attack on privatization in general. The appropriate response is to raise anew what Charles Wolf correctly calls "one of the cardinal issues of public policy: namely, 'who should do what?' as between government and the private sector?"[28]

Public and Private Sectors: Allies or Adversaries?

Today a single, highly competitive world economy is emerging. National boundaries are less effective barriers as ideas, monies, and people flow rapidly and easily from one country to another. All nations, including communist nations, are adapting to this new market-oriented economic order. The United States, thanks in part to the privatization movement, is well under way in its own adjustment to new economic realities.

Those promoting privatization in the United States tend to accept the premise that the interests of the public and private sectors are in inevitable conflict. Although rarely stated directly, the assumption appears to be that this international competition is largely and properly between the private sectors of the respective countries.

With respect to the United States, the prevailing political model is akin to a zero-sum game. That is, the smaller and less effective the federal government, the larger and more effective the national private sector. The public and private sectors are viewed as natural adversaries where the prosperity of one sector is achieved largely at the expense of the other sector.

The author rejects the zero-sum game model as the model most likely to make the United States competitive in the new world economic order. Competition between nations is not confined to private sectors, but is equally pervasive between public sectors. Public sectors are responsible for developing and protecting the infrastructure that permits private-sector growth and stability. For instance, private securities markets must be kept honest and efficient through governmental supervision, or capital transactions will take place in other national markets. Private security interests, therefore, have a stake in building the capacity of the Securities and Exchange Commission to regulate their activities. Similarly, if foreign airlines are going to have confidence in the safety of American-made passenger planes, the domestic aircraft industry has a stake in building the capacity of the Federal Aviation Administration to monitor its activities. The list of private and public congruence of interests is endless.

The private sector does not benefit from an adversarial attitude toward the public sector. The two sectors, although fundamentally different, are nonetheless tied together in a symbiotic relationship. Neither sector can prosper while the other is weakened. The prosperity of both is linked in a mutually beneficial relationship. Privatization, however defined, will require energetic and creative public sector management and oversight to be successfully implemented.

The United States is reviewing many of its public functions to determine where these functions, in whole or in part, are best assigned to contribute to the growth of the nation's competitive position. This assignment process is critical to America's future and should be guided by theory leavened with experience.[29] The choice is not whether there will be public management of privatization; such management is a given as long as public (governmental) authority or public funds are necessary to implement a public policy or program. The choice is whether or not that management will be enlightened by sound doctrine and implemented by public managers endowed with adequate resources and discretion to ensure that the objectives are achieved. To complete the assignment process successfully, the two sectors must be viewed as allies, not adversaries.

Acknowledgment

Although the name Charles Levine does not appear in the text of this chapter, the reader should know that his spirit guided my pen. Charles thought about public-sector management in innovative ways. We had many conversations on the future of public-sector management in a world increasingly subject to the international discipline of the marketplace. It was Charles who first suggested to me that I consider writing on the implications of the privatization movement on public administration and public law theories. He also piqued my interest in the problem of how public-sector managers might oversee and hold accountable third-party contractors performing governmental activities. This chapter, hopefully, provides some insights on these issues. I miss Charlie very much. Not only could we share our thoughts on how to make government work better, we shared a common sense of humor that sought to bring perspective to the absurdities that determine so much of the human condition.

Notes

1. Ronald C. Moe, "Exploring the Limits of Privatization," *Public Administration Review* 47 (November/December 1987): 453–60.

2. Harold Seidman, "The Quasi World of the Federal Government," *Brookings Review* 6 (Summer 1988): 23–27.

3. National Academy of Public Administration, *Privatization: The Challenge to Public Management* (Washington, D.C.: National Academy of Public Administration, 1989), x.

4. Daniel Guttman and Barry Wilner, *The Shadow Government: The Government's Multi-Billion-Dollar Giveaway of Its Decision-Making Powers to Private Management Consultant, "Experts," and Think Tanks* (New York: Pantheon Books, 1976); Daniel Guttman, "Organizational Conflict of Interest and the Growth of Big Government," *Harvard Journal on Legislation* 15 (Spring 1978): 297–364; James T. Bennett and Thomas J. DiLorenzo, *Underground Government: The Off-Budget Public Sector* (Washington, D.C.: CATO Institute, 1983).

5. Mark L. Goldstein, "Hollow Government: The Incapacitating Consequences of Continuing Austerity," *Government Executive* 21 (October 1989): 12–22.

6. Alan Pifer and Forrest Chisman, "Putting Out a Contract on the Government," *The Wall Street Journal*, 15 October 1984, 28.

7. A recent book in this genre is Randall Fitzgerald, *When Government Goes Private: Successful Alternatives to Public Service* (New York: Universe Books, 1988); E.S. Savas, *Privatization: The Key to Better Government* (Chatham, N.J.: Chatham House, 1987).

8. Testimony of Harold Seidman. U.S. Congress, House Committee on Post Office and Civil Service, Subcommittee on Human Resources, *Hearings: Contracting Out and Its Impact on Federal Personnel and Operations*, 101st Cong., 1st sess. (Washington, D.C.: Government Printing Office, 1990), 125.

9. OMB Circular A-76, paragraph 6e.

10. OMB Circular A-120, paragraph 7B.

11. Letter from Comptroller General Charles Bowsher to Senator David Pryor, chairman, Federal Services, Post Office and Civil Service Subcommittee, Senate Committee on Governmental Affairs. General Accounting Report B-237356, 29 December 1989. See U.S. Congress, Senate, Committee on Governmental Affairs, Subcommittee on Federal Services, Post Office and Civil Service, *Hearings: Use of Consultants and Contractors by the Environmental Protection Agency and the Department of Energy*, 101st Cong., 1st sess. (Washington, D.C.: Government Printing Office, 1990).

12. For an insightful discussion of how this process, called by some "interest-group liberalism," works, consult Theodore Lowi, *The End of Liberalism* (New York: Norton, 1979).

13. Donald F. Kettl, "Third-Party Government and the Public Manager: The Changing Forms of Government Action," *NAPA Proceedings* (Washington, D.C.: National Academy of Public Administration, 1986), 33. See also Donald F. Kettl, *Government By Proxy: (Mis?)Managing Federal Programs* (Washington, D.C.: CQ Press, 1988).

14. Lester M. Salamon, "Rethinking Public Management: Third-Party Government and the Changing Forms of Government Action," *Public Policy* 29 (Summer 1981): 255–75; Lester M. Salamon, *Beyond Privatization: The Tools of Government* (Washington, D.C.: Urban Affairs Press, 1989).

15. Ronald C. Moe, *Privatization from a Public Management Perspective*, Congressional Research Service, Report 89-160, 1989, 75–76.

16. Harold Seidman and Robert S. Gilmour, *Politics, Position, and Power:*

From the Positive to the Regulatory State, 4th ed. (New York: Oxford University Press, 1986), 134–35.

17. Ronald C. Moe and Thomas C. Stanton, "Government-Sponsored Enterprises: Reconciling Public Law with Private Management," *Public Administration Review* 49 (July/August 1989): 321–29; Thomas H. Stanton, *A State of Risk: Will Government-Sponsored Enterprises Be the Next Financial Crisis?* (New York: HarperCollins, 1991).

18. Clayton P. Gillette and Thomas P. Hopkins, "Federal User Fees: A Legal and Economic Analysis," *Boston University Law Review* 67 (November 1987): 451–531; Michael W. Bowers, "The Expansion of User Fees to Finance Government Programs: An Area to Watch," *Federal Bar News and Journal* 34 (January 1987): 21–36.

19. For further discussion by this author of the current status of the president's managerial capacity, consult "Traditional Organizational Principles and the Managerial Presidency: From Phoenix to Ashes," *Public Administration Review* 50 (March/April 1990): 129–40.

20. U.S., Congress, Senate, Committee on Governmental Affairs, Subcommittee on Federal Services, Post Office and Civil Service, Report to the Subcommittee Chairman by Majority Staff, "The Department of Energy's Reliance on Private Contractors to Perform the Work of Government," in *Hearings: Use of Consultants and Contractors,* 65.

21. U.S., Securities and Exchange Commission, *Self-Funding Study* (Washington, D.C.: Securities and Exchange Commission, January 1989).

22. Philip J. Hilts, "A Guardian of U.S. Health Is Failing under Pressure: The FDA and Safety," *New York Times,* 4 December 1989, A1; Enrique J. Gonzales, "A Rudderless FDA Drifts, Awaits Congressional Action," *Washington Times,* 8 December 1989, B6.

23. Peter Grier, "Has Privatization Gone Too Far?" *Military Forum* 5 (April 1989): 30–35.

24. Louise D. Walsh, "IRS Loses Two Million Tax Documents Yearly," *New York Times,* 19 February 1989, A16.

25. National Academy of Public Administration, Charles A. Bowsher, The James E. Webb Lecture, "An Emerging Crisis: The Disinvestment of Government," National Academy of Public Administration, Washington, D.C., 1988, 6–7.

26. "According to a [1979] *National Journal* survey, their [DOD, HEW] budgets support four workers who do not work directly for the federal government for every one who shows up on the payroll." Barbara Blumenthal, "Uncle Sam's Army of Invisible Employees," *National Journal,* 5 May 1979, 730.

27. Jeff Gerth, "Regulators Say 80's Budget Cuts May Cost U.S. Billions in 1990s," *New York Times,* 19 December 1989, 1.

28. Charles Wolf, Jr., in the Preface to Randy L. Ross, *Government and the Private Sector: Who Should Do What?* (New York: Crane Russak, 1988), x.

29. John D. Donahue, *The Privatization Decision: Public Ends, Private Means* (New York: Basic Books, 1989).

7

The Politicization of Bureaucracies in Historical and Comparative Perspective

Hans-Ulrich Derlien

The politicization of bureaucracy has become a practical concern and a theoretical issue in a number of countries during the past two decades.[1] While there are three meanings commonly given to the term *politicization* (functional, role understanding, and personnel), only one of them has been the predominant concern. Functional politicization of government bureaucracies is reflected in active involvement in the political decision-making process, but public administration probably has nowhere and never been separated from politics, as the classical dichotomy of politics and administration would have it. As to role understanding of bureaucrats, concern with the emergence of politically sensitive[2] as opposed to a classical "apolitical" type also has not been great; indeed, it has sometimes been applauded. When the profession expresses concern over politicization, it is addressed to a tendency to recruit civil servants into leading positions increasingly on the grounds of party membership, political loyalty, political conviction, or ostensible sympathy and not solely on the ground of previous professional performance.

In the following sections I trace how this topic of party politicization has emerged in various countries during the past twenty years. It turns out that in Europe the concern is primarily with civil service neutrality and impartiality, while in the United States it is perceived as an impairment of professional expertise. This difference in emphasis will be historically explained by turning to the roots of Western political-administrative systems; it is argued that the perception of the problems emerging from party politicization depends on what came historically first: bureaucracy or democracy. In western Europe, where "the state" was first institutionalized in a professional bureaucracy, the subsequent introduction of democracy made nonpartisanship a key issue. In the United States, where democracy historically preceded bureaucracy, establishing and securing professional expertise appeared to be of primary importance.

Despite these differences in tradition, from a systematic point of view all modern political systems are confronted with the problem of preventing bureaucracy from becoming politically self-controlling because of the very fact of its overwhelming expertise. Politicizing or neutralizing the bureaucracy are two basic options. Various national systems are inspected as to the personnel policy mechanisms they provide for securing political responsiveness to political authority and the extent to which they invite party politicization. Hence I arrive at three kinds of civil service systems based on the degree to which they manage to balance expertise and political responsiveness—the British model putting the highest premium on expertise, the U.S. model most strongly of all Western countries emphasizing political loyalty, and the German system reaching an equilibrium of both functional imperatives. Finally, some unintended consequences of the inevitable party politicization are addressed that reflect specific U.S. and European traditions of the state apparatus and its functional problems.

The Emergence of the Issue

Complaints about party politicization were voiced in Finland,[3] Canada,[4] and West Germany[5] in the 1970s and in France after 1981,[6] when social democrat, liberal, or socialist governments came to power after a long reign of conservative governments.

Despite the apparent ideological bias that suggests that party politicization is a new phenomenon associated with leftist governments, empirical evidence shows in these instances that the personnel policy of the incoming administrations displayed an overt tendency to use legal bureaucracy to an unprecedented extent. There is, however, strong evidence that the same need to control the bureaucracy through the appointment of politically loyal bureaucrats has also been felt by conservative governments. Richard Nixon's "administrative presidency"[7] reacted to "clashing beliefs" originating from the persistence of Democratic officials in some departments.[8] After 1979, Margaret Thatcher also interfered with the previously self-controlled process of appointing top civil servants in Whitehall.[9] Further, after the return of the conservatives to power in Bonn in 1982, the extent of party-political streamlining was at least as great as in 1969, when the Social Democrats came to power.[10] While articulating party politicization as an issue seems to be mostly the preserve of conservatives, the actual personnel policy of conservative governments follows the same imperative of patronage. They will follow this imperative more strongly the more the predecessor government itself has sought to politicize the bureaucracy by party. Also, the more an incoming government conceives of itself as a "conviction" government, the more it too will seek to redirect the permanent government and to weaken the grip of the "directionless consensus" that Richard Rose claimed characterized Whitehall.[11]

While there is a common scientific discussion in the United States and Europe about party politicization, this discussion is accented differently. Europeans focus on the phenomenon either in a normative way as conflicting with the norm of civil service neutrality and nonpartisanship as such or interpret it in a functional way following Max Weber's concern with political control over bureaucracy. The work of the late Charles Levine[12] reveals a peculiarly American viewpoint: while party politicization is not a problem per se, owing to the tradition of elective officeholders and the institution of political appointees, it is the extent of politicization, the implicit challenge of the legitimacy of the professional civil service, and ultimately the danger of erosion of expertise that Levine worried about. Although in Europe, too, party politicization is perceived as a violation of the achievement principle in recruitment and promotion, there is less concern with securing expertise in the bureaucracy as an institution and fewer concerns about the problem of a "government of strangers,"[13] noted by Hugh Heclo, than is the case in the United States.

Historical Background

This distinct emphasis derives from differences in political history in Europe and in the United States. Whereas for continental Europe bureaucracy is the creature of the absolutist state and is considerably older than democracy, in the United States a professional civil service long postdated the development of democracy. While the 1883 Pendleton Act, establishing a merit system and a professional civil service, served to complement Andrew Jackson's ideal of the elected lay administrator and the resulting democratic spoils system with the expertise secured in a permanent career civil service, the functional imperative on the Continent was to make the absolutist civil service politically more responsive to the democratic institutions that had emerged after 1848. In this context, the norms of neutrality, universality, or of standing above parties can be interpreted as reminders of the authoritative state, in which the civil service identified with the crown and had become accustomed to viewing societal and political forces as potentially dangerous to the state and to the commonweal that the state organs, including the bureaucracy, claimed to define. In particular, the German nineteenth-century notion of a state-society dichotomy was directed against democratic political forces above which the bureaucracy ruled in a mythical nonpartisan way, relying solely on its expertise. The American politics-administrative dichotomy, in contrast, presupposes politics but wants to foster the new professional civil service. Thus the difference in emphasis on securing expertise in the United States and on neutrality in Europe.

Systematically, in all Western countries the politics-administration dichotomy derives from the doctrine of separation of powers as a system of political checks and balances, in which the executive branch draws its legitimacy from parliament. It is, however, not merely a normative theory, which had a strong bearing on most civil service codes and in particular implied that the neutral (impartial, impersonal, noncorrupt) execution of written law should guide administrative decision making, but it also reflects the historically new legitimation needs and problems of politically accountable control of bureaucracy: the coming into existence of parliaments and political parties, organized interest groups, and mass media transformed the absolutist state on the Continent and differentiated the polity into various subsystems, among which bureaucracy remained but one, albeit an important power center exposed to an increased number of conflicting interests and rival expectations. With the advent of constitutional monarchy and even more with republican states and competitive party systems, the relationship between "political master and staff of domination," to put it in Max Weber's terms, became more complicated. Whereas under absolutist rule top administrators often were politicians and ministers juridically civil servants, roles became formally differentiated as (at least prime) ministers were elected and supported by a parliamentary majority and stayed in office for a limited number of years. The new tenured, professionally trained, appointed, and salaried full-time continental civil servant, who went through a career to the top of the administrative hierarchy, faced the elected, transitory amateur as his political master, who after the introduction of equal suffrage might well be from a working-class background.

The structural differentiation of the polity coincided at least after revolutionary constitutional changes with a social differentiation of politicians and higher civil servants, when, for example, republican governments under Social Democratic leadership had to work with a ministerial bureaucracy predominantly recruited from nobility and still monarchist in orientation, as in Germany after 1918.[14] Both groups of politico-administrative actors subsequently have become assimilated, because, as Max Weber observed, politicians increasingly tended to "live from politics instead of living for politics."

Despite this professionalization of politicians, the career path of both elite groups remained quite distinct with a predictable career and job security in the case of civil servants and more entrepreneurial, competitive, uncertain transitory careers in the case of politicians. The central functional problem then became how to govern the bureaucracy. Politicizing or neutralizing it were the two basic strategies.

Neutralizing the Civil Service

There are marked national differences in the degree to which horizontal mobility occurs between the realms and arenas of politics and administration, and vice versa, depending basically on the institutional safeguards developed to secure neutrality of the civil service. Whereas some countries by law (United States) or by norm (Great Britain) forbid formal affiliation with political parties, others allow public servants to become members of political parties and even to run election campaigns while formally in office (e.g., Germany, France) as their civil right. The norm of incompatibility between office and mandate on the same level of the (federal) political system is a standard in most countries, however, and the civil servant elected to office is suspended from his duties while serving as a member of parliament. Some countries have a relatively high percentage of civil servants in local, state, and national parliaments, although these are not top administrators. France is the exception to the rule; ministers have frequently gone through administrative careers and are part of the bureaucratic state elite.[15] In any event, in systems in which they are eligible to do so, civil servants tend to become members of political parties. In such systems, it is also more likely that politicians have a civil service background, as in France and Germany, thus clouding the structural differentiation between politics and administration. In these countries, which also have a strong "state tradition,"[16] politicians' interest in public affairs seems to be mediated more through civil service tradition than through democratic institutions.

Mobility from politics into top administrative positions, in contrast, is always less frequent and, when it occurs, presupposes that there are legal (or normative) holes in an otherwise closed civil service career system. Again, we observe national differences as to the degree to which administrative positions may be and are actually staffed with external recruits from politics or other elite sectors. The motives for allowing exceptions to the career system are twofold: on the one hand, external recruitment is justified by the functional need to bring special expertise into an administrative system, particularly where it is normally staffed with generalists. Second, in the United States, top executive positions are filled with candidates formally politically appointed. This is not just a remnant of the old spoils system but can be functionally interpreted as a consequence of far-reaching attempts to neutralize the civil service politically, (e.g., in the Hatch Act of 1939, making political activity for federal civil servants unlawful, and subsequent amendments). A supposed lack of internal civil service responsiveness could be compensated for by importing loyalty from the outside. In Europe, even with the possibility of external recruitment for top positions, we seldom find prominent party or parliamentary politicians in administrative positions; in systems of party government they enter the executive as cabinet politicians. It is often forgotten that in the U.S. presidential system there are no ministers with a political power basis of their own, but merely "secretaries" appointed by the president.

It should therefore be recalled that in Europe the notion of separation of powers, at least as far as the relationship between parliament and government is concerned, has tended to become weak, since in reality most European countries are characterized by party government with ministers regularly being members of parliament; the boundary weakened yet further as additional positions, such as parliamentary secretaries of state (Germany) or junior ministers (Britain), were institutionalized. The notion of linkage rather than separation of powers applies better in the parliamentary systems, and the actual threshold between politics and administration increasingly is located somewhere below the top executive position; the exact borderline depends on the extent to which political criteria are actually applied in staffing executive positions, including those in the bureaucracy proper. From a bird's eye view, the U.S. practice of having political appointees far down the administrative hierarchy is not so completely different from the European practice of party-politicizing the executive bureaucracy. Are there functional imperatives that press for structural convergence across nations?

Mechanisms of Political Control

If bureaucracies are functionally politicized anyway, and institutional arrangements to keep them distinct from politics are established to varying degrees, how can executive politicians today preserve responsiveness to their policies, keep the huge bureaucracy politically under legitimate control, and prevent it from emancipating itself from its political master? Even when excluding insubordination or sabotage, withholding information from a minister, or information leakage, political control by a minister cannot be fully exerted as the complexity of tasks and openness of the decision-making process prevent a minister from knowing everything that goes on in his department. The law of requisite variety[17] limits his attention and information-processing capacity vis-à-vis an apparatus of overwhelming expertise, renders political control necessarily selective, and gives the bureaucracy a potential to become politically self-controlling, as Max Weber observed in imperial Germany. The politician, therefore, is bound to broaden his control capacity over the apparatus.

One way of doing so is to build up staff units; the French *cabinets ministériels*[18] are the prototype of a structural arrangement for increasing the political control capacity, resulting, however, in an impairment of the top administrators' line authority. In most European countries and the United States, furthermore, staff units can mostly be observed on the level of the chief of government, used in order to secure interdepartmental coordination.[19]

Another arrangement practiced in a number of countries consists of implanting more genuine politicians onto a closed civil service career system where top bureaucrats cannot be removed from office on political grounds. The politically neutralized, although not apolitical, Whitehall bureaucracy then might function quite smoothly because a great number of MPs are regularly appointed to political executive positions: the sixty subcabinet positions and thirty-six unpaid parliamentary private secretaries do serve patronage functions within the parliamentary faction,[20] but they also enable the minister to delegate external relations and to broaden the internal political control capacity. Increasing the number of politicians in the executive branch may, however, create problems of balancing and coordinating the division of labor in departmental management.

An additional means of enhancing the control capacity of ministers over their bureaucratic staff is the selective promotion of political trustees within the civil service career system. Whether in staffing the French ministerial cabinets or in appointing top-line administrators, ministers all over the world try to select candidates whom they regard as valuable collaborators in the policy process, because they supposedly share normative convictions with the minister. This congeniality reduces the need to communicate political decision premises and allows the politician to rely on the candidate's political self-control. Selective, politically motivated promotion is possible even in a closed career system, as the change in personnel policy in Whitehall indicates.[21]

The widest range of politically motivated staffing is in the notoriously open American (spoils) system, where political appointees as well as senior executive civil servants can be removed from office or specific positions, respectively, and new trustees appointed to vacancies from within and outside the career service. Other countries, such as France and Germany, merely know of "political civil servants," career civil servants who can be temporarily retired, an institution that is particularly made use of after changes in government.[22] Of course, with public employees instead of tenured civil servants (as mostly holds for the personnel in French cabinets), it is even easier to purge important positions. The most modest form of gearing top career civil servants to the political requirements of the day is to reshuffle them and put those looked at with disgrace into less politically sensitive positions. If reshuffling is not possible, new positions might be established and filled with trustees in order to circumvent or control untrustworthy office holders.

Not merely are these the basic mechanisms for substituting in practice communicated political decision premises by socialized convictions; in my view they also contribute to explaining why top administrators on average fit into a functionally politicized environment and exhibit a role understanding that is compatible and partly congruent with that of politicians. The wide range of informal devices available for political control by personnel policy could also help explain why there are fewer cross-national differences in subjective role understanding of top civil servants than might be expected[23] given the different formal prescriptions for recruitment into top administrative positions and for neutralizing the civil service. Even the formally most extreme cases of staffing top executive positions, Whitehall and Washington, actually can converge toward a "whitewash" system combining, to varying degrees, political responsiveness with expertise.

Combining Expertise and Responsiveness

While party politicization obviously serves to strengthen political loyalty and responsiveness, it is often believed to conflict with the second major goal of personnel policy: securing expertise. In particular, in administrative systems structured strongly by the achievement principle, it is feared that the intrusion of party political criteria of recruitment could impair the career system and the expertise it is supposed to breed.

In systemic perspective one can distinguish three main kinds of civil service systems according to the way in which they match political loyalty and expertise. The Washington model, owing to its democratic historical roots, tends to maximize loyalty at the expense of expertise, because turnover in top positions is high, and external recruitment for staffing these positions is frequent. This is not to suggest that U.S. political appointees do not possess policy knowledge; on the contrary, they are regularly part of a policy network in which they move in and out of the center.[24] What they often lack is administrative experience.[25] In the other extreme case, the Whitehall model, a pure career civil service with solely internal recruitment, maximizes expertise. Here, as was pointed out above, political loyalty has long been taken for granted, relying on the comprehensive party-political neutralization of the British civil service. Reshuffling and selective promotion are the ultimate mechanisms activated to enhance political responsiveness.

The German civil service combines elements of both Washington and Whitehall. Elsewhere I have characterized it as a closed career system with loopholes.[26] While in principle top positions can be staffed only with candidates who have advanced through the hierarchy of offices in a career, an element of openness is introduced by the possibility of recruiting candidates from equivalent civil service ranks in the Länder and local governments; furthermore, with the approval of the Federal Personnel Commission, candidates from other societal and economic sectors may be recruited into top positions of the federal departments, especially if they promise to bring in expertise not normally found in the traditionally juridically trained civil service. Overtly applying party political recruitment criteria would be unconstitutional, however. While German civil servants enjoy the constitutional right to be members of a political party, incumbents of the two highest federal civil service ranks also can be temporarily retired at any time and on any ground, especially if they are deemed not to be in full political consent with the ruling government. The so-called institution of the political civil servant was introduced in Prussia in 1852, after the 1848 revolution, when a parliament came into being, and thus conflicts of loyalty arose. Thus the German model, while heavily relying on internal recruitment for top positions, at the same time provides a mechanism for quick political adjustment.

Party membership among the German administrative elite has dramatically increased in the past two decades and party politicization is recognized by the civil service elite.[27] At the same time, temporary retirement has more often come into use, especially after government changes. External recruitment, however, to staff the vacant positions is still an exception. Not surprisingly, the formal qualification of the German civil service elite has not changed in response to party politicization. Contrarily, the German civil service is still a career system insofar as top positions are staffed from within the ministries, although it has gradually ceased being a traditional career system. Although relying on internal recruitment and expertise, (new) governments are in a position to secure loyalty and responsiveness by selectively appointing party members to top positions. Obviously, the internal reservoir of candidates is large enough to find the required combination of expertise and explicit political loyalty for both of the traditionally leading government parties.

Compared to Whitehall, with its strict prohibition of party membership and (thus) permanence in office even after government changes, temporary retirement and the growing supply of party members among senior civil servants in Germany allows for quicker political adjustments to new governments than can be achieved by selective promotion and reshuffling alone. At the same time, the German system avoids the dysfunctional consequences associated with the U.S. practice of political appointment of newcomers to leading positions.

Unintended Consequences of Party Politicization

So far, the universal trend toward party politicization has been explained historically and functionally by referring to needs for political control of the career civil service, especially in countries where the civil service predates democratic political institutions. The various devices for politically neutralizing the civil service at best buffer patronage motives. It is further argued that the expertise inherent in a career civil service system is hardly impaired by party politicization, if recruitment draws on the internal reservoir of political sympathizers. Reality, though, is not that simple. There are signs and warnings from practitioners that unrestrained party politicization can become counterproductive and even degenerate the historically developed professional civil service structures.

A recent German study detected a "politicization paradox":[28] even top civil servants who have themselves joined political parties to an unprecedented extent and might have profited from their party membership in career terms increasingly complain about the politicization trend. In making personnel decisions they are exposed to growing pressures from party headquarters and subordinates to promote people whom they do not believe to have the necessary professional qualification. A practice of domination patronage may induce zealots to gain personally from such a partisan system, thus driving it ultimately toward alimentation patronage, where rewarding deserved followers is the dominant motive for party-politicized staffing.

It is also reported that civil servants who owe their position to party-political considerations tend to forgo an essential advantage that tenured civil servants have over elected politicians: without risking their careers, they may and often are even legally obliged to remonstrate, that is, to tell politicians which policy does not work or is too costly. Party-political streamlining can thus jeopardize the built-in administrative potential to correct unfeasible political wishes. Precisely because it is so difficult to distinguish serious remonstration from political obstinacy and to close the gap between administrative and political rationality, civil servants are tempted to avoid internal controversies if they are supposed to behave overtly politically loyal. Furthermore, civil servants, who feel obliged to a certain government for advancing their career for other than professional reasons, may be likely to engage in illegal activities to keep the parliamentary opposition out of government.[29]

The more political patronage by the ruling parties becomes obvious or is even merely suspected (it regularly fails to be proved in appeals to administrative courts) and is exercised irrespective of professional performance, the more aspiring civil servants who either do not belong to a party or belong to the "wrong" party lose motivation because they cannot envision further career prospects. In Germany it is also reported that subdivision heads occasionally prefer not to be promoted into the "catapult seat" of division head, where they could be temporarily retired.

Excessive party patronage might also induce opportunism, by joining a specific party, and ultimately not only paralyze the patronage system but also introduce a kind of neofeudalism, wherein life chances no longer would be structured by performance but by a modern form of ascription.

All these consequences of maximizing political loyalty used as a way to manage the control of the government bureaucracy obviously impair its professional competence. Seen from a European point of view, the deterioration of a formerly competent apparatus, engendered by the imbalance of political control motives, was Charles Levine's basic and, as I see it, typically American reference point of strengthening professional expertise vis-à-vis the well-established political control strategies in Washington.

Over the past few years Charlie had elaborated on a further aspect of the politicization phenomenon, beyond those I already have discussed: functional politicization, politicization of subjective role understanding, and party politicization. He dealt with what could be termed *status politicization*. By this, he meant individual or collective reactions of the civil service to political reforms or policies that threaten their social prestige or material status. As a result of the 1978 Civil Service Reform Act, pushed by President Carter, the 1984 Grace Commission Report, and the salary problems under President Reagan's tenure, Charles Levine saw a decline in the attraction of the U.S. civil service for future recruits and an erosion of the existing human capital of the administration.[30] Not only is the U.S. civil service obviously lacking competitiveness vis-à-vis the private sector as far as salaries are concerned, and therefore appears to suffer from a brain drain to the private sector, but the bonus system of the 1978 reform, which was to stimulate performance, appears also to have been politically manipulated. Combined with spreading political appointments, the deficiencies of the reward system seem to have engendered a critical situation for the U.S. civil service. For only slightly different reasons, Britain is facing a similar situation, where civil servants react with "exit" to status politicization and status deterioration.[31] One can probably generalize from these two cases that politicization of personnel policy, demotivating as it may be in individual cases, becomes threatening for the system's expertise if the status of the service as such becomes politicized, whether because of attacks on its prestige or its material rewards. In both respects, though, the higher civil service in France and Germany, countries with a strong bureaucratic state tradition, is unchallenged and even privileged to the extent that party politicization has not yet resulted in a loss of its attraction.

Notes

1. François Meyers, ed., *The Politicization of Public Administration* (Brussels: International Institute of Administrative Sciences, 1985).

2. Robert D. Putnam, "The Political Attitudes of Senior Civil Servants in Western Europe: A Preliminary Research Report," *British Journal of Political Science* 3 (1973): 253–90; Joel D. Aberbach, Robert D. Putnam, and Bert A. Rockman, *Bureaucrats and Politicians in Western Democracies* (Cambridge: Harvard University Press, 1981.)

3. Krister Ståhlberg, "The Politicization of Public Administration: Notes on the Concept, Causes and Consequences of Politicization," *International Review of Administrative Sciences* 53 (1987): 363–82.

4. Colin Campbell, "The Higher Civil Service in Canada," in *The Higher Civil Service in Europe and Canada: Lessons for the United States*, ed. Bruce L.R. Smith (Washington, D.C.: Brookings Institution, 1984), 53.

5. Hans-Ulrich Derlien, "Politicization of the Civil Service in the Federal Republic of Germany—Facts and Fables," in Meyers, *Politicization of Public Administration*, 3–38.

6. Jean-Luc Bodiguel, "Les Relations entre Administration et Partis Politiques dans la France Contemporaine," *European Group Public Administration*, Occasional Paper 4 (1986): 15; Jean-Luc Bodiguel and Jean-Luis Quermonne, *La Haute Fonction Publique sous la Ve République* (Paris: Presses Universitaires de France, 1983), 223–35; Klaus-Werner Schmitter, *Das Regime Mitterrand: Regierungsstruktur und Haute Administration im Wandel* (Berlin: Quorum, 1986), 116–24.

7. Richard Nathan, *The Plot That Failed: Nixon and the Administrative Presidency* (New York: Wiley, 1975).

8. Joel D. Aberbach and Bert A. Rockman, "Clashing Beliefs within the Executive Branch: The Nixon Administration Bureaucracy," *American Political Science Review* 70 (1976): 456–68.

9. Yvonne Fortin, "Madame Thatcher et la Politisation des Échelons Supérieurs de l'Adminstration Centrale," in *Grand-Bretagne 1979–1984, Mythe ou Réalité?* 50 (1984): 337–54; Frederick F. Ridley, "Politics and the Selection of Higher Civil Servants in Britain," in Meyers, *Politicization of Public Administration*, 153–77.

10. Hans-Ulrich Derlien, "Repercussions of Government Change on the Career Civil Service in West Germany: The Cases of 1969 and 1982," *Governance* 1 (1988): 50.

11. Geoffrey K. Fry, "The Development of the Thatcher Government's 'Grand Strategy' for the Civil Service: A Public Choice Perspective," *Public Administration*, 62 (1984): 325.

12. Michael G. Hansen and Charles H. Levine, "The Centralization-Decentralization Tug-of-War in the New Executive Branch," in *Organizing Governance: Governing Organizations,* ed. Colin Campbell and B. Guy Peters (Pittsburgh, Pa.: University of Pittsburgh Press, 1988), 259–65.

13. Hugh Heclo, *A Government of Strangers: Executive Politics in Washington* (Washington, D.C.: Brookings Institution, 1977).

14. Wolfgang Runge, *Politik und Beamtentum im Pateienstaat: Die Demokratisierung der Politischen Beamten in Preussen zwischen 1918 und 1933* (Stuttgart: Klett, 1965).

15. Ezra N. Suleiman, "From Right to Left: Bureaucracy and Politics in France," in *Bureaucrats and Policy Making: A Comparative Overview,* ed. Suleiman (New York: Holmes and Meier, 1984), 107–35.

16. Kenneth Dyson, *The State Tradition in Western Europe: A Study of an Idea and Institution* (Oxford: Robertson, 1980).

17. W. Ross Ashby, *An Introduction to Cybernetics* (London: Chapman and Hall, 1963), 206–18.

18. Guy Thuillier, *Les Cabinets Ministériels* (Paris: Presses Universitaires de France, 1982).

19. Richard Rose and Ezra N. Suleiman, eds., *Presidents and Prime Ministers* (Washington, D.C.: American Enterprise Institute, 1980).

20. Richard Rose, "British Government: The Job at the Top," in Rose and Suleiman, *Presidents and Prime Ministers,* 6.

21. Some observers contend that Mrs. Thatcher was looking for style rather than partisanship in her civil servants. The managerialist attitude favored in civil servants should, though, be viewed as an element of her political philosophy.

22. Derlien, "Einstweiliger Ruhestand Politischer Beamter des Bundes 1949–1983," *Die Öffentliche Verwaltung,* 37 (1984): 689–99.

23. Putnam, "Senior Civil Servants in Western Europe"; however, he showed that the Italian case deviated due to frequent government changes.

24. Hugh Heclo, "In Search of a Role: America's Higher Civil Service," in Suleiman, *Bureaucrats and Policy Making,* 18–20.

25. Max Weber distinguished between *Fachwissen* ("academic knowledge") and *Dienstwissen* ("office knowledge," or administrative experience); the latter can be accumulated only inside bureaucracy.

26. Derlien, "Repercussions of Government Change," 55.

27. Renate Mayntz and Hans-Ulrich Derlien, "Party Patronage and Politicization of the West German Administrative Elite 1970–1987—Towards Hybridization?" *Governance* 2 (1989): 384–404.

28. Ibid.

29. A German case in point was the abuse of the bureaucracy by the minister president of the Land Schleswig-Holstein during the elections in 1988. The affair ended with his suicide and revealed parallels to the Watergate affair.

30. Charles H. Levine, "Human Resource Erosion and the Uncertain Future of the U.S. Civil Service: From Policy Gridlock to Structural Fragmentation," *Governance* 1 (1988): 115–43; Charles H. Levine, ed., *The Unfinished Agenda for Civil Service Reform: Implications of the Grace Commission Report* (Washington, D.C.: Brookings Institution, 1985), and his introduction therein.

31. Richard Rose, "Loyalty, Voice, or Exit? Margaret Thatcher's Challenge to the Civil Service," in *Jahrbuch zur Staats- und Verwaltungswissenschaft*, ed. Thomas Aloin et al. (1988) 2: 189–218.

8

Conclusion

BERT A. ROCKMAN

In the introductory chapter of this book, Guy Peters portrayed with great acuity both the scholarly concerns and the public passions of Charles Levine. Charlie believed that effectiveness, excellence, and commitment to the commonweal were the core ingredients of a top-notch civil service. These ingredients were vital because a high-quality civil service was necessary both to running the public's business and to the arts of government. As a motivating force, Charlie thought that while pecuniary incentives were never unimportant, they simply were no match for dedication to public service. If this sounds naïve, it is not. Individuals like to optimize their utilities. It is just that different individuals have different utilities. And for the most part, Charlie thought that civil servants were different.

The state and quality of the civil service for Charlie was therefore a matter of passionate concern—and because it was, it was also a matter to which he devoted his great intellectual talents. Two dangers became prominent in Charlie's later work, as both the public sphere and the civil service came under attack during the 1980s. One of these dangers was the politicization of the civil service and its potential deterioration.[1] Another danger was the erosion of the public sphere and with that a loss of accountability and democratic control.

In the long run, the unity and neutrality of the civil service, Charlie contended, were essential to effective service in the public realm.[2] Privatization, to some extent, endangered unity, whereas politicization imperiled neutrality. Yet Charlie was no doctrinaire. Charlie's creed was antidogmatism. He understood well the conditions necessary for managerial efficiency and those of political responsiveness. He knew full well that an unabashed apologia for the public sphere was sheer statism and that an equally irrational defense on behalf of elevating the status of the civil service was unadorned elitism.

In extending the themes of Charlie's later concerns in this chapter, I want to focus especially on the conditions and problems of neutrality, competence, and responsiveness, and the implications of how the growth in privatization affects the principal responsibilities of the civil service.

Civil Servants and Their Roles

In his introduction, Guy Peters noted that the idea of civil servants as policymakers, while certainly realistic, violates some preconceptions of the role of the civil service and its political neutrality. These notions follow from the Wilsonian dichotomy between politics and administration, hardened in turn by the scientific management ideas of Frederick Winslow Taylor and the rules of administration set forth by Luther Gulick.[3]

The mythology that civil servants are not, and should not be, policymakers is most persistent in the United States, where populism is strongest and where the development of democratic politics preceded the rise of bureaucratic institutions. Nowhere, of course, is it permissible for civil servants to be partisans in the most overt meaning of the term. But in most settings, formally or informally, civil servants are expected to be participants in the policy-making process. There are two senses in which this is so. Frequently, civil servants are the first line of defense in mediating relations between governmental agencies and the interest groups that form their clientele. In this context, they handle political negotiations until problems in those negotiations require resolution at a higher policy level. The second sense is that top civil servants also are expected to provide advice to political decision makers.

In most political settings these expectations of the role of top civil servants arise in part because the political leaders form a thin icing over the bureaucratic organizations that carry out governmental programs. Proximity to political power enhances the civil servant's role. Whatever the historical reasons for this proximity, the American system, by contrast, does not grant that condition. So, advice giving is difficult, and political negotiation is both suspect and circumscribed, which does not so much eliminate it as drive it underground.

Ironically, given this elaborate effort to wedge leadership-friendly officials between the political heads of departments and the career service, the American style of governing is better equipped to deal with civil servants as neutral competents than are the systems in which civil servants are nearer to the political authorities. Why? One reason is that U.S. civil servants are increasingly thought of as public managers in ways that seem to fit the Wilsonian distinction between the hurly-burly world of politics and the well-organized one of management and administration. By marginalizing the policy roles of civil servants and micro managing their activities, the main function of civil servants is reduced to managing clearly defined tasks well.[4] If the political officials provide sufficiently clear direction and the micro managers in central clearance agencies dictate the terms of management, then civil servants need be only "smart tools."

If, however, civil servants are expected to handle interest-group relationships and render advice, then the political leaders of the day may have a greater interest in the capacity of the civil service elite to be responsive to them. Americans frequently do not realize the extent to which gaining the currency of power also bears the risk of having achieved it only momentarily. In many European continental systems, a distinctly political class of civil servants exists near the top. Changes in political regimes create risks for them. In other settings, such as Japan (where there has been no regime change in nearly forty years), the ministerial vice-director leads a charmed but brief life in that role before retiring.

Before Charles Levine's untimely death, he had come to be an active participant in the Research Committee on the Structure and Organization of Government of the International Political Science Association. The former group, known to its aficionados by the acronym SOG, utilized its frequent international meetings to explore what was different and similar across national systems. It was meant to get beneath structural divergencies to examine frequent functional parallels. And it was designed to track developments in various systems that might lead to changes in the roles of civil servants and political leaders and in their relationships. It is precisely through this form of international comparison that we can draw or modify generalizations. Otherwise we fall into idealized comparisons. In his perceptive article comparing Whitehall and the White House, Richard Neustadt illustrated how important it was to probe beneath the structural distinctions to see many underlying functional parallels between the U.K.'s senior careerists and the American in-and-outers.[5] Similarly, Charles Levine came to believe that comparison was necessary to both understanding the American system better and exploring the variety of relationships taken between political leaders and civil servants.

Forms of Relationship

Of one thing there is little doubt, and that is that political leaders and civil servants inevitably have certain points of tension between them. These may be overcome by confidence between them individually (a short-lived phenomenon), politically (a regime-dependent condition), or culturally (a relatively long-lived equilibrium).

Personal chemistry helps any relationship. Particular civil servants can be quite effective in gaining the confidence of particular political leaders. The more that relationship is seen to be based on ties between personalities, however, the more it takes on the appearance of a patronage connection. Understandably, the more any civil servant is connected to a particular political leader, the more that civil servant's fortunes will fluctuate with the fortunes of his or her principal. This also means that when the political patron or matron is replaced, connections that rest on the personal compatibility of the principal and the agent may prove to be fragile. A good working relationship requires closeness and openness between civil servant and political overseer, but too much of a good thing will produce the appearance of a bad one for the civil servant.

Similarly, relationships resting on the compatibility of political parties or outlooks may persist only as long as the present regime does. How stable that is may depend on the stability of the political coalitions or dominant party at the top. One thing is certain: a regime that has been in power a long time will have created an expectation of its durability and, consciously or not, a civil service that is politically compatible, or at least sufficiently comfortable, with it that the prospect of change is likely to be unsettling. The prevailing policy inertia may be embedded in the collective mentality of the civil service, and that inertia, by definition, will be incompatible with programs that seek to reverse the prior directions.

When regimes turn over more routinely, identification with a departing one may be ruinous for any individual's career. Collectively, it endangers the expectation of neutral competence in the civil service. This concern provokes public administration professionals and scholars alike. Will the civil service be thought of as merely the tool of any given regime and responsive only to its interests? And will that mean that every new administration will seek ways to mold the civil service to its interests and goals? This is, of course, an entirely legitimate concern. Of equal concern is whether the civil service is made irrelevant by the importation of outsiders and the erosion of their functions to strictly managerial ones. And even these managerial functions often carry with them diminished discretion.

The outsiders, of course, may be every bit as competent as (and perhaps more competent than) the inside careerists. That was Neustadt's observation in comparing the staffs serving the White House and the servants of Whitehall. The outsiders are likely to be more policy responsive. They also carry fewer of the organizational interests, commitments, and memories than the careerists do. But they will be seen, fairly or not, as the instruments of the political wishes of the departed administration when new political leaseholders take over the governmental property. The value of continuity inevitably is lost in the wholesale changeover of regimes. The modest place of the civil servant's role in the American system makes such changeovers both more complete (since a whole new team of people can be appointed to the noncareer positions) and riskier for continuity.

Finally, confidence based on cultural compatibility is perhaps most beneficial to both sets of actors, for it promises a long-term relationship irrespective of party or political outlook. Johan P. Olsen, for example, notes in his study of Norwegian democracy that what makes the system work at forging consensus comes down more to a matter of shared norms than of any lack of structural complexity or division.[6] Similarly, the ability of the Swedish civil service, which was generally more conservative than the governments it had been serving, to work within the context of the welfare and social equality goals of the ruling Social Democrats seems largely to have been a product of the culture of pragmatism and social harmony.[7]

All that said, even in Sweden there is nonetheless a band of policy-initiating civil servants who are more politically responsive and sympathetic to the elected government. In the heyday of the celebration of Swedish political culture, these officials were crafting Social Democratic ideas. More recently, they had crafted Conservative ones. It helps, of course, that Swedes like to reach agreements regardless of the diversity of their preferences. But whatever stripe a Swedish government has, it still feels the necessity of "responsive competence" close to it.

There are conditions, of course, that drive the normal level of tension between political leaders and civil servants to greater heights. When does this happen?

Tensions between Politicians and Civil Servants
RADICAL DEPARTURES FROM THE STATUS QUO

One of the most obvious sources of tension between newly crowned leaders and career officialdom occurs when sharp change lies on the horizon. At a minimum, this raises the level of uncertainty among civil servants to a considerable degree. All change is at least moderately unsettling. The shifting of personalities requires new relationships to be constructed even when policy shifts may be incremental. Old networks have to be rethreaded. Predictability is inherently diminished.

Nonetheless, when big policy changes loom on the horizon, anxieties on the part of civil servants are likely to increase greatly. Not all changes are anxiety producing, of course. Sometimes civil servants are interested in changes that help make their programs work better. When the changes threaten the foundation of their programs, however, tensions are clearly raised, and the network of alliances that civil servants have generated may be eroded. Beyond program changes, alterations in personnel policy, explicit or implicit, also present a major source of threat to civil servants. People who have earned their spurs through one process are unlikely to see the virtues of having the process of certification substantially changed, and certainly they are likely to resist personnel policies that place them at greater risk. Early studies of the Senior Executive Service in the United States, for example, indicated that civil servants saw more potential for threat than for opportunity.[8]

Big change without adequate preparation always presents a threat to those commanded to implement it. How the civil servants react varies with the options available to them. To use Albert Hirschman's terminology, exit may be a viable option either to other, less controversial sites in the bureaucracy or from the system altogether. There were some intimations of this during the early period of the Reagan administration in the United States, when in several agencies officials were charged with having to fulfill an entirely different set of priorities from those they had been working on in the previous administration. Data that Joel Aberbach and I collected indicate, for example, that a substantial transformation in the political identities and ideologies of senior civil servants in the social services departments took place between 1970 and 1986–87.[9] Although we cannot discern whether these changes were a consequence of voluntary departures hastened by the radical policy shifts initiated by the Reagan administration or whether they were the result of manipulations of the personnel system by the political leadership (or indeed the result of other factors), it is clearly the case that those most predisposed to resist the Reagan administration's social policies were no longer in place. The moral of this story seems quite clear. When the political leadership has an agenda of radical change, it needs also to have a personnel strategy for its implementation. When it does, its plans stand a greater chance of being consummated. Typically, these circumstances create problems for both public administration professionals and scholars because they result in the displacement of one set of values—continuity, stability, and expertise—with another set—democratic renewal, policy change, and the rule of the elected over the selected.

Naturally enough, not all civil servants connected to the ancien régime will exit. No personnel system allows wholesale instantaneous replacements of civil servants (as distinct from carefully selected ones). Some may respond, in Hirschman's terms, with the voice option. There are two versions of this option. One is overt and the other covert. The overt option normally requires resignation as an accompaniment. The covert option has greater possibilities, especially in such a loosely jointed political system as the American one, where members of congressional staffs and the news me-

Conclusion

dia are eager recipients for signs of disharmony in the executive and for evidence of political or legal wrongdoing. American civil servants occasionally speak of the possibility of sabotage against their political superiors in the executive. They do so when they believe they are being asked to do something illegal or contrary to the intent of the laws they enforce. To be less charitable, they do so when their preferences and those of their superiors may be irreconcilable. Yet they could hardly do this at all were it not for the numerous opportunities offered by the American political system to find ready recipients for internal executive information.

The problem of large change in government bureaucracies is endemic to the beast itself, whatever the specifics of the political system. Partly this is so because of the very different perspectives through which civil servants and politicians see the world.[10] Bureaucrats complexify while politicians simplify, among other of their distinctive traits. And partly, as William Plowden suggests, this reflects the failures of political leaders to manage change or, put differently, to think through the strategic implications for the civil service of desired changes in the culture of governance.[11]

In any event, one thing is entirely clear. Bureaucracies are not the birthplace of revolutions, and civil servants make improbable revolutionaries. Change unsettles the ground on which bureaucracies like to be settled.

DIVIDED GOVERNMENT

It is precisely the opportunities given to civil servants in the American system to sabotage the plans of their would-be superiors that heightens the tension between political leaders and civil servants. The looseness of the system counts for much. There is no "government" there. Instead, there are coequal branches of government, each independent of the other yet necessarily sharing power with the others. Independence is dictated by the Constitution. Interdependence is dictated by the realities of governing.

While unified government is no picnic for the political leaders of the executive, divided government makes things even worse for them. For when government is divided, policy preferences are also divided across institutions. Similarly, different constituencies are apt to come into and go out of favor depending on whether the domain is the executive or the legislature. Norton Long once posed the central problem of American public administration as being that of "who is the boss?"[12] Since Long well knew that the answer to that question was not singular, he also knew that American public administration suffered from the effects of being buffeted by different authorities who had constitutionally derived rights to hold agencies and civil servants accountable. Yet Long wrote when divided government was relatively rare, implying that even under unified government the problem of multiple legitimacies and authorities created complications for

American administration. The problem, of course, was magnified by the struggles for control of agencies and programs that took place in the latter stages of the Nixon administration and then again during the Reagan and Bush administrations.

Indeed, Terry Moe has advanced the argument that the different institutional perspectives and interests of the presidency and the Congress lead to strenuous efforts on the part of each institution to control the administration of programs and to define the terms of their implementation.[13] While Moe does not say so directly, the implication clearly is that divided government makes these normal tendencies much worse.

The consequences of this struggle are meaningful, for they create both powerful constraints as well as significant opportunities for civil servants. The constraints are that civil servants are caught in a crossfire between two, all too frequently, warring camps, each trying to optimize their preferences through administrative implementation. The presidency, through its central clearance functions, seeks to control the agencies by minimizing their discretion and bringing decision making into the White House and the Executive Office of the President (EOP). An important method of doing this is to rewrite administrative regulations and control the activities of agencies by imposing greater regulatory controls from the center of government on the latitude of its operating agencies. Alternatively, the Congress seeks greater control over the process by writing legislative amendments to laws that become increasingly confining and specific and thus minimize agency discretion. This process of micro management goes on at both ends of Pennsylvania Avenue. In the midst of this crossfire, it behooves civil servants to hunker down rather than rise up. They are buffeted from both ends and are increasingly made marginal to the policy process.

Of course, amid the powerful constraints imposed by divided government, there also are opportunities for maneuver. The existence of divided authorities presents opportunities for civil servants to appeal decisions made within the executive. The well-timed leak to congressional staffers or others who might influence the policy process provides one of a variety of ways by which the political leadership of the executive might be sabotaged. When civil servants resort to these tactics (high-risk ones to be sure), they are engaged in parrying the initiatives of others rather than advancing their own. The room for maneuver is largely defensive because civil servants can best propose ideas within the executive setting. Yet because executive control is limited by the potential for legislative intervention, civil servants are prime suspects as potential saboteurs in the eyes of any presidential administration intent on using administrative processes to attain its policy goals.

The separation-of-powers system tends to inhibit the close proximity to executive power that civil servants in other systems enjoy. Divided government makes loyalties even more suspect and distances civil servants from the sources of executive power. It exacerbates the tension that would normally exist and makes life for civil servants a lot more complicated and, in all likelihood, less desirable than in systems with more settled definitions of governmental authority.

Opportunities for Alliance Formation

The extent to which civil servants have opportunities to form alliances is bound to create suspicions among their political overseers. As noted, the American setting provides ample opportunities for that to happen, and the condition of divided government reinforces those opportunities dramatically. As a general matter, the more loosely jointed the political system, the more such opportunities for alliance formation present themselves. A loosely jointed political system—in which political authority is both fragmented and accessible—reduces the cost of seeking political support outside the "chain of command" precisely because that chain is so loosely concatenated.

Alternatively, the closer civil servants are to sources of authority and the more political authority is centralized, the greater the costs of seeking external alliances. Proximity to influence is an asset that U.S. civil servants tend to lack relative to their peers in more centralized parliamentary systems. But the losers in policy debates under the latter systems lack avenues of appeal. Interest groups, congressional staffs, and the media are all willing consumers of leaked information that can serve their interests or needs or that can be used to embarrass opponents or targets. The independence of Congress, its fragmented structure of authority, and its frequent divisions over policy with the executive grant numerous opportunities for policy supplicants to seek redress.

Ironically, one of the burdens that civil servants carry in the American setting is that they typically are removed from direct policymaking influence so that higher political decision makers and civil servants rarely mix. Yet the political system, being so loosely jointed, is one in which the political decision makers are bound to feel that civil servants may try to work around them when they are in disagreement, thus breeding further suspicions and generating greater distance between the two.

As with other proponents of the professional civil service, Charlie Levine saw this estrangement between politicians in the executive and civil servants as a worrisome matter for the quality of government and for democracy. The need to reduce suspicion between the politicians and the civil servants was vital because politicians needed the experience and advice of civil servants if they were to avoid big problems that might otherwise have been anticipated. On the other side, bureaucrats require realistic direction and guidance from politicians. The two can and ought to influence the thinking of one another.[14] But the American system sometimes makes that difficult. And the onset of political leadership during the Reagan administration that was uninterested in facts or analytics that might interfere with its policy directions made that even more difficult.

New Dimensions of the Civil Service Role

As we move into the twenty-first century, what, if any, notable trends appear on the horizon regarding redefinitions of the role of civil servants in the process of governing? Citing "trends" is always an endeavor filled with some presumption, but let me suggest a few that seem at least plausible.

FROM NEUTRAL COMPETENCE TO RESPONSIVE COMPETENCE

The assumption behind neutral competence is that civil servants are fundamentally disinterested in the fate of their political overseers. They will seek to implement the directions and analyze the options of whatever political leadership happens to be in power with an equivalent level, or lack, of vigor. The notion of neutral competence implies something that political leaders have difficulty fathoming, namely, that someone can be genuinely neutral even if they have no ostensible partisan ties. To some politicians, the idea of neutral competence is suspect because they find it difficult to imagine officials who have been implementing a policy suddenly having to implement something diametrically opposed to it.

The idea of responsive competence borrows in some degree from the old Chinese Communist maxim of "red and expert." When the competence side is emphasized, more attention is given to the "expert" side than the "red" side. In fact, what may be emphasized is less that one is "red" than that one is not anti-red (or whatever color). The conundrum of competent responsiveness is twofold: (1) more attention may be given to the responsiveness side than to the competence side, in which case bureaucrats become merely compliant tools of the political leadership; and (2) bureaucrats become identified with an existing regime and thereby lose their legitimacy when there is a change of political leadership.

In Britain particularly, the notion of neutral competence has been dearly held. That partly reflects a relationship in which ministers often have seemed dependent on their top civil servants. In the United States, to the contrary, responsiveness historically has played a major role in the administrative system and in the councils of policy advice. Politically appointed positions abound in the federal government and so does "political" staffing in both the White House and the Congress. All of this is a means of building in responsiveness, and most of the time only a relatively few executive appointees might be regarded as being overtly incompetent. On the European continent, frequently a political class of civil servants is identified at the top of the system with the personal status of its members (though not their civil service status) dependent on political patrons in the governing party.

How the tension between responsiveness and competence is sorted out still remains to be seen, and there is little evidence that either the British or the American models will be adopted in whole. But my guess is that in view of the growth of politically responsive agents in government and indeed of the fears of some British students of public administration, it is likely that other democracies will move more in the American than the British tradition.[15] The move toward responsive competence, assuming that there is a trend in that direction, ironically is a sign of just how central the functions of public administration have become, rather than how remote they are to the concerns of political decision makers.

CENTRAL VERSUS DEPARTMENTAL BUREAUCRATS

Joel Aberbach and I have argued earlier that financial stringency brings central agencies to the fore.[16] That assessment appears to be only partially correct. Certainly tight times place greater emphasis on financial review, managerial efficiencies, and even the internal regulation of government. The emphasis of tight times is to control the supply of governmental resources in the face of what appears to be an insatiable demand from the spending departments. In this regard, a Reagan policy adviser noted that the Reagan administration did not treat all agencies or civil servants alike in spite of its antigovernment themes. Instead, it gave the civil servants in OMB a preferred status to allow them to do what their natural inclinations would lead them to do, that is, cut budgets.[17]

But, not all systems fit the same mold. While financial stringencies compelled a more activist Finance ministry role in budget negotiations during the 1980s in Australia, for instance, Campbell and Halligan, in their recent book on this process, portray under the Hawke government a more cooperative and mutually adjusting role between spending ministries and the financial watchdog.[18]

Moreover, central agencies also can become important as a stimulant to a more activist policy-planning government. That certainly is the message that Campbell and Szablowski relate in their book on the growth of central agencies and the "superbureaucrats" who led them during the Trudeau government in Canada.[19]

In fact, what the growth of central agencies does reflect—and it is a growth that is far from universal—is the interest of central political leaders in exerting control over the affairs of government, whether this be expressed as rolling back the state or enhancing its policymaking and planning capacities. Left to their own devices, the line agencies will tend to follow the path of the prevailing inertia. Their links will be to their program clienteles. Central agencies thus become the stimulants and goads for change and are more closely linked to the central political leadership. The more important the challenges to government, in all likelihood, the more important central agencies are likely to become.

Advising versus Managerial Roles

Once again, the United States and the United Kingdom provide paired and starkly contrasting portraits. The relative remoteness of the U.S. civil service from the corridors of ostensible power diminishes its capacity to play a major policy-advising role. This condition is reinforced by the classic distinction between politics and administration, so that civil servants formally are supposed to be neutral managers of a process under which decisions are made by the appointed agents of the president. The realities, of course, are not so neat, but for the most part, American civil servants are expected merely to be the efficient instruments of decision makers representing the presidential administration.[20] Reflecting this and the American penchant for managerial gadgets in both the public and the private sectors, the heavy emphasis in the United States is on the management rather than the advisory role of civil servants.

In sharp contrast, precisely the opposite condition obtains in Britain. Indeed, the British public sector (and sometimes the private sector as well) has been imbued with the spirit of amateurism in management. What elite British civil servants want is their minister's ear. The "next steps" program of administrative reform introduced in Britain moves in almost exactly the direction opposite that which has been prevalent in the United States. In America, the emphasis has been to bring in outsiders as policy advisers and give the civil servants a well-defined managerial role. Under the "next steps" program, managerial supervision can be given to people brought in from outside the system, whereas the role of policy counsel will continue mostly to be the province of the civil servants.

Although it is not entirely clear how this relationship between advisory and managerial roles is playing out in other systems, two things seem to be developing. The first is a greater emphasis on the professionalization of management. The second is, as indicated earlier, an emphasis on a political class of civil servants who work intimately with their political overseers. Civil servants are thus expected to be policy advisers, but they may equally be expected to be responsive rather than neutral competents.

Privatization and Public Accountability

One of the great trends of recent times has been the divesting of state enterprises and even services into the private sphere. Yet this divestiture still requires public accountability inasmuch as the services or enterprises that have been transformed from public to private tend to form natural monopolies. What are the means by which private suppliers of essentially public services can be held accountable?

To most public administration theorists, privatization is apt to bring skepticism. And, certainly, as Kettl's volume on this subject demonstrably shows, there is plenty of reason to greet the nostrum of privatization with skepticism, since in too many cases, the ability to hold the private supplier accountable is lacking and the inefficiencies operative under nonmarket conditions are often greater than when the same services are supplied through the public sphere.[21]

Nevertheless, it is as reasonable to ask, "What services cannot be supplied by private sources?" as it is to ask, as the General Accounting Office (GAO) had, "What is an inherently governmental function?" The question for students of public administration is not to defend public supply as such but through what procedures accountability can be managed when the supply of public goods is performed by the private sector, and, as is mostly the case, market conditions fail to prevail. These are new challenges for public administration in a world where both public and private suppliers of public goods are increasingly prevalent.

In Search of Public Administration

Few disciplines are as introspective about themselves as is public administration. Part of the reason, as Guy Peters pointed out in his introductory chapter, lies in the bifurcation of the field between practitioners and theorists. To the practitioners, public administration is more an art than a science, more a matter of savvy and experience than formalistic rules or applications. The theorist, however, is trying to figure out, among other things, what is the role of the public administrator? How much and what kinds of discretion should be granted? What is the nature of accountability and how can it be organized? What do civil servants bring to the process of governing? How ought the worlds of civil servants and politicians and of administration and politics mix? New approaches, such as political economy, have unsettled the field. In their wake, battle lines have formed between the defenders of the public administration tradition and those regarded as hostile to it. But this is the wrong battle. For the discipline of public administration to advance, it needs to refine its questions, sharpen its answers, and investigate that which by assumption has been previously unquestioned.

Inevitably, there will be tension between practitioners and scholars. That is precisely as it should be. The practitioners can tell us when theories fail to guide them and what the limits of theories are. Not all theories have immediate "engineering" applications. Alternatively, the scholars can point to the broader but sometimes unrecognized generalizations that stem from the practitioners' experiences. We need to lower our defenses and increase our inquisitiveness. That is how a discipline advances. And that, of course, would be a proper legacy to the memory of Charles Levine.

Notes

1. See Peter M. Benda and Charles H. Levine, "Reagan and the Bureaucracy: The Bequest, the Promise, and the Legacy," in *The Reagan Legacy: Promise and Performance,* ed. Charles O. Jones (Chatham, N.J.: Chatham House, 1988), 102–42.

2. In one of his last articles, Charlie expressed deep concern over the fragmentation of personnel policy in the civil service with different pay scales applying to civil servants inside the General Schedule classification and to others outside it. The symptom here was salary, but the deeper malaise was the undermining of a common identity. See Charles H. Levine, "Human Resource Erosion and the Uncertain Future of the U.S. Civil Service: From Policy Gridlock to Structural Fragmentation," *Governance* 1 (April 1988): 115–43.

3. See Woodrow Wilson, "The Study of Administration," in *Classics of Public Administration,* 2d ed., rev. and expanded, ed. Jay M. Shafritz and Albert C. Hyde (Chicago: Dorsey, 1987), 10–29; and Luther W. Gulick, "Notes on the Theory of Organization" in *Papers on the Science of Administration,* ed. Luther W. Gulick and Lyndall Urwick (New York: Columbia University Institute of Public Administration, 1937).

4. Bert A. Rockman, "Tightening the Reins: The Federal Executive and the Management Philosophy of the Reagan Presidency," *Presidential Studies Quarterly* 23 (Winter 1993): 103–14.

5. Richard E. Neustadt, "White House and Whitehall," *Public Interest* 2 (Winter 1966): 55–69.

6. Johan P. Olsen, *Organized Democracy: Political Institutions in a Welfare State—The Case of Norway* (Bergen: Universitetsforlaget, 1983).

7. See Thomas J. Anton, *Administered Politics: Elite Political Culture in Sweden* (Boston: Martinus Nijhoff, 1980).

8. See, for example, Lloyd G. Nigro, "CSRA Performance Appraisals and Merit Pay: Growing Uncertainty in the Federal Work Force," *Public Administration Review,* July/August 1982, 371–75; Patricia W. Ingraham and Charles Barrilleaux, "Motivating Government Managers for Retrenchment: Some Possible Lessons from the Senior Executive Service," *Public Administration Review,* September/October 1983, 393–402; and Naomi B. Lynn and Richard E. Vaden, "Bureaucratic Response to Civil Service Reform," *Public Administration Review,* July/August 1979, 333–42.

9. Joel D. Aberbach and Bert A. Rockman with Robert M. Copeland, "From Nixon's *Problem* to Reagan's *Achievement:* The Federal Executive Reexamined," in *Looking Back on the Reagan Presidency,* ed. Larry Berman (Baltimore: The Johns Hopkins University Press, 1990), 175–94.

10. See Joel D. Aberbach, Robert D. Putnam, and Bert A. Rockman, *Bureaucrats and Politicians in Western Democracies* (Cambridge: Harvard University Press, 1981).

11. William Plowden, "What Prospects for the Civil Service?" *Public Administration* 63 (Winter 1985): 393–414.

12. Norton Long, "Power and Administration," *Public Administration Review* 9 (1949): 257–64.

13. Terry M. Moe, "The Politicized Presidency," in *The New Direction in American Politics,* ed. John E. Chubb and Paul E. Peterson (Washington, D.C.: Brookings Institution 1985), 235–72; and, especially, Terry M. Moe, "The Politics of Bureaucratic Structure," in *Can the Government Govern?* ed. John E. Chubb and Paul E. Peterson (Washington, D.C.: Brookings Institution, 1989), 267–330.

14. See Aberbach et al., *Bureaucrats and Politicians in Western Democracies.*

15. See, for example, Claes Linde and Gunnar Wallin, "After the Tide? Patterns of Politicization among the Swedish Administrative Elite," paper prepared for the IPSA-SOG Conference on Governance in an Era of Skepticism: Administrators and Politicians, Stockholm, Sweden, 16–18 September 1992. For the fears of a prominent British student of administration about the evolution of his country's administration, see F.F. Ridley, "Career Service: A Comparative Perspective on Civil Service Promotion," *Public Administration* 61 (Summer 1983): 179–96.

16. See, for example, Joel D. Aberbach and Bert A. Rockman, "Political and Bureaucratic Roles in Public Service Reorganization," in *Organizing Governance: Governing Organizations,* ed. Colin Campbell and B. Guy Peters (Pittsburgh: University of Pittsburgh Press, 1988), 79–98; and Joel D. Aberbach and Bert A. Rockman, "On the Rise, Transformation, and Decline of Analysis in the U.S. Government," *Governance* 2 (July 1989): 293–314. Charlie Levine, alternatively, saw the role of central agencies and the emphasis on technical rationality in American public administration to be a function of the weak status and legitimacy of the civil service in the United States. See Michael G. Hansen and Charles H. Levine, "The Centralization-Decentralization Tug of War in the New Executive Branch" in Campbell and Peters, *Organizing Governance,* 255–82.

17. Martin Anderson, *Revolution: The Reagan Legacy,* expanded ed. (Stanford, Calif.: Hoover Institution Press, 1990), esp. 246–48.

18. Colin Campbell and John Halligan, *Political Leadership in an Age of Constraint* (Pittsburgh: University of Pittsburgh Press, 1993).

19. Colin Campbell and George J. Szablowski, *The Superbureaucrats: Structure and Behaviour in Central Agencies* (Toronto: Macmillan of Canada, 1979).

20. This conception was especially realized during the Reagan administration. See Rockman, "Tightening the Reins," and Hansen and Levine, "The Centralization-Decentralization Tug of War."

21. Donald F. Kettl, *Sharing Power: Public Governance and Private Markets* (Washington, D.C.: Brookings Institution, 1993).

About the Contributors

Hans-Ulrich Derlien is a professor of public administration at the University of Bamberg, Germany. His research interest is the political aspects of local and national government in general and the administrative elite in particular. His English-language publications include contributions to *Governance*.

Richard T. Green is an associate professor at the University of Wyoming, where he teaches in the Master of Public Administration Program within the Department of Political Science. He is the author of many journal articles and book chapters pertaining to public administration history, ethics, law, and personnel.

Lawrence F. Keller is an associate professor in the Public Administration Program at the Levine College of Urban Affairs at Cleveland State University. He has written extensively on urban and legal aspects of public administration and developed city charters in several states.

Wendy Laird is the director of the U.S.-Mexico Borderlands Program at the Sonoran Institute in Tucson, Arizona. She received her MPA from the University of Arizona.

H. Brinton Milward is a professor and director of the School of Public Administration and Policy at the University of Arizona. His research focuses on the relationship between interorganizational networks and the state on issues of governance. He recently edited *The State of Public Management* with Donald F. Kettl.

Ronald C. Moe is the Specialist in Government Organization and Management at the Congressional Research Service of the Library of Congress and also a Fellow at the Center for the Study of American Government at Johns Hopkins University. He has published extensively on executive management in scholarly journals.

B. Guy Peters is Maurice Falk Professor of American Government and chair of the Department of Political Science at the University of Pittsburgh. He previously taught at Emory University, Tulane University, and the University of Delaware; he has held visiting positions in Norway, Sweden, Mexico, and the Netherlands. Peters has published widely in the field of public policy; he is the past editor of *Governance* and the current editor of the *International Library of Comparative Public Policy*.

Bert A. Rockman is University Professor at the University of Pittsburgh, where he teaches in the Department of Political Science and the Graduate School of Public and International Affairs. He is the author of *The Leadership Question: The Presidency and the American System*.

Bernard H. Ross is a professor and chair of the Department of Public Administration, School of Public Affairs at The American University. He is the coauthor of *Urban Politics: Power in Metropolitan America*, and *How Washington Works*.

Irene S. Rubin is a professor in the Public Administration Division at Northern Illinois University. She is the author of *The Politics of Public Budgeting* and editor of the journal *Public Budgeting and Finance*, and, beginning in May 1996, editor of *Public Administration Review*.

James A. Thurber is a professor of government and director of the Center for Congressional and Presidential Studies at The American University. He is the editor of *Divided Democracy: Cooperation and Conflict Between the President and Congress* and coauthor of *Setting Course: A Congressional Management Guide*. He is a former professional staff member of the Senate Committee on Committees and the Commission on the Administrative Review of the U.S. House of Representatives.

Gary I. Wamsley is the founding director of the Center for Public Administration and Policy at Virginia Polytechnic Institute and State University. He is best known for his work as editor of and contributing author to *Reforming Public Administration* and for his book with Mayer Zald, *The Political Economy of Public Organizations*. He has been editor of *Administration and Society* since 1979. His expertise covers selective service, national security, emergency management, and budgeting.